W9-DCN-560

United States
Diplomatic
History
Volume II

Edited by
Walter V. Scholes

UNITED STATES DIPLOMATIC HISTORY
VOLUME 2

READINGS FOR THE
TWENTIETH CENTURY

EDITED BY
WALTER V. SCHOLES
DEPARTMENT OF HISTORY
UNIVERSITY OF MISSOURI

HOUGHTON MIFFLIN · BOSTON
ATLANTA · DALLAS · GENEVA, ILL. · HOPEWELL, N. J. · PALO ALTO

FOR MARIE

Cover photograph by Donald Dietz.

Furniture courtesy of The Workbench,
Cambridge, Massachusetts.

Library of Congress Catalog Card Number: 72-6699

ISBN: 0-395-14057-9

CONTENTS

INTRODUCTION

Political, social, economic, and strategic factors have all played a role in shaping American foreign policy in the twentieth century. American policy has been political in the international sense in that the United States has insisted on stability and peaceful coexistence among nation states, opposing any serious threat to the status quo from the right or the left, from Hitler or Stalin. And since the United States has resisted revolution in other nations around the world, its policy has also had social implications. Economic matters too have influenced foreign policy, in that the government has desired to promote foreign trade and American investments abroad. Strategic considerations have required the United States to broaden its horizons: In the past American domination of the Caribbean was sufficient; after World War II the United States became concerned with controlling the Atlantic and Pacific oceans as well.

To implement its policies the United States has used political pressure, non-recognition to weaken undesirable governments, loans and aid programs to strengthen acceptable governments, and on occasion, military intervention to avert a situation that would be intolerable to American interests. The case of Mexico presents a good example of American diplomacy in action. When Mexican political leaders refused to follow United States' advice, as happened under Presidents Wilson and Harding, recognition was withheld. In the early 1920s, when Mexico began pursuing land and oil policies unfavorable to American interests, the Secretary of State would not sanction private loans to the Mexican government. And President Wilson so heartily detested the Huerta government that he finally sent troops to occupy the port of Veracruz.

To protect its interests the United States became involved in this century's two world conflicts. In 1917 most Americans entered World War I with enthusiasm, in that they believed that the survival of democracy depended on an Allied victory over Germany. More sophisticated Americans, like President Wilson, regarded United States participation as an opportunity to preserve the American concept of liberal internationalism. Wilson believed that a viable world order had to embody principles basic to the American system: freer trade, world peace under the aegis of international institutions, and the disappearance of colonial empires through self-determination. Only if America went to war could it sit at the peace conference that would determine the shape of the postwar world. Although Wilson failed to achieve his objectives, many responsible American political leaders, among them Franklin Delano Roosevelt, never relinquished these ideals. When these ideals were gravely threatened after 1939 by Adolf Hitler's attempt to submit all Europe to German control, the United States entered World War II.

But Hitler's defeat did not provide an opportunity for setting up a new world order, for American and Western European leaders perceived a new threat to the liberal international system—this time from the Soviet Union and Stalinism. In a bold move to shore up the weak and battered democratic nations of Western Europe, the United States, by implementing the Marshall Plan, funnelled abroad massive financial aid for reconstruction and, in a truly precedent-breaking step, committed itself as well to the defense of Western Europe.

Until the Cold War the United States advocated self-determination and opposed empires, and thus encouraged free governments based on free elections. Americans, with their traditional antipathy to political alliances, also opposed the balance of power concept and gave at least token support to international and regional organizations designed to maintain peace. Although the United States has continued to support the United Nations and the Organization of American States, under Presidents Truman and Eisenhower fear of the Soviet Union led to radical changes in American foreign policy attitudes. To stop Communism the United Sates devised the policy of containment, which recreated the old balance of power system through a series of alliances dependent largely on American military strength.

An overwhelming majority of the American people supported the containment of Russia and Communism. In 1950 United States entry into the Korean War proved their determination to stop Communist expansion, at gun-point if necessary. Now however, as several protests enlisting the sympathies of many people against the Vietnam War have indicated, that war has caused many Americans to reconsider the assumption on which United States policy was based. Never before in American history has the country been so divided on a question of foreign affairs. No one can yet say whether this criticism will be limited to attacks on military spending and armed intervention or whether it will become a far-reaching and profound critique of American policy.

Although Americans had stubbornly refused during the first four decades of the 20th century to make any political commitment to another nation, they were convinced that if all countries adopted the American economic and political system, the world would be a richer and happier place for everyone. While some vestiges of that belief still prevail, its basic assumptions have increasingly been challenged by criticism from abroad and at home. The American goal now seems to be to secure its current position through detente with the Communist powers.

PART 1
PRELUDE TO
WORLD POWER:
ROOSEVELT
AND TAFT

INTRODUCTION

The industrial revolution was developing in nineteenth century Europe as technological innovations greatly expanded the productive capacities of the industrial nations, fostered in the last quarter of that century the "new" imperialism. By the 1880s the rival European powers were pushing into Africa, Asia, and the Pacific Islands, seeking both raw materials for their factories and markets in which to sell their products. The European nations either annexed territories outright, assumed protectorates, or created spheres of influence (thereby acquiring exclusive economic control). But other motives figured in this expansion: the drive for power, the desire to enhance national prestige, and the need for strategic security. The European nations could also justify their exploitation of alien peoples, by their assumption that it was the white man's burden to tutor and uplift the backward.

Since the Civil War and reconstruction absorbed the national energy and attention for over a decade, the United States was late in joining the expansionist drive, but when it did, its motives and justifications paralleled the Europeans'. Americans, however, were more inclined to refer to "Manifest Destiny" than to the "white man's burden." With the closing of the frontier in 1890 and a succession of economic depressions, culminating in a serious economic collapse in 1893, many farmers and manufacturers became convinced that the country's prosperity depended on overseas markets; at the same time members of the ruling elite began to advocate expanding the navy and acquiring key strategic areas to complement the required economic expansion. The annexation of Hawaii in 1898 and the results of the "splendid little war" with Spain which gave the United States the Philippines, Puerto Rico, and a protectorate over Cuba, provided the United States the opportunity to take its place among the world's leading powers.

After President McKinley's death in 1901, the United States acquired a leader supremely attuned to the expansionist mood. Theodore Roosevelt's personality—his ability to project a strong character—his innovations in domestic affairs, and his concept of the United States as an international force, all combine to make him one of the most interesting men in American political life. By continuing most of the old policies and advancing new initiatives of his own, Roosevelt involved the United States in the affairs of Latin America and Asia. What were the overall concepts which influenced his foreign policy? David H. Burton, in Reading No. 1, suggests that Roosevelt was prompted chiefly by considerations of geopolitics and race.

Historically, American foreign policy had concerned itself chiefly with Latin America, especially the Caribbean region. Both Roosevelt and Taft believed that the Caribbean area was of vital economic and strategic importance to the United States. Economically, the area served as an outlet for capital investment, particularly in Cuba and Mexico. Strategically, the Caribbean had always played a large role in the defense plans of the United States, and with the decision to build the Panama Canal, it assumed even greater significance.

Although President Monroe had announced in 1823 that the United States would never tolerate the acquisition of territory in the Western hemisphere by a European power, the United States had always recognized the right of any nation to intervene to collect debts owed its nationals and to protect their lives and property. Since all the small Caribbean countries seemed afflicted by the "malady of revolution" and were prone to bad debts accruing in Europe, and because Roosevelt believed that such indebtedness and constant revolutionary instability would endanger America's economic and strategic interests by leading to European intervention, he insisted that the countries establish stable—though not necessarily democratic—regimes. Chronic wrongdoing and continual internal disturbances, Roosevelt warned, would force the United States to act as an "international police power" to restore solvency and tranquility. To the Monroe Doctrine's original intent of preventing Europe from taking advantage of the Latin Americans' difficulties in governing themselves, Roosevelt added the corollary that the United States might intervene whenever it decided that a country was botching the job of governing itself.

In 1905 the new American policy found its first practical test in Roosevelt's intervention in the Dominican Republic. After stopping a civil war, Roosevelt arranged a private American loan so that the Dominican government could pay off its old debts. To guarantee repayment of the new loan, Americans took charge of the customhouses and paid the debt installments before turning any money over to the Dominicans. In addition to insuring that the Americans would get their money, this procedure had a further advantage. By controlling what was, in all the Latin American countries, the most lucrative source of domestic revenue, the United States could eliminate the biggest incentive to revolution. Americans thought that with no chance for sizeable boodle at the customhouses, the Latin Americans would not bother to overthrow their governments.

The American management of customs brought economic and political stability to the Dominican Republic for a time, and the country became the "show case" of American policy in the Caribbean. The Taft·administration, impressed by this success, tried to extend Roosevelt's policy to other Caribbean countries. The United States made a special effort in Nicaragua and finally got that government to accept American control of the customhouses but the Americans had to use force to support their policy. Historians continue to dispute the reasons for Taft's action. Some insist that American economic interests were largely responsible for the intervention. Others, like Dana G. Munro in Reading No. 2 believe that the United States intervened for political reasons—that a stable government would ultimately bring democracy and economic development.

Until the 1890s American interest in Asia had been more romantic than practical, but with the new urgency to expand foreign trade, Asia, and especially the four hundred million potential customers in China, assumed greater economic significance. In Asia, however, there could be no question of direct American military intervention, since the United States was at a disadvantage, in comparison with the strategic position of the European nations and Japan.

In China, for the first time in history, all the major powers confronted one another in one place. All but the United States had railroad concessions, leased territories, or spheres of influence from which they derived special privileges. Fearful that the powers would exclude

American traders from areas under their control, Secretary of State John Hay promulgated the Doctrine of the Open Door: that all nations had an equal opportunity to trade in China and that therefore, by implication, China's territorial integrity would be preserved.

Although President Roosevelt knew that American opinion favored maintaining the Open Door, he realized that the courses open to him were limited. China was too weak to defend herself, and the American people were not willing to fight—either alone or with allies—to preserve the territorial integrity of China. Since Manchuria was the chief source of Sino-American trade, American attention focused on the three northern provinces that make up Manchuria. Originally, the antagonist was Russia, but after her defeat by Japan in 1905, Russia had to surrender much of her influence to the Japanese, who became the greatest threat to Chinese integrity and American interests. But Roosevelt did not consider these interests vital enough to defend at the risk of clashing with Japan. Rather, he believed that by eliminating the sources of Japanese-American friction, the United States could avoid war and still keep the door ajar for American trade.

Roosevelt strongly advised his successor to follow the same course, but Taft paid no heed. Instead, the Taft administration chose to regard the liberation of Manchuria from Japanese control as essential to the independence of China and therefore vital to American interests. But preserving equality of commercial opportunity was not all that was at issue; forcing Japan out of her privileged position was the more intractable problem. Political neutralization of Manchuria, which the United States hoped to achieve through capital investment in order to eliminate Japanese control of the railroads, became the American objective. (Reading No. 3) The priorities of the Roosevelt administration were reversed; the preservation of China became more important than the conciliation of Japan.

1

THEODORE ROOSEVELT: CONFIDENT IMPERIALIST

DAVID H. BURTON

In the antithesis of Western imperialism and colonial nationalisms and the still uncertain synthesis the United States has had a significant and in some ways a determining role. By the extension of its frontiers into the Caribbean and the Pacific at the turn of the century, the United States found itself an imperialist power. American imperialism consciously endeavored to bring what was best of the Western way of life to its colonial peoples. Nevertheless, it depended on the conventional instruments of military force and colonial-civil government imposed by the conqueror. For the United States the Philippines became the fittest subject for this Westernizing process for which Theodore Roosevelt was the outstanding spokesman and apologist. Under President Roosevelt's direction the work of civilizing a backward people received a full American expression, and from a consideration of that enterprise the temper of American imperialism may be sounded. Drawing from the Philippine experiment and from experience with the Caribbean countries Roosevelt combined practical judgments with certain intellectual and emotional attitudes to elaborate a comprehensive doctrine of imperialism.

His doctrine was compounded of a sense of the superiority of the white race, particularly the Anglo-Americans, and the persuasions of democracy; of the Western individualist's urge to dominate and his wish, often more than a pious one, to be the preceptor of lesser civilizations and the protector of unfortunate human beings. For Roose-

From "Theodore Roosevelt: Confident Imperialist," *The Review of Politics*, July 1961, pp. 356–377. Reprinted by permission. Footnotes omitted.

velt the justification of imperialism consisted in the opportunity for human improvement that it afforded subject peoples. There are, in consequence, two critical, distinguishing norms for interpreting his philosophy of imperialism: the resources and the means whereby the process of civilization was carried forward by the powers, and the benefits accruing to backward peoples measured by their adaptability to Western institutions in general and to principles of self-government in particular.

Theodore Roosevelt was a nationalistic patriot and an imperialist in his very bones. On July 18, 1918, he wrote to the like-minded Albert J. Beveridge that ". . . nationalism is the keynote of your attitude and mine—just exactly as it was of Marshall's and Hamilton's. I have never known a professional internationalist who was worth his salt."

While touring British Africa (1910) he had confided to his friend, Arthur Hamilton Lee: "I am, as I expected I would be, a pretty good imperialist." Such attitudes were part of Roosevelt's temper and era. Though of Dutch extraction he felt himself a conscious and living part of Anglo-American culture. Pugnacious by instinct "TR" believed implicitly in the benefits of competition, concluding that human progress was its ordained end and viewing the Anglo-Americans as the embodiment of progress in the race. The times that Theodore Roosevelt moved in were shot through with the thought of Darwin, and, though he refused to apply "Darwinian" postulates to social situations without considerable refinement, a competitive mood colored much of his imperialist doctrine. Roosevelt held firmly to the position that it was a "natural process" that these people best fitted for expansion and self-government should control the backward regions of the world. Pre-eminent among such peoples were the English-speaking races. Evidence of this historical perspective is written large in the opening paragraph of Roosevelt's early study, *The Winning of the West*:

> During the past three centuries the spread of the English-speaking peoples in the world's waste spaces has been not only the most striking feature in the world's history, but also the event of all others most far reaching in its effects and its importance.

The colonial migrations of European settlers and the westward movement of American pioneers were expressions of the superior energy and the higher civilization of the West. The British settlers in Africa reminded him so forcefully of his "beloved westerners" that he felt entirely at home among them. Roosevelt, therefore, readily likened the conquest and control of the Philippines to the taming of the American Great Plains. He justified the wrestling of land from the barbarian Indians as a service to humanity and saw the American experiment in the far Pacific in a similar light. The American record in Minnesota and the Dakotas was not without mistakes nor would it be in the Philippines but, whatever the errors, Americans were justified in their conquests because civilization was advanced. This apologia for imperialism Roosevelt had first proposed in *The Winning of the West*. It mattered little whether the American whites had won the land by fair treaty or by force, or by a mixture of these methods, "so long as the land was won. It was all-important that it should be won, for the benefit of civilization and in the interests of mankind." To oppose such action as immoral or unjust argued a "warped, perverse, silly morality." Roosevelt maintained that conquest, even involving war and its barbarities, American over Indian, Boer over Zulu, Cossack over Tartar, and New Zealander over Maori had "laid deep the foundations for the future greatness" of mighty peoples.

In the conquest of vast stretches of the earth inhabited by backward peoples Roosevelt claimed a leading role for Americans and for himself, if possible, direct involvement. "The only job which I think I would really like to do," he told Maria Longworth Storer (Dec. 2, 1899) as the United States prepared to take up the administration of colonies, "is a job I shall not be offered, *viz.*, the Governor-Generalship of the Philippines with a free hand. That would be a job worthwhile undertaking. . . ." Shortly thereafter, he complained to his good friend, Henry Cabot Lodge, that the Vice-Presidency, were he nominated and elected, would cut him off from all chances of governing the Philippines, "a job emphatically worth doing." Less than two years later he became President and, thus, attained an unrivalled position for directing the civilizing of the Philippines. But the presidential eminence did not provide him with the sense of participation and accomplishment that would have been his as a great American proconsul.

In his admiration for William Howard Taft and Leonard Wood as successful, proconsular administrators appears his own unfulfilled ambition to serve the outposts of empire. He spoke of Taft as a man "who knows the [Philippine] Islands like a book and cares for the Islanders not merely as if they were his little brown brothers but his little brown children. . . ." Wood, he believed, had encountered more difficulties in the Moro country and had overcome them more satisfactorily than British administrators had done under less onerous conditions in the Malay Settlements. To his son, Kermit, he (Nov. 23, 1906) described an American official in Puerto Rico as "a perfect trump and such a handsome athletic fellow and a real Sir Galahad. Any wrong doing and especially any cruelty makes him flame with fearless indignation." Letters of later years reveal his frustration at not having had personal direction of colonial administration. Drawing upon observations of British rule in Egypt and the Sudan where he had visited in 1910, Roosevelt wrote to Whitelaw Reid: "There are plenty of jobs for which I am not competent, but I must say, I should greatly like to handle Egypt and India for a few months. At the end of that time I doubtless would be impeached by the House of Commons, but I should have things moving in fine order first.

To the task of civilizing backward folk Theodore Roosevelt brought certain preconceptions which are the core of his imperialism. An enduring conviction that the white race was destined to spread its culture across the world was its first tenet. This white race, defined by European geography, the Christian religion, a cultural link with Greece and Rome, and a kinship of blood, furnished the superior peoples of the modern era, ordained to rule because they possessed the energy and ability to control other races. Their superiority had been won, it was not innate. Roosevelt recognized that only in the last twenty-five hundred years had the Europeans, the "higher races," been dominant, prospering "only under conditions of soil and climate analogous to those obtaining in their old European homes." In ancient times the fair-skinned inhabitants of northern Europe had been the barbarians in need of culture and law from the Mediterranean.

Expansive energies might vary from epoch to epoch. In the modern era Roosevelt drew little distinction between English conquests in Egypt and the Sudan, French Algerian exploits, and Russian advances in Turkestan. In each case the expansive energies of a superior people worked for progress. These centrifugal movements, similar to earlier Roman, Carthaginian, and Spanish expansion, would leave a heritage of similar improvements in the life of the conquered barbarian tribes. He discounted the argument that these nations expanded only to die, for "the universal law of death . . . is part of the universal law of life.

In the end the man who works dies as surely as the man who idles; but he leaves his work behind him." Thus, it was important to expand and influence history. "Rome expanded and passed away but all western Europe, both Americas, Australia, large parts of Asia and Africa to this day continue the history of Rome. But what slightest faint trace of Rome's ancient rival Etruria is now to be found in living form? None, for Etruria was stationary while Rome expanded." The Anglo-Americans were the contemporary Romans upon whom fell the double mantle of opportunity and responsibility for shaping the history of modern man.

What mattered was not expansion simply for conquest but what that expansion underscored: the higher culture of the energetic races. It was Roman influence on language, law, literature, governmental system, and the whole way of looking at life that counted: the civilizing process for the benefit of the barbarians that Rome—or the United States—brought under its yoke. Linked inseparably to civilization was the peace of the world. "The object lesson of expansion is that . . . peace can not be had until the civilized nations have expanded in some shape over the barbarian nations." Peace and order had followed Russian penetration of Turkestan, French expansion into Algiers, English conquests in Burma, the Malay States and Egypt, and would attend possession of the Philippines. Occupation of the barbarian reaches of the world reduced the risk of international war by bringing more areas under the influence of the civilized states. These states, Roosevelt believed, were unlikely to start a conflict which could only injure civilization.

Roosevelt did not even require a democratic government from superior races, for he favored the expansions of Czarist Russia. Not the form of government, though he obviously had the strongest preference for democracy, but expansive quality distinguished a nation as superior. Indeed, in spite of all his pre-occupation with the white race, he recognized the contemporary Japanese as a superior race because they were capable of conquests. The Koreans and the Chinese appeared to be stationary races and Roosevelt was not minded to help them against Japanese domination. A country without the spirit or force to defend itself deserved to go under. Roosevelt called this the "natural process." The Koreans and Chinese were not racially equal to the Japanese. Of the Chinese "TR" observed wryly to John Hay (Sept. 2, 1904): "They are of the same race [as the Japanese] only in the sense that a Levantine Greek is of the same race with Lord Milner." Roosevelt's racism was, then, flexible enough to keep pace with time and tide and the fortunes of war. Nonetheless his emphatic concern was with the white race, and, primarily, with the Anglo-Americans.

The greatest bequest of a civilized nation to barbarians in ancient or modern times was government under law, of which self-government was the ultimate in evolution and in justice. For nationalities capable of self-government Roosevelt felt kinship, while a people given to chaos and banditry earned his contempt. Human progress required the more politically sophisticated races to rule people unable to govern themselves until they had sufficiently matured. Men must have government, and must govern themselves or submit to government from without. Should they, because of lawlessness, fickleness, folly, or self-indulgence refuse to rule themselves, then subjugation would be their lot. The only way to escape this domination was to demonstrate a capacity for self-rule. Self-government could not be a gift; it had to be earned, unfolding from the capacities of the social body.

> It is no light task for a nation to achieve the temperamental qualities without which institutions of free government are but an empty mockery. Our people are now successfully governing themselves, because for more than a thousand years they have been slowly fitting themselves, sometimes consciously, sometimes unconsciously, toward this end. What has taken us thirty generations to achieve we can not expect to see another race accomplish out of hand, especially when large portions of that race start very far behind the point which our ancestors had reached even thirty generations ago.

As the self-governing Western powers fashioned their empires, democracy in some form, attenuated perhaps, would inevitably find its way into the colonies and into the thinking of the subject peoples anxious to use it to advance their burgeoning nationalisms. The resulting problems were difficult. The typical Western legislature was, as Roosevelt well knew, composed of members usually quite unfamiliar with conditions prevailing in Burma or Puerto Rico. Thus, there was little likelihood that it could devise the necessary colonial laws. Such imperialist irresponsibility might have been acceptable when the paramount interest was in exploiting colonial areas. That day had passed. But a subject people was almost certainly unprepared to govern itself and this condition was further complicated by the tendency of democratic politicians to indulge the fancies of native nationalist demands. Colonial administration must avoid exploitation and "mawkish sentimentality." Hoping that any general departure of Europeans from colonies was many decades distant he nevertheless recognized that dominion over many colonial areas was unlikely to be permanent. This judgment reveals a sturdy realism in Roosevelt's imperialism, for he argued that the overwhelming numbers of aborigines would eventually assimilate the white population, and that "men of our stock do not prosper in tropical climates."

Roosevelt agreed that conquest usually meant the use of force. So long as conquest meant progress for mankind it was good. "It is only the growth of European powers in military efficiency," the president wrote to Carl Schurz (Sept. 8, 1905), "that freed it [Europe] from the dreadful scourge of the Turk. Unjust war is dreadful," he went on, but "a just war may be the highest duty." "If England had disarmed to the point of being unable to conquer the Sudan and protect Egypt, so that the Mahdists had established their supremacy in northeastern Africa, the result would have been a horrible and bloody calamity to mankind." Similarly Roosevelt supported American-British military cooperation in the Yangtze valley, suggested by A. T. Mahan in *The Problem of Asia*, as in the interests of Asia and the world. Military conquests meant some bloodshed; "but to withdraw from the contest for civilization because of the fact that there were attendant cruelties," was in his opinion, "utterly unworthy of a great people."

Only the civilized nations could participate responsibly in international affairs. Backward races unable to maintain domestic order could not be expected to assist in the maintenance of international law. To think otherwise struck Roosevelt as "mere folly," "the silliest kind of silliness," "absolutely feebleminded on our part." To ask Mexico or Venezuela, for example, to guarantee the Monroe Doctrine was "like asking the Apaches or Utes to guarantee it." Perhaps the most striking evidence of the Rooseveltian faith in the influence of civilization is to be found in his conviction that war between civilized peoples might soon become extinct. ". . . More and more civilized peoples are realizing the wicked folly of war and are attaining that condition of just and intelligent regard for the rights of others which will in the end, as we hope and believe, make worldwide peace possible." Thus, if any colonial people did achieve in a national form the industrial or military prosperity to compete with the Western Powers, the very process of achievement would have seen the civilization of that people. Thereafter, they could be dealt with not by recourse to war, but peacefully as in the case of a civilized state.

.   .   .

Dangers for the world lurked wherever ill-prepared people fumbled with self-government, as was illustrated in Haiti, Venezuela, Santo Domingo, Colombia, and Cuba. Writing in 1914 Roosevelt observed that democracy, "the highest ideal of government," "is an ideal for which only the highest races are fit." In the countries south of the United States more trouble had come from failure to recognize this fact than from all other causes put together. For example, the French Revolution enabled Haiti to become an absolute democracy, the first West Indian island to live under what was intended to be a free government. The results had amply shown that it would have been infinitely better for the Haitians to have suffered anything else, even years of slavery, than to have been handed a democratic form of government for which they simply were not fitted. If the Haitians were to learn self-restraint, respect for law, and civilization, they needed an apprenticeship such as the Filipinos were serving under the United States. The irregular behavior of Venezuela and Santo Domingo caused Roosevelt to affirm his belief that some nations were not ready to take up the responsibilities of freedom. Interference by the superior nations to police these countries was fully warranted. On July 12, 1901, he told his friend Speck von Sternburg: "If any South American state misbehaves toward any European country let the European country spank it." As President, Roosevelt defended American intervention in both countries. United States action not only meant the prevention of misery and chaos, but served to protect American national interests from the ambitions of other superior, expansive nations. This intervention was described by the President as an honest policy from which no gain was expected. As for United States pressure on Colombia during the Isthmian canal crisis Roosevelt defended his diplomatic war of nerves on the grounds that construction of a canal was in the interests of human progress. The "bandits of Bogota," "homicidal corruptionists," by their unprincipled efforts to delay or prevent the canal had given another warning of the dangers of independence for countries to whom the advancement of civilization was a matter of secondary importance.

These views were the lessons of imperialistic adventures. Earlier, without this experience, Roosevelt had been enthusiastic for the unconditional independence of Cuba. After the destruction of the *Maine* he insisted that "the one possible solution of a permanent nature" for the Cuban affair was the independence of the island. "The sooner we make up our minds to this, the better," he wrote John Ellis Roosevelt (March 9, 1898). But the removal of Spanish control left a power vacuum that the Cubans themselves were unable to fill. At first, Roosevelt appeared confident that America's part in Cuba's destiny was to adopt a hands-off policy. In a letter to Elihu Root published in *The New York Tribune*, May 21, 1904, he explained that the United States had driven out tyranny and had remained in Cuba until it had established civil order and laid the foundations of self-government and prosperity. But he shortly learned the lesson that the foundations of self-government and prosperity must be deeply laid and slowly aged. Revolutionary outbreaks in independent Cuba made Roosevelt realize that the Cubans there were unable to measure up to their newly acquired political responsibilities. Armed intervention by the United States followed in 1906. Even then the President did not favor annexation of the Island; "emphatically we do not want it," he explained to George Otto Trevelyan. Nonetheless the Cubans had failed to govern themselves, the need for American direction and guidance remained, and "TR's" chagrin was considerable. He described himself to Henry White as "so angry with that infernal little Cuban republic that I would like to wipe its people off the face of the earth." But, after all, Cubans were not sprung from Anglo-Saxon stock and American guarantee for Cuban good behavior became another phase of our destiny as a great nation. In each of these episodes the failure of Central American peoples to achieve what Roosevelt considered a proper degree of political stability had given rise to remedial action by a superior state whose duty it was to promote the interests of civilization, if necessary, by the imperialistic methods of armed intervention and military occupation.

The span of Theodore Roosevelt's imperialist experience extended from the plains of the American west to the battlefields of Europe, coinciding with the years when Western control of the world's backward regions was at flood-tide. Conquests of large areas of Africa and Asia which had struck him as "natural," marked a rivalry that ended in a general war menacing many of his most cherished values. At this point he drew back instinctively. As attracted as Roosevelt had been to the tenet of the expansive superiority of the white race, his final judgment was characteristic of the man. Granting that his estimate of what constituted human progress was highly personalized and sometimes jaundiced, Roosevelt's dedication to the promotion of progress was more meaningful to him than the superior race thesis. His doctrine of imperialism was a stern one that included war, misery, and bloodshed, for Roosevelt was a stern and serious public man. It was a doctrine tempered however by a civilized heart, for Roosevelt accounted himself a civilized human being. The expansive quality of the Western peoples might well be the source and means of civilization. But it was the upward curve of progress that counted most to him.

2

THE FALL OF ZELAYA AND
THE NICARAGUAN CIVIL WAR
DANA G. MUNRO

The revolution of October 1909 was the work of a group of conservative leaders from the interior and of Zelaya's own governor at
Bluefields, General Juan J. Estrada. Estrada and his brother Aurelio
were influential liberal leaders who had apparently been hostile to
Zelaya for some time, and it is probable that Zelaya had left the governor at his post only because he feared to break with his faction.
The governor was in a position to give the revolutionists immediate
control of the east coast, and he was promised the presidency in return for his assistance. Money for the movement was obtained from
a number of local Americans and from some of their associates in the
United States.

It was later charged that the United States government instigated
the revolt. The conspirators, who of course knew of Zelaya's bad
relations with the State Department, certainly hoped for its help.
They had had little success, however, in their earlier efforts to obtain assurances from American officials. In May 1909, for example,
an American who said that he was an emissary of the conservative
leader Adolfo Díaz told the commander of the U.S.S. *Marietta* that
the conservatives and Estrada were ready to revolt if they could be
assured that the United States would not interfere, but the plan was
abandoned when the commander refused to give any assurances. In
July, Estrada himself told the American consul that he would start a

---

Selections from Dana G. Munro, *Intervention and Dollar Diplomacy in the
Caribbean, 1900–1921* (copyright © 1964 by Princeton University Press). Omission of footnotes. Reprinted by permission of Princeton University Press.

revolution if he could be promised the disinterested moral support of the United States and could be given $50,000 in cash and 2,000 rifles. He apparently got no such promises, for his army was handicapped in the early stages of the war by its failure to receive arms from any source. It is possible, of course, that the State Department's local representatives encouraged the revolutionists. Vice Consul Caldera, who was the only representative of the United States at Managua, was a Nicaraguan who was hostile to Zelaya, and Consul Moffat at Bluefields was later characterized by an American Admiral as "less an American consul than an agent for the Estrada faction."

A careful study of the files, however, makes it seem doubtful that the State Department at Washington had any connection with the revolution in its earlier stages. . . . There was no suggestion of partisanship in the formal action that the American government took. When Moffat reported from Bluefields on October 8 that a revolt was about to begin, Adee as Acting Secretary instructed all of the consuls in Nicaragua to "observe strict neutrality and abstain from any action or expression of opinion that might be imputed or construed as an indication of this government's opinion." Later, Moffat was told "to do nothing whatever which might indicate the recognition of the provisional administration." The commanders of the numerous war vessels that were sent to both coasts of Nicaragua to protect American interests seem to have understood that it was their duty to be neutral.

Zelaya's own reckless action caused the American government to abandon its formal neutrality. Estrada's forces took control of the east coast with little trouble, but Zelaya foiled a plan for a simultaneous uprising in the interior by arresting the leaders. He then sent a force down the San Juan River to attack the rebels on the coast. Two Americans, Lee Roy Cannon and Leonard Groce, who were captured while allegedly trying to blow up a troop ship, were shot by Zelaya's forces, at his order, despite the efforts of the American consul to obtain a reprieve. Zelaya's action was especially exasperating because two Frenchmen who had been taken under the same circumstances were spared.

Zelaya asserted that Nicaraguan law authorized the death penalty for rebellion, but the State Department thought that regularly commissioned officers in the revolutionary army were entitled to be treated as prisoners of war. It was not disposed to tolerate the murder of American citizens, even though it frowned on the participation in the revolt and knew that Cannon, at least, was a ne'er-do-well who had been involved in other Central American revolutions. Before deciding on a course of action, however, the Department spent several days making sure that it had accurate information and discussing the legal aspects of the case and the questions of policy involved. Wilson wanted to announce that the United States would occupy Corinto, the chief port of Nicaragua, and possibly Managua also, until a government able to maintain order and assure respect for the 1907 conventions should be established, but this idea was apparently abandoned because it was felt that any such action should be approved in advance by Congress. Instead, the United States broke off all formal relations with the Nicaraguan government.

. . .

The turning point in the war proved to be the failure of a liberal attack on Bluefields, which began in May 1910. Bluefields was then the only important place still held by Estrada, and its fall would have meant the end of the war. Madriz' forces proposed to move against the city from the land side, while their warship, the *Máximo Jerez*, blockaded and bombarded it, but their plans were frustrated by a series of actions taken by the American naval commanders.

When the *Máximo Jerez* threatened a bombardment if the revolutionists did not surrender within twenty-four hours, Commander Gilmer of the U.S.S. *Paducah* told both sides that there must be no fighting in the city and landed 100 men to enforce his demand. The revolutionists were required to withdraw all but a small part of their forces from the city, but they profited from the situation because they could send all of their army to meet the attackers without worrying about protecting their base. Soon afterward, Madriz' forces took the bluff, where the Bluefields customhouse was, in order to cut off the supplies Estrada was receiving by sea, but the American commanders, at the request of the State Department, forbade them to interfere with the passage of ships to the new customhouse set up in territory under Estrada's control. Finally, the liberals' whole plan was disrupted when the American government refused to permit the *Máximo Jerez*, their one formidable warship, to blockade Bluefields. By the end of May it was clear that the attack on the city was a costly failure, and the liberal army withdrew into the interior.

What was done at Bluefields has frequently been criticized as an improper intervention in Nicaragua's internal affairs. It was no unusual for foreign naval officers to forbid fighting in towns where there were so many foreigners and so much foreign property as there were at Bluefields, and there was some justification for preventing interference with American merchant ships entering the port in the absence of a blockade.

. . .

Discouraging as the prospect for peace seemed in June, the end of the civil war was not far off. The reverse at Bluefields and the continued hostility of the United States hurt Madriz' prestige more than the American officials realized, and it encouraged his enemies to stage small uprisings in regions which he had hitherto controlled. Disorders in western Nicaragua in July encouraged the rebels to undertake another invasion of the interior. One of their armies won a decisive victory at Tipitapa on August 18, and a day or two later, when the liberals were again defeated at Granada, Madriz' regime collapsed. The leaders of the revolution entered Managua on August 28.

With the victory of the revolution, Knox and his advisers could be more hopeful for the success of the Central American program which the Secretary had presented to the Cabinet in March 1909. Zelaya's fall had eliminated one of the chief obstacles to peace, and it seemed probable that customs collectorships, from which so much was expected, could now be set up in the two countries that seemed most in need of their stabilizing influence. Negotiations for a loan to Honduras were already well advanced . . . and the State Department confidently expected the new government in Nicaragua to ask for the same sort of help. The basis for this expectation is not clear, but the plan had probably been discussed with Salvador Castrillo, who was Estrada's agent in Washington, and there is a suggestion in one memorandum that some sort of assurance had been received from Estrada himself.

The State Department's ideas were set forth in a cable that Castrillo sent to Estrada on August 28, giving the precise language that the Provisional President should use in a request for recognition. Estrada was to give assurances that he would hold elections within six months and that he would contract a loan secured by the customs. He should also promise to prosecute the murderers of Cannon and Groce and to pay a reasonable indemnity, and he was to ask the United States to send a commission to deal with any matter that might require a formal agreement between the two governments.

Estrada was at first reluctant to commit himself to this program. For the moment he was not desperately in need of money because Madriz had left a considerable sum in the treasury. Probably neither he nor the other revolutionary leaders were anxious to accept outside financial control or to pledge themselves to early elections. Nevertheless, the new government desperately needed the recognition and the moral support of the United States, and on September 10 Estrada asked for recognition in virtually the language that Castrillo had suggested, except that he promised to hold elections within one year. When the State Department made a friendly reply to Castrillo's note, the latter cabled that he had obtained recognition, and the provisional government celebrated by firing cannon every hour through the day. This caused some embarrassment, because the State Department had only intended to enter into *de facto* relations with the new regime pending the establishment of a constitutional government. The Department nevertheless sent Dawson to Managua as special agent to help the new government carry out the policies to which Estrada had committed it. . . .

Dawson was instructed to urge the reestablishment of constitutional government "at the earliest possible date," through an election in which "absolute freedom" should be guaranteed. But he soon realized that a popular election would be "dangerous to peace" and also probably that absolute freedom could not be expected in any election which the Nicaraguans might conduct. He therefore accepted the traditional Central American device of a constitutional convention to give legal effect to the agreements that he persuaded the principal revolutionary leaders to sign. Under these, Estrada was to be elected as president for a two-year term and Adolfo Díaz, who was an influential conservative leader but a personal friend of Estrada, was to be Vice President.

The "Dawson Agreements" provided that the new constitution would abolish monopolies and that Estrada's administration would cooperate with the United States in setting up a commission to adjudicate all unsettled claims against the Nicaraguan government, including those resulting from the cancelation of monopolistic concessions. The new administration would also ask the American government's help in obtaining a customs-guaranteed loan. The murderers of Cannon and Groce were to be punished. All of these undertakings were formally communicated to Dawson on November 5 as an expression of the new government's policy. A separate agreement, signed by

Estrada, Díaz, Chamorro, Mena, and the prominent conservative Fernando Solórzano, provided that Estrada would not be a candidate for reelection and that all the signers would support as his successor the candidate favored by a majority of them. The constitutional convention was chosen late in November at an election in which *zelayista* liberals took no part, and its members unanimously voted for Estrada and Díaz as president and vice president.

The United States formally recognized the new government when it was inaugurated on January 1, 1911, and Elliott Northcott was sent to Managua as American minister. Northcott was instructed to see that the Nicaraguan government carried out the full program contemplated by the Dawson Agreements. He found, however, much opposition to the most important features of the program and reported that "an overwhelming majority of Nicaraguans" were "antagonistic to the United States." The idea of a foreign customs collectorship was especially obnoxious, and the proposal for a claims commission became less palatable when the State Department changed its original plan and insisted that the Secretary of State of the United States should designate two of the three members. Estrada, who knew that he must have the moral support of the United States and appreciated the need for a loan, was willing to go forward with both projects, but his cooperative attitude made him increasingly unpopular and gravely weakened his government's prestige.

. . .

Northcott endeavored to persuade Estrada and Mena to work together, and at Mena's request he obtained Estrada's promise not to make any hostile move against the Minister of War. Nevertheless, on May 8, 1911, Estrada suddenly had Mena arrested and began to arm the liberals of Managua. The attempted *coup* failed when the conservative army officers refused to obey the President's orders, and, when Northcott intervened to save Mena's life and insisted that the prisoner be transferred to the British consulate, Estrada realized that the situation was hopeless and left the country. Northcott insisted that Mena recognize Vice President Díaz as the new head of the government, and at the same time persuaded Díaz to continue Mena as Minister of War.

Adolfo Díaz was to play an important role during two periods when the United States was intervening in Nicaragua's affairs, but when he took office in 1911 the officials in the State Department apparently knew little about him. He had been one of the civilian leaders in the Bluefields revolution, and his relations with some of the North American businessmen on the coast had been useful in raising funds for the movement. In politics, he was a moderate conservative, but not a member of the Granada group. He had little personal following, but his astuteness and his tolerant disposition, which made him less feared by opponents, gave him a special position in Nicaraguan politics. It was these qualities, and his sincere belief that Nicaragua would benefit from close relations with the United States, that later won him the confidence of most of the North American officials who dealt with Central American affairs.

The new President found himself in a difficult situation. With Mena in control of the army, he had little authority in his own government. He could not prevent arbitrary arrests or other discreditable acts by his subordinates, and even the members of his Cabinet paid little attention to his wishes. To retain Mena's support, he was compelled to promise in writing that he would permit Mena to make himself president for the next term. . . .

The State Department was far less interested in the political situation than in the realization of its program of financial reform. . . . The plan was to negotiate a treaty providing for an American customs collectorship and at the same time to . . . look into the republic's financial situation and outstanding debts in order to determine how large a loan was needed. When this study was completed, a contract would be drawn up and the loan would be awarded to the bankers who offered the best terms. The negotiation of the loan treaty went ahead rapidly after Díaz became President, and on June 6, 1911, the treaty was signed at Washington.

The treaty was similar in every respect to an agreement which had been signed five months earlier with Honduras and which was already in the hands of the Senate Committee on Foreign Relations. It provided that Nicaragua should negotiate a loan to refund its internal and external debts and to provide funds for the development of the country's resources. The two governments would take note of the provisions of the loan contract and would consult with one another if difficulties arose. The bonds were to be secured by the customs duties which were to be administered by a Collector General appointed by the government of Nicaragua from a list of names presented by the fiscal agent of the loan and approved by the President of the United States. The customs duties were not to be changed during the life of the loan without the agreement of the government of the United States. Both governments would give the Collector General of Customs any necessary protection in the exercise of his duties. The treaty differed from the Dominican convention of 1907 in the arrangement for the appointment of the Collector General and also in the omission of any provision requiring the consent of the United States for further increases in Nicaragua's public debt. The treaty was at once approved by the Nicaraguan Assembly, and President Taft submitted it to the United States Senate to be considered at the special session which had been convened in May. . . .

When the Foreign Relations Committee voted on both treaties on May 8, however, the result in each case was a tie, which defeated the motion for a favorable report. This practically ended any hope for ratification, although it was some time before the officials in the State Department were willing to admit that the projects were dead.

In the case of Nicaragua, it was too late for the bankers or the State Department to withdraw from the commitments that they had undertaken on the assumption that the treaty would be ratified. Instead of selling bonds to the public, the bankers had tied up a considerable amount of their own money in stopgap loans to a government that was still on the verge of bankruptcy. They could not refuse further help or give up the management of the National Bank and the Pacific Railroad without risking the loss of this investment. The American government was also committed to a new relationship with Nicaragua, through the customs collectorship and the Mixed Claims Commission, and it had at least some moral obligation to help the bankers solve their problems. The State Department had achieved some of its objectives in Nicaragua, but the failure of the loan treaty would prevent the rapid economic advance for which it had hoped.

. . .

By June 1912 a showdown between the rival conservative factions was imminent. Díaz had somewhat more control over his government after he reorganized the Cabinet in October, but he still had little personal following. Emiliano Chamorro's influence had increased, so that he now had most of the conservatives behind him. In June 1912, *chamorrista* was elected President of the assembly, which had continued to function as a legislature after it finished work on the constitution. This impaired Mena's influence, but the Minister of War still controlled the police and practically all of the army except the garrison at Managua, which was commanded by officers personally loyal to Díaz.

The crisis came on July 29, when Mena brought a band of his followers to Managua and attempted to occupy the fort of La Loma. Díaz gave orders to resist and appointed Chamorro General in Chief. In the fighting that ensued, the government clearly had the upper hand. Mena would probably have been captured and killed if Weitzel, at Díaz's request and at great risk to himself, had not gone to Mena to propose that he resign. Mena agreed to do so, but in the night, under cover of darkness, he slipped out of the city, taking the police force with him. Since he had already taken the precaution to ship most of the government's arms and ammunition to places under his control, and since much of the army still followed him, Díaz was at a serious disadvantage. The situation became worse when many liberals began to join the revolution.

North Americans were in real danger because Mena's followers as well as the liberals were resentful toward the United States. Other foreigners were also alarmed, and Weitzel was beset by demands for protection. In the first days of August, when Mena seized the lake steamers which belonged to the railroad company and were thus under the management of the New York bankers, the Minister formally asked Díaz for assurances that American property would be protected. The President replied by requesting that the United States "guarantee with its forces security for the property of American citizens in Nicaragua and that it extend its protection to all the inhabitants of the Republic"; and Weitzel immediately arranged to have 100 bluejackets from the U.S.S. *Annapolis* come to Managua as a legation guard. At the same time the State Department arranged to have substantial additional forces sent to Nicaragua.

. . .

The intervention in Nicaragua in 1912 marked a turning point in American policy in the Caribbean. Before 1912, the navy had frequently made a show of force to prevent fighting which would endanger foreigners or to discourage revolutionary activities. Sometimes, as in Nicaragua in 1910, such measures had influenced, or decided, the outcome of a civil war, but there had been no case before 1912 where American forces had actually gone into battle to help suppress a revolution. American public opinion, as reflected in the press, seemed on the whole to approve what was done, but many voices were raised in protest. Senator Bacon, who had criticized previous actions of the State Department in Central America and had presented a resolution denying the right of the President to use the military forces in operations in a foreign country without the express consent of Congress, again spoke out when the marines first began to arrive in Nicaragua, pointing out that the State Department had gone ahead with its financial projects in spite of the Senate's refusal to approve them and that the power of the United States was being used to support private interests in profitable, speculative operations. The Senate unanimously approved his resolution for an inquiry.

The intervention intensified the already prevalent fear and mistrust of the United States in the other Central American countries. On the other hand, for several years after 1912 the recollection of what had happened to Mena's rebellion discouraged potential revolutionists throughout the isthmus. Except for a *coup d'état* staged by the Minister of War of Costa Rica in 1917, there was no case where a government was overturned by force in Central America between 1912 and 1919. When disturbances threatened, the appearance of an American warship was enough to restore tranquility. The belief that the United States would intervene to uphold constituted governments helped the groups in power in each country to remain in power with little regard for the rights of their opponents, but it at least gave Central America an era of much needed peace.

In Nicaragua, the continued presence of the legation guard was interpreted to mean that no revolution would be tolerated. This meant that the conservatives would stay in power, though everyone, including the State Department, knew that they were a minority party. The arguments advanced in defense of this policy: the assertion that the liberals included a large proportion of the "ignorant mob," and that most of their leaders represented the evil *zelayista* tradition, were perhaps put forward in all sincerity by officials who had little contact with any except the conservatives, but they made little sense to anyone who had friends in both parties. The support of a minority government was inconsistent with the principles that governed American policy in the Caribbean, but for more than ten years no Secretary of State wanted to assume responsibility for the revolution that would almost certainly follow the legation guard's withdrawal.

3

THE OPEN DOOR:
AN IDEA IN ACTION,
1906-1913
CHARLES VEVIER

Commentators have long held open season on the open door policy of
John Hay. Although it has been regarded as the basic idea of American policy in China, few writers have accepted the doctrine at its face
value. The open door has been charged with a lack of principle, indicated as an excuse for intervention, and shrugged off as an old approach to new problems. These, however, are criticisms of the open
door as a tactic rather than as an idea of policy. Viewed in this way,
the open door as an idea proves to be less durable than the use of the
open door as a means to another end.

In the years 1906 to 1913, Hay's policy was employed to justify an
attempt at American financial supremacy in China and Manchuria.
This effort was first influenced by the American railroad king, Edward
H. Harriman, and Willard Straight, an American consular official
stationed in Manchuria after the Russo-Japanese War. It was later
taken over by the first American banking group for China. Although
it was sponsored by financiers, the policy in these years drew upon
Hay's emphasis on the open door as a means of protecting and
extending American trade in China. In addition, a substantial number
of businessmen, publicists, and politicians dreaded the prospect of a
glut of manufactured goods in the home market as well as declining
profits and interest on capital invested at home. A nation whose

popular ideology exalted the vitality of the American economic system easily made the mental transition necessary to view China as a lucrative market that would absorb the threatened surplus of goods and capital.

From 1899 to the end of the Russo-Japanese War, the United States concentrated on that aspect of the open door which sought to protect American commercial privileges. Despite his note of 1900, Hay did little to preserve China's territorial integrity. He even made a clumsy attempt to acquire a naval base for the United States at Samsah Bay. Difficulties with Russia over American trade in Manchuria convinced him that China would not be able to retain control over the area. He believed that the best and only course of action was to safeguard American commercial interests regardless of whatever nation controlled the territory. Thus Washington linked the Chinese-American Trade Treaty of 1903, which provided for the open door in Manchuria, to American support of Japan against Russia in the war of 1904–1905. President Theodore Roosevelt agreed to Japan's control over Russia's former holdings in Southern Manchuria on condition that China's sovereignty would be recognized. In this way, Peking's grant of the open door in Manchuria to American trade in 1903 would be guaranteed by Tokyo.

But in his zeal to balance off Russia and Japan, Roosevelt overlooked the fact that the safety of the open door in Manchuria now depended on Japan's performance in that region. At the same time, his concern for Manchuria became secondary to the immigration issue and the talk of war that plagued Japanese-American relations in his administration. As a consequence, the United States relinquished the diplomatic initiative in Manchurian questions to Japan and entrusted to Tokyo the supervision of the open door in that area.

But American critics dissented with Washington's policy toward Japan and deplored the lack of stronger measures to insure the open door at the end of the Russo-Japanese War. American businessmen, diplomats, and consular officials warned that Tokyo had little respect for the open door in Manchuria and accused the Japanese of attempts to monopolize Manchurian trade and railroad transportation. In their view the protection of the open door was the stated end of American policy. It was at this juncture of affairs that Edward H. Harriman and Willard Straight attempted to install the United States in a position of financial leadership in Manchuria and China proper.

Harriman drew up a plan for an international transportation system that included the use of Japanese steamship lines and Tokyo's newly acquired South Manchurian Railroad. Intent upon the development of its own stake in Manchuria, Japan rejected Harriman's bid for co-operation. Even the influence of Jacob Schiff, the American banker and Japan's financial friend during the Russo-Japanese War as well as Harriman's close business ally, failed to move the Japanese. It remained for Willard Straight to set the American magnate's railway plans in motion.

Ambitious, strongly anti-Japanese, and devoted to the interests of the United States, Straight was a constant critic of Japanese activity in Manchuria. As American consul general in Mukden from 1906 to 1908 he was impressed with the attitude of European observers in the Far East who declared that the United States was regarded as the "champion" of the open door. In order to give some substance to American claims for the maintenance of the open door, Straight worked ceaselessly to introduce American goods and capital into Manchuria.

In his letters to Harriman, Straight described Manchuria as another American frontier, a "new West" ripe for exploitation. He sent Harriman a proposal for a Manchurian bank which would be financed by American funds and under joint Chinese-American control. Aware of China's determination to strengthen itself in face of the threat posed by the powers, Straight viewed American financial participation in China's reform effort as a means of extending the American stake in Manchuria. Once this was accomplished, the way would be open for American loans to finance the great railroad projects then being planned for China proper.

In 1908 the State Department recalled Straight from Mukden. The action was taken at the direct request of Harriman, who was interested in Straight's Manchurian projects. At the same time a feeling began to grow in the inner circles of the State Department that the open door was merely a theory. If Americans were not interested enough to take advantage of it, their denunciations of Japan's action in Manchuria were academic. "We would welcome a more tangible position," Acting Secretary of State Robert Bacon stated after honoring Harriman's solicitation for Straight's recall.

Straight returned to Washington with the Manchurian bank project, a plan for the purchase of the Chinese Eastern Railway from Russia and the construction of a railroad from Chinchow in South Manchuria northward to Aigun on the Russo-Chinese frontier. Under American control, these lines would contribute important links to Harriman's transportation network. Through Kuhn, Loeb and Company, Schiff agreed to finance the Manchurian bank and take the lead in lending money to China for the purchase of the Chinese Eastern Railway from Russia and the South Manchurian Railroad from Japan. This would have made Schiff the "stakeholder" of Manchurian transportation. If Japan refused to sell, Schiff covertly threatened to build the Chinchow-Aigun Railroad as a competing line which would cut into the business of the South Manchurian Railroad. With the approval of President Roosevelt, Secretary of State Root sanctioned Straight's efforts to bring the Harriman-Schiff interests in contact with Manchurian officials. Root was particularly interested in a large loan to China for currency reform, tariff revision, and abolition of an old transit tax that hindered trade. Straight, who acted as intermediary between the Chinese representative in the United States and the Harriman-Schiff group, transformed Root's and Roosevelt's approval of this project to his own determination to bolster the United States in Manchuria.

Tokyo, however, was well aware of the possible consequences of the Straight-Harriman-Schiff plan and had no intention of surrendering its own aspirations. In order to create the "tangible position" in Manchuria that Bacon had requested, the United States was obliged by the logic of its desire to take a strong diplomatic stand with regard to Japan. This Washington refused to do. The State Department rejected Straight's pleas to use Boxer indemnity funds remitted to China as security for a Manchurian loan; Washington called off an anti-Japanese propaganda campaign launched unofficially by Straight; and the Root-Takahira Agreement of 1908 demonstrated Washington's determination not to antagonize Tokyo although it still insisted upon respect for the open door.

Through its encouragement of Straight and Harriman, however, American open door policy was bound to clash with Japan. By seeking to employ a financial interest to make good a diplomatic profession, American diplomacy became subservient to its instrument. Attracted by Straight's grandiose scheme and Harriman's plans, American bankers hoped to dominate the economic development of Manchuria and China proper. The assertion of the open door as a diplomatic policy in this context operated as an advance guard for an attempt at American economic supremacy. During the Roosevelt administration, however, it was obscured by the immigration question and Roosevelt's reluctance to antagonize the Japanese. It remained for William Howard Taft to clarify the direction already taken by the State Department and the Schiff-Harriman financial interests.

Taft understood the Manchurian situation very well. As Roosevelt's heir apparent and with an obvious reference to Japanese ambitions in Manchuria, he promised American merchants in Shanghai that their government intended to protect them against the political preferences accorded their commercial competitors. When he became President in March, 1909, Taft informed Congress that American capitalists and manufacturers sought overseas markets and that it was the government's duty to assist in this enterprise. Within his official family he gathered about him men who would hew to that line.

The Secretary of State, Philander C. Knox of Pennsylvania, had been an early supporter of Albert J. Beveridge's imperialist oratory and was anxious to make the open door a practical policy. The Assistant Secretary of State, Francis M. Huntington Wilson, was delighted with Straight's apparent success in attracting American capital to Manchuria. William Phillips, Third Assistant Secretary of State, knew of Harriman's connection with Straight. As chief of the Division of Far Eastern Affairs toward the end of Root's tenure as Secretary of State, he had permitted Straight to approach the American railroad king with his Manchurian schemes. Appointed acting chief of the Division of Far Eastern Affairs when he returned home and then detained in Washington by the Taft administration, Straight brought the Secretary of State up to date on the Harriman-Schiff negotiations. William W. Rockhill, American Minister to China and an important original influence behind the open door policy, was the only important casualty. Because of his lack of aggressiveness in pushing American economic interests in Peking, he was sent to a new post in St. Petersburg. It is no surprise then that the signature by Anglo-German-French bankers of the Hukuang Railway loan contract in May, 1909, caused consternation in Washington.

Since the end of the Spanish-American War, American interests had claimed rights to build some of the Hukuang lines that were to be located in China proper, connecting Hankow with Canton and Szechuan. Assistant Secretary of State Phillips had quickly informed the House of Morgan of rumors about the impending Hukuang loan, for as the last American holder of the Hankow-Canton Railroad concession, J. P. Morgan and Company was thinking of sending a representative to China. The International Banking Corporation, an organization with close working ties to the National City Bank, had previously asked for Washington's aid in getting a share of the loan. It was eager to take up Chinese railroad business if the government would lend its support. Meanwhile, early in May, 1909, Schiff had offered Straight a position as Kuhn, Loeb's representative in China in order that business discussions with the Chinese, inaugurated by Straight in Mukden, would be continued.

Throughout these developments, the State Department remained convinced that it was its duty to extend American economic interests in foreign areas. It also understood the relationship between Chinese railway construction and the creation of a demand for American manufactured goods and capital. With Straight acting as the link between the bankers and the State Department, the next step was obvious.

Aware that J. P. Morgan and Company and Kuhn, Loeb and Company were already actively interested in Chinese loans, the State Department "invited" them to form the American Banking Group for China and demanded entrance into the Hukuang loan. With pointed references to the open door, the United States claimed prior rights to the Hukuang concession. If the powers were to lend money to China, Washington asserted, then the principle of the open door required the participation of American bankers on an equal basis. And even though the American group expressed willingness to enter the arrangement on an unequal basis, the State Department refused its approval.

The Hukuang loan, however, was an expedient seized by the State Department to make a substantial move into the China loan field. Indeed, the opportunity appeared a month after a disruption of Chinese internal politics had temporarily cancelled negotiations between the Harriman-Schiff interests and China's representative in the United States. In view of the emphasis placed on Manchuria by Straight as well as Harriman's contention that he had "originated the China business," the Hukuang loan assumed a less important role at the outset.

Shortly before the formation of the American group, Harriman, who received a separate share in the enterprise, went to Europe and reopened negotiations with the French agent of the Russian Finance Ministry for the sale of the Chinese Eastern Railway. At the same time, he sent Straight to China to seek the construction rights for the Chinchow-Aigun Railroad, a line which would threaten the Japanese-controlled area in Manchuria. Through a combination of these two lines, Harriman hoped to force Tokyo to sell the South Manchurian Railroad. He had no illusions about the attempted combination of American and European banks in the Hukuang loan. Intent upon his own affairs, he identified his project with American enterprise in the Far East, in order to gain, as he wrote, "purely American influence in some one thing, so we can show them how to do it right and thus get a real and lasting American influence."

Harriman's death in September, 1909, however, shifted the direction of the scheme to Straight who promptly enlarged it to a plan for American economic control of Manchuria, Mongolia, and the Russian Far East. He proposed that the American group take over Harriman's Chinchow-Aigun railroad project and admit Russia to a minor share in this road and to the International Banking Consortium that would operate in China. If this were done, Straight thought, then Russia would be willing to sell the Chinese Eastern Railway to the same American-controlled Company that was to operate the Chinchow-Aigun Railroad. This action was certain to force Tokyo's capitulation. As a capstone to the whole idea, Straight suggested that the American group take up the old scheme for a Manchurian Bank. The result would be the development of Manchuria and Mongolia principally under American auspices. It would create an atmosphere of friendship between the United States and Russia that would open Siberia and the Russian Far East to the investment of American capital and the sale of American goods. And, once Russia had abandoned its railroad in Manchuria, it would force Japan into a similar course of action.

If all went well, China would receive uncontested sovereignty over Manchuria. The American bankers would enjoy a great financial advantage because of the lead they had taken in moving Russia and Japan out of the region, thus, as Straight used the word, "neutralizing" Manchuria as a factor in international politics. When the American group authorized Straight to proceed with the scheme, the financial structure of American activity in China was reshaped. Now Harriman's idea, modified and expanded by Straight, was taken over by the American group. And the support given to the group by Washington was carried along in the mechanics of the transfer.

These developments occurred at a time when Washington was sorely troubled. Since the spring of 1907, the United States had contested Russia's claims for control of the railroad municipality of Harbin in northern Manchuria. The State Department argued that the open door was being violated through Russia's assumption of civil rule in Chinese territory. The American objection was indirectly aimed at Japan which had a similar position in southern Manchuria. In addition, through agreements signed with China, Japan appeared well on the way to dominance in Manchuria. The situation alarmed Assistant Secretary of State Huntington Wilson and members of the Division of Far Eastern Affairs. But the State Department was well informed of Straight's plans for the Manchurian-Mongolian-Siberian enterprise and it knew of Straight's negotiations with the Chinese for the Chinchow-Aigun Railroad. Fearing that Tokyo would threaten the success of the venture, it was impressed with Straight's contention that Japanese opposition would be a violation of the open door.

Washington was also aware of a strong feeling held by influential Russians who advocated a tie with the United States against Japan in the Far East. State Department officials brought Secretary of State Knox up to date on Harriman's negotiations with Japan in 1905 and Russia's attempts to sell the Chinese Eastern Railway. Confident that the American bankers had written confirmation from the Chinese establishing the American rights to the Chinchow-Aigun Railroad, Knox launched his proposal for the neutralization of Manchuria's railroads in November, 1909.

The Secretary invoked the open door, but the context of economic affairs in Manchuria made his action a bid for American financial supremacy in the area. The American Banking Group felt secure in its possession of rights to the Manchurian Bank and the Chinchow-Aigun Railroad. It was this that impelled the Secretary of State to believe that he now could argue from a position of power by claiming the existence of a substantial American stake in Manchuria. He hoped to force Tokyo to accept the political neutralization of Manchuria in order to permit the economic exploitation of the region, and if Japan accepted his political overtures, it would be forced to accept business terms laid down by American bankers. This was also true of the alternative scheme proposed by Knox for Anglo-American support of the Chinchow-Aigun Railroad. Stripped of political rights to economic concessions in Manchuria, Japan would have to play the game according to American rules.

At least from the American point of view, neutralization, as Huntington Wilson declared, was truly a "practical policy." Its greatest weakness was in seeking the achievement of an economic end through diplomatic means without admitting this to be its purpose. Hamstrung by this handicap, the policy was defeated by diplomacy, for the powers were able to turn aside Knox's thrust by pretending that the surface issue was the real issue. Japan had diplomatic ties with Russia and the British had diplomatic ties with both Russia and Japan. Straight's estimate of the possibility of American-Russian diplomatic cooperation overlooked these vital circumstances. Heading the list of diplomatic tragedy, however, was the fact that the American-Chinese agreement for the Chinchow-Aigun line was not binding when Knox made his move. Thus at the outset, the secretary of state had no bargaining power because he lacked an important economic interest in Manchuria with which he could justify his claim to a voice in Manchurian affairs.

The criticism directed against the American Secretary's diplomacy that led to the Russo-Japanese pact of 1910, is justified but not extensive enough. It overlooks the essential hypocrisy of Knox's use of the open door. He was not bluffing as Hay was in 1899 and 1900. On the contrary, he thought that the open door had derived substance through the American Banking Group's activity in Manchuria. It was a fateful error.

From that point down to 1913, the American effort concentrated on China proper. Manchurian affairs still attracted the bankers and the State Department but the Hukuang loan, the currency reform loan, and the negotiations for the reorganization loan revealed the overriding necessity for compromising with the other powers in China. Once having joined the International Banking Consortium and agreeing to the admittance of Japan and Russia because of their Manchurian interests, the United States cast the open door aside, as it had in the past, for the sake of expediency. It was time to give up the idea of being "regarded as champions of the 'Open door'," Straight declared. He favored admittance of Russia and Japan to the International Banking Consortium, an act which would "enable the four Groups to do business in their respective spheres of influence." Washington followed suit. The open door could be asserted from time to time whenever necessary, but the emphasis was to be placed on the virtues of international cooperation in China via the Six Power Consortium. In this way, the open door would no longer be an embarrassment,

China would have to take measures to save Manchuria herself; and the Six Power Group would concentrate on strengthening its own position in China proper. In June, 1912, when the American minister in China suggested that there was little hope for international co-operation in China, particularly with the emergence of Russia and Japan, Huntington Wilson revealed the true direction of American policy. "If you can't get what you want, you'll take nothing?" Thus far had Washington travelled in its excursion into the realms of international finance.

Chinese reluctance to deal exclusively with the Consortium and tensions within the Consortium spurred the American group to take stock of its position late in 1912 and early 1913. In November, 1912, moreover, the Progressive ferment in the United States split the Republican party and brought the Democrats to control in Washington. Woodrow Wilson's party, depending heavily upon its anti-big-business crusade, did not appear likely to offer a receptive atmosphere for the continuance of the American group's operations in China. By February, 1913, it looked to Wilson's assumption of the presidency "with apprehension."

Affairs within the American group were far from tranquil. Kuhn, Loeb and Company had a long record of hostility toward Russia. When it became apparent that the other American bankers would accept Russian participation in the Consortium, Schiff's firm withdrew from the arrangement on June 30, 1912 in protest. The next day it returned. In December, however, Kuhn, Loeb and Company withdrew again because of its opposition to giving China any further loan advances. By February, 1913, it demanded that the American group withdraw from the Consortium. These difficulties were compounded by the general instability of the financial situation.

Reports arrived in Washington and New York indicating a crisis in China's credit. In December, 1912, the American group's European agents sent word that the international money market could not absorb a large amount of Chinese bonds. New York continued nego-tiations with Peking but with no intention of floating a loan until the financial picture cleared.

Shortly afterward, the American group came up with more evidence of financial difficulty. American troubles with Mexico "badly chilled" prospective purchasers and the underwriters, who had been pledged to take Chinese bonds, refused to be committed beyond the middle of February, 1913. If the situation deteriorated further, the American group warned, it would be forced to withdraw. Uncertain of financial conditions and doubting that the new administration would lend its support, the American group sought to conclude the loan by March 1, 1913, or give it up entirely.

The group's decision was a blow to Knox's China policy. Pressed by public opinion to recognize the recently formed Republic of China, yet determined not to move ahead of the other powers, Knox was rocked by the group's determination to leave the China loan field. He called Henry P. Davison of J. P. Morgan and Company, who was acting as chairman of the American group, and urged him to delay the action until the Taft administration had left office. Davison assured the harassed Secretary that no change would be made that would embarrass the out-going administration but complained that the negotiations were difficult and the "time must come" when they had to conclude "one way or the other."

The American group was as good as its word. Nothing was done until Wilson had assumed power on March 4, 1913. Six days later, the bankers marched on Washington. They found Secretary of State William Jennings Bryan "courteous and open-minded," but the "administration was asked almost brutally to declare its position." The American group insisted that the government request it to continue its participation in the Six Power Consortium negotiations for the reorganization loan; that it receive Washington's assurance that no other American financiers would be permitted to enter the loan; and that the American group would control future loans. As Bryan recalled it, the group also demanded that the security of the loan be linked to Chinese government revenues and that, if necessary, the United States would use force in cooperation with the other powers if China refused to live up to the terms of the contract. "I rather gather we will not be requested to go on," Straight noted dryly four days after the meeting.

Under the circumstances the President had no choice but to accept the challenge thrown down by the bankers. He condemned the terms of the reorganization loan, refused to bear the responsibility for the possible use of force in support of the American group, and implied dark motives to Wall Street's activities in China. The demand made of Wilson—that he ask the American bankers to continue—was symbolic of the evolution of open door policy from 1906 to 1913. As a tactic, it was a failure; as an idea, it was nonexistent.

PART 2
WILSONIAN
DIPLOMACY

INTRODUCTION

When Woodrow Wilson became President of the United States in 1913, he anticipated devoting most of his time in office to domestic affairs. As it turned out, foreign affairs dominated Wilson's years in the White House, and when he left office in 1921, America had become, if not the greatest, at least one of the major powers. From the outbreak of hostilities in Europe in 1914, Wilson, and most of his countrymen as well, tended to favor Great Britain and France over Germany, and ultimately the United States entered the war on the side of the Allied powers. Too much the liberal to accept the old empire system, Wilson wanted to refashion the world in the image of American capitalism and democracy.

Although Woodrow Wilson's liberalism led him to denounce dollar diplomacy, he did not retreat from Taft's position. Indeed, he sent troops into Latin America more often than any other President, and when World War I turned the Caribbean Sea into an American bay, Wilson made free use of the marines in the hopes of preventing revolutions. To the various elements usually decisive in shaping American foreign policy, Wilson added a new dimension, which Howard Cline has labeled "moral imperialism." (Reading No. 1) Wilson invoked this notion in order to justify his intervention in Mexico.

For approximately a quarter of a century, while President Porfirio Díaz silenced dissent, Mexico had appeared to be the most stable of the Latin American states, but in 1910 Francisco Madero initiated a revolution that forced Díaz from office. Since Madero's ideological baggage included some liberal ideas, the conservatives early in 1913 responded by compelling him to resign. These events were in no way abnormal and of themselves need not have affected Mexican-American relations. Trouble arose, however, when Madero and his vice-president were brutally murdered by forces under the command of General Victoriano Huerta, who had assumed the presidency. All of this happened in the last days of the Taft administration, and thus President Wilson inherited the problem of dealing with the new Mexican regime.

Of course other presidents had moral standards too, but for none was the Christian precept to help one's fellow man so compelling as for Wilson. Professor Arthur Link has emphasized that Wilson's compulsion to guide Latin Americans to a better way of life was partly responsible for his military intervention in Haiti. Unfortunately, however, Wilson's efforts to do good reflected a disembodied idealism, as the Wilson administration lacked sufficient knowledge of Caribbean affairs and showed little wisdom in dealing with small quasi-protectorates. Although American troops did move into Haiti (and did not leave until 1934) the Haitians fared better than the Dominicans. The Haitians at least kept a semblance of control over their own affairs; in the Dominican Republic the United States armed forces removed local politicians from office and ran the country until 1924.

In Asia Wilson faced an increasingly powerful Japan. When the Japanese sought in 1915 to take advantage of Europe's preoccupation with World War I in order to expand their influence in China, and presented China with the Twenty-One Demands, the United States found that it could do little to thwart these designs. Although China's acceptance of the Demands would have given Japan a dominant position on the mainland, Wilson (like his predecessors) refused to commit American troops to the Asian land mass, nor could he count on the warring Europeans to intervene militarily in any allied venture. All that the United States could do was to make clear that it did not intend either to surrender any treaty rights or to ask China to do so. Fortunately, however, the Japanese were constrained by British pressure to modify some of their claims.

In an attempt to reach an understanding about China, the United States and Japan concluded the Lansing–Ishii Agreement in 1917, and this seemed to satisfy both countries. (Reading No. 2) The United States recognized that Japan had special interests in China, particularly in the areas contiguous to Japanese possessions, and Japan promised to adhere to the Open Door policy desired by the United

States. But for Wilson, however, the arrangement was merely a temporary expedient, and after the end of World War I, he attempted to checkmate Japan by organizing an international banking consortium to control all major loans to China. He thereby hoped to eliminate Japan's independent lending operations, since he believed that Japan was using loans as an instrument to acquire special privileges which would ultimately enable her to close China off to American trade. With the help of American financiers Wilson hoped to keep China at least partly open to American interests.

In contrast to Roosevelt and Taft who had confronted Europe only in Asia, Africa, and Latin America, Wilson entered European affairs directly when he declared war on Germany in April 1917. From the start of the war in 1914, Wilson held the Germans to strict accountability for submarine activities, and his stance did not vary right up to 1917. Since this kind of warfare imperiled the American notion of freedom of the seas, such naval activity soon involved, as Ernest R. May points out in Reading No. 3, the prestige and influence of the United States and led ultimately to the declaration of war.

In entering the war, Wilson had other aspirations, as N. Gordon Levin, Jr. makes clear in Reading No. 4. The President wanted to establish liberal, international capitalism throughout the world, and he believed that he could best export American liberalism by expanding American trade. Two new laws helped Americans to expand: Congress allowed bankers engaged in foreign activities to establish foreign branch banks; and the Webb–Pomerene Act allowed competing firms to divide a foreign market for purposes of developing it under American auspices. Thus, the domestic antitrust laws did not apply to foreign involvements.

In 1918–1919 towering European problems confronted Wilson and the Allies: a defeated Germany and the new Bolshevik government in Russia. After bitter disputes at the Peace Conference the powers deprived Germany of her colonies and from Germany herself France gained crucial territory. Furthermore, the powers pinned the guilt of war on the Germans and imposed heavy reparations. Wilson, convinced that the world must have a League of Nations if it were to have peace, succeeded in getting his Covenant embodied in the Treaty of Versailles, only to discover that the United States Senate would not accept the League. As Arno J. Mayer points out in Reading No. 5, the deliberations and decisions of Wilson and the other world leaders at the Peace Conference were affected by domestic considerations. The conservatives in both Europe and America wanted harsh terms for Germany and got them; the left achieved a negative victory by thwarting the conservatives' demand for further intervention in Russia. The peace of 1919 proved a seedbed of future international conflict. The political settlement left Germany sullen and vindictive, France frightened, and colonial peoples frustrated in their hopes for greater independence.

1

NEW CRUSADES
HOWARD CLINE

It is interesting but fruitless to speculate about what might have happened to the Mexican Revolution had President Taft recognized Huerta, as Ambassador Wilson so vehemently urged. But he did not. Taft left the thorny situation to his successor, Woodrow Wilson, whose administration was to take office on March 4, 1913. For more than eighteen months thereafter relations with Mexico were the most serious international problem facing the United States. Mexico itself was again split into warring factions in the familiar nineteenth-century pattern. The Mexican Revolution of 1910, which seemed to have closed with Madero's successes, was in fact just beginning as his political heirs set about reversing the Huerta stroke. The Revolution was reborn.

In widening ripples, the difficulties arising from Huerta's anachronistic *coup* spread as domestic and international forces formed and combined to support or oppose him. Nearly all semblance of order disappeared from Mexico as a result. The provisional president in February 1913 found an empty treasury and a demoralized bureaucracy, a riven society and a shattered political apparatus.

Huerta, therefore, promised to restore the Golden Age of Díaz. After two years of constant bloodshed and upheaval many now ap-

Reprinted by permission of the publishers from pp. 135–36, 139–42, 144–47, 155–60 of Howard F. Cline, THE UNITED STATES AND MEXICO, Cambridge, Mass.: Harvard University Press, Copyright, 1953, 1963, by the President and Fellows of Harvard College.

proved of his program. Like any well-trained Latin-American *caudillo,* Huerta began replacing elected state governors with his own trusted military men. At first the Church was distrustful, but gradually moved toward his support. The Huerta regime evolved toward the classic form of Latin-American dictatorship. But opposing forces, within Mexico itself and from the United States under Woodrow Wilson, thwarted the successful operation of Huerta's plans. The interaction of pressures in Mexico and around it forms one of the most complicated eras of domestic politics and an even more complex tale of its relations with the United States. There is still no general agreement about the success of Woodrow Wilson's Mexican policy during these turbulent months following the fall of Madero. Fortunately Wilson's reputation does not rest wholly on his generally poor handling of this thorny problem.

One of the first needs of the new Huerta government was money. To obtain it, internal peace was essential. The United States and Europe were the sole sources of funds, but until foreign governments officially recognized his government, their bankers would make no loans to Huerta. His diplomatic objective was at first very simple: to secure recognition of his government. Domestically his policy was to pacify the country and to consolidate his shaky hold on the National Palace. The two aims were intertwined.

Response at home came in the historical Mexican pattern. . . . From the North came immediate revolt against Huerta's plans for a Neo-Porfirian regime. Venustiano Carranza, governor of Coahuila, and Abram González, governor of Chihuahua, immediately refused him the allegiance of their states. . . . On March 26, 1913 Carranza published the Plan of Guadalupe. It was a short, simple political statement that constitutional government must be restored to Mexico in accordance with Madero's earlier (1910) Plan of San Luis Potosí. From his state troops and willing guerrillas Carranza organized a politico-military Constitutionalist Army of which he became "First Chief."

Some of the most crucial decisions that determined the ultimate fate of Mexico and its Revolution were not made within the area at all, but in Washington, London, Berlin, and Paris. Perhaps the single most critical constant element of the whole era was the varying attitudes and actions taken by Woodrow Wilson, President of the United States from 1913 to 1921. The position of the United States vis à vis Mexico and the European crises that led to the first World War affected all parties, and formed the context in which relations with Mexico were carried on for nearly a generation.

Neither avowedly a pacifist nor an imperialist, Wilson was an idealistic nationalist. His political creed drew heavily on the stern Christian morality his Presbyterian father had inculcated in him as a youth. He sought the truth, and once he believed he had found it, rarely did he change his mind. He seemed intolerant of criticism, and often considered opposition to his views the result of insufficient study by his opponents.

. . .

For many months before and after March 1913 Woodrow Wilson believed that Mexicans were fully prepared for democracy in the American style. He assumed that the Mexican nation, though at a less advanced stage, was basically the same as the Anglo-Saxon ones; by some quirk of circumstance Mexicans spoke Spanish instead of English and lived outside the United States rather than in it, but their problems and outlook were parallel to the ones with which he was familiar through study or experience. Wilson acted as though the differences were superficial rather than fundamental. His early policies were predicated on the belief that if Mexicans would hold a free election and follow constitutional practices their troubles would evaporate. He learned that such was not the case.

Wilson was slow to voice a Latin-American, much less a Mexican, policy. He early issued a prepared statement, March 11, 1913, which assured the world that in Latin America the United States had no sympathy with those who "seek to seize the power of government to advance their own personal interests or ambition." The windy and unclear sentiments puzzled everyone. The pronouncement was widely interpreted to serve notice on Central American revolutionists that Wilson would not favor their attempts to overthrow existing governments and that he was displeased with Huerta. That was true.

The larger significance of the initial statement was that it heralded a new and deviant policy of recognition when changes in form and personnel broke continuity. When a government succeeds by overturn, recognition is required; since that has happened often, the United States had by mid-nineteenth century established a policy to guide its actions. Writing in 1848, Secretary of State Buchanan had summed up the historic policy by saying that the United States always recognized *de facto* governments—ones that really had come into control. "We do not go behind the existing Government to involve ourselves in the question of legitimacy. It is sufficient for us to know that a government exists, capable of maintaining itself; and then its recognition on our part inevitably follows." To this time-tested formula had been added the ability of governments formed by revolution to comply with international obligations, especially the protection of foreign interests. If it existed and was stable, recognition merely registered that fact; it carried no cachet of approval or of disapproval. It was almost a routine diplomatic operation. Wilson proposed to change that.

For the mere fact of existence—*de facto*—and occasionally a pledge that it would protect third parties, Wilson substituted a new doctrine to decide whether a new government should be recognized by the United States. He thus reversed the settled policy. His was the test of "constitutional legitimacy." It implied the right of the United States to inquire fully into whether the new government was complying with its own national constitution and even to go behind its existence to scrutinize whether it had come to power because its leaders were motivated by personal interests and ambition, or whether they were really trying to pry off despotism by the historic right of revolution. Scrutiny and inquiry seemed to most Latin-American nations the same as meddling in their internal affairs.

Thus there were "good" revolutions and "bad" revolutions in the Wilsonian view. The latter brought only venal, unidealistic people to power, while the former put the particular nation back on the constitutional track by overthrowing an unconstitutional tyrant. As events in Mexico and elsewhere ultimately showed, the test of "constitutional legitimacy" was unworkable, especially in Latin America. The United States once renounced it as a national policy in 1921, though its shades rise constantly to plague international affairs since Wilson's time. In the case of Mexico, Wilson had to decide whether Huerta's was a "good" revolution, worthy of recognition, or a "bad" one, unworthy. If the latter, some "good" revolution had to overthrow Huerta to win the coveted accolade which Wilson now had made of recognition.

· · ·

The President had decided that he would never recognize Huerta, and he did not swerve from that view, no matter what obstacles loomed. Privately he stated, "I will not recognize a government of butchers." Since in Wilson's mind recognition was tantamount to approval, to bestow that favor on Huerta would be condoning murder, countenancing unconstitutional practices, encouraging other barracks-uprisings in Central America, but above all, be taking the advice of Henry Lane Wilson, who represented everything President Wilson deeply distrusted—unprincipled opportunism, Big Business, Dollar Diplomacy, Republicans. In addition, recognition of Huerta would mean the defeat of the Constitutionalists, whose very name hypno-tized President Wilson. In short, Huerta's revolt was "bad"; that of the Constitutionalists was "good."

He believed the Mexican problem to be a political one, to be solved by free elections which would put into power a government that would govern constitutionally. Since Huerta was both unscrupulous and unconstitutional—double damnation—he must go. Discreet hints by the British that perhaps a joint intervention was needed to bring peace to troubled Mexico made it clear to the President that he must abandon his "do nothing" attitudes on Mexico.

THE LIND MISSION

Wilson determined to "mediate," but in such a way that Huerta would be eliminated and so that the Constitutionalists, by default, would be favored. Wilson showed himself the veriest tyro in diplomacy by not first taking the elementary precaution of finding out whether the Con-stitutionalists were willing to have such "mediation." Wilson named John Lind as his special presidential agent to dicker directly only with Huerta.

Lind knew nothing of Mexico, Spanish, or diplomacy. He was a tall, gaunt Swede who was a Democratic party power in Minnesota where as governor he had battled the trusts. . . . The Lind Mission was well-meaning, but doomed almost from the outset when newspapers in the United States and Mexico headlined a story that he was going to get Huerta's resignation.

His instructions were not quite that drastic. He was directed to tell Huerta that the United States was "acting on the behalf of the rest of the world" (whom Wilson had not let in on the secret) and to demand as the price of mediation, four things: an armistice between the gov-ernment and the Constitutionalists, an early election, Huerta's prom-ise not to be a candidate, and his assurance that he would accept the results.

Lind's orders closed with a novel plea, "Can Mexico give the civilized world a satisfactory reason for rejecting our good offices? If Mexico can suggest any better way in which to show our friendship, serve the people of Mexico, and meet our international obligations, we are more than willing to consider the suggestion." Huerta made such a suggestion: friendship and all these other matters could be unmistakably shown by recognizing his government, the traditional symbol of amity. Otherwise he refused to consider this unwarranted series of proposals to bring peace to the land. He viewed the Constitutionalists as troublesome bandits.

Lind wrote Wilson that Huerta needed money and suggested a loan. Wilson approved, and on his second attempt, Lind offered American presidential help in arranging such a New York loan if the General would call an armistice and hold early elections. Huerta refused this bare-faced bribe. Lind, with permission, threatened that President Wilson would recognize the Constitutionalists or intervene directly in Mexico, but Huerta knew it was a bluff. The Constitutionalists had not even formed a provisional government, and in the United States Senate a resolution fathered by Republicans asking for armed intervention in Mexico had been snowed under by presidential orders to the Democratic faithful.

But in answering Lind's notes, Huerta's Secretary of Foreign Affairs wrote that the Mexican Constitution prevented the provisional president from standing for reëlection. Lind took this back-handed comment as agreement that Wilson's terms for mediation had been accepted, and wired the President on August 27, 1913 that the mission was a success. It was not. Huerta had agreed to nothing, let alone resignation or mediation.

JOINING THE ISSUES

Upon receiving Lind's overoptimistic news, Woodrow Wilson went before Congress to explain his Mexican policy, his first major public statement on the matter. Part of Wilson's motivation was to quiet persistent demands for action, part to put public opinion against Huerta and on Wilson's side. He explained that patience was necessary and claimed that with his mediation efforts the United States had done its international duty; the next move was up to Huerta, to accept them, that is, resign. If he did not, he was an ingrate. Fighting might continue in Mexico, said Wilson, and therefore United States citizens were urged to leave, though the executive promised to protect those who did not. In a burst of rhetoric that was more emotional than logical, Wilson claimed that the United States was going to be "neutral" by embargoing arms both to the rebels and to Huerta; this, he said, was following the "best practices of nations," an untrue statement.

For about a month there was a honeymoon period, when tension relaxed. In September Huerta announced "his ardent desire to turn government over to a constitutional successor" and when Catholics named his Secretary of State as candidate for the forthcoming elections, Bryan privately wrote to Wilson "I feel that we have nearly reached the end of our trouble." The State Department announced it would recognize Gamboa if he were elected, even though the rebellious states of northern Mexico did not take part in the elections. Entrance of a new element, the British, disturbed the tranquillity.

Wilson sat back to await the outcome of Mexican elections called for October 26. They might liquidate the whole matter. If Huerta lived up to his tacit acceptance of Wilson's terms of mediation, constitutional government would return to Mexico. But from the Embassy in Mexico reports flowed to Washington that Huerta was busily rigging the election. News of Constitutionalist victories raised the President's hopes that the "good" revolution would triumph. The Constitutionalists had captured the rail center at Torreón and had cut Huerta off from his northern outposts. Huerta support began to wane rapidly.

Then on October 12 Huerta reacted understandably to the crisis. He scattered Congress (which had been elected with Madero) and imprisoned 112 deputies, exempting only the Catholic bloc. This action was termed "lawless" by Wilson, who immediately dropped all thoughts of recognizing the results of any election held while Huerta was still in power. On election day Huerta announced that so few people had turned out to express the nation's will that, though a new (Huertista) Congress would be seated, he himself would remain as provisional president—which he did until April 1914.

Wilson now bent his whole effort to ridding Mexico of Huerta so that the Mexican people could hold a real plebiscite and form a constitutional government that the United States could recognize. Appeals to Huerta's patriotism and cupidity had failed, as had bluffing. Wilson began a long feud with Huerta, who proved an agile and re-

sourceful opponent to the very end. Wilson's difficulties are an elo-
quent rebuttal to those who think it is a simple matter to dislodge even
a small-time Strong Man, under optimum circumstances. Short of
armed invasion, a last resort, nothing worked. Wilson tried nearly
every other trick in the book before that. Even armed force proved no
major success, but rather was a tragic accident.

.   .   .

Strung along the Panuco River that empties into the Gulf at Tampico were foreign-owned oil installations—wells, storage tanks, and a
little refining apparatus. The petroleum colony, chiefly British, were
apprehensive that purposely or accidentally Mexicans might set these
strategic properties afire in an engagement between Federalists or
Constitutionalists. British, French, German, and even Spanish war vessels converged to protect the threatened interests of their nationals.

Since Taft's day, at least, the American Navy had been patrolling
Gulf waters. One battleship was permanently at Tampico, while
others hung off Veracruz. As Secretary Knox once said, the purpose
of the battlewagons was to keep Mexicans "in a salutary equilibrium,
between a dangerous and exaggerated apprehension and a proper degree of wholesome fear." Wilson's feelings about the danger of the
Mexican situation could be gauged by the number of vessels hovering
in Gulf waters. With a major battle for Tampico looming, he had the
Navy outnumber and out-gun the combined European units there.
Admiral Mayo commanded at Tampico, while Admiral Fletcher, with
a smaller force, stayed at Veracruz.

Various national naval commanders warned both Constitutionalists
and Federalists away from the oil installations. None had qualms
about enforcing their warnings with action. With a critical battle
going on, Tampico was tense. It was in this atmosphere that a German gasoline salesman rushed aboard Admiral Mayo's flagship and
reported that seven American sailors and an officer had been arrested
and jailed by Huerta's men.

From a dock that everyone had been forbidden by Huerta's Federalists to use, these Americans had been loading gasoline into a
whaleboat flying the American flag. Ordered out of their boat by the
government patrol, they had been marched off to the Tampico prison.
Immediately Admiral Mayo sent his aide to the Huertista commander
and demanded the release of the men. Apologetically General Zara-

gosa explained that his subordinate had made a mistake, and the Americans were released. The whole incident from beginning to end had not occupied an hour.

Admiral Mayo, however, decided that the Mexican explanation was an inadequate recompense for the indignity to the United States Navy. He sent his chief-of-staff (in full uniform) to the commander with an ultimatum: by six o'clock the following evening General Zaragosa was to "hoist the American flag on a prominent position on shore and salute it with twenty-one guns, which salute will be duly returned by this ship." Moreover, the Mexican officer responsible for the "humiliating arrest" of American personnel was to be court-martialed, and a written apology from General Zaragosa was to be sent to Admiral Mayo. Thus spake the Navy for the United States.

Almost simultaneously two other aggravating Mexican incidents occurred. In Veracruz one of Admiral Fletcher's mail orderlies had been arrested and taken to jail by an overzealous Mexican soldier; there had been a Navy reward posted for an AWOL sailor and the optimistic Mexican had hoped that this was the right one. Then, unaccountably, cable messages from Mexico City to the United States were held up for nearly twelve hours by the Mexican censor, just at a time when wires were buzzing to straighten out the Tampico and Veracruz incidents. These matters were lifted from local handling to the hands of the respective national leaders. Huerta faced Wilson.

Huerta was willing to apologize in written form to Mayo and to court-martial the unfortunate officer, but he would not salute the American flag with twenty-one guns, the main issue at stake. It would have been political suicide to do so, since he was buoyed up to a great extent by posing as the stalwart defender of Mexican nationalism; even if he did fire the salute, he was running the risk that the United States might not return it—disastrous to his prestige! With alarming incidents coming so close together, Wilson's mind linked them together as a plot to discredit the United States. He had no realization of the intense anti-foreign atmosphere and the normal minor peccadilloes of Mexican life.

On April 13 Wilson spent the whole day studying what he ought to do. He had convinced himself that Huerta was deliberately launching a campaign to lower the dignity of the United States. Wilson delayed his decision until John Lind returned on April 14. As Lind was a heated proponent of intervention his advice did little to weaken the

President's determination. Here was an issue that warranted intervention, unsullied by dollars or issues over property. Nobody could vote against an insult to the flag.

INTERVENTION

At his cabinet meeting on April 14 Wilson announced that he was going to make a strong naval demonstration against Huerta. The whole Atlantic fleet was then ordered to Tampico, an additional seven battleships and six smaller vessels to complement the units already there. The three at Veracruz were to remain. The Navy warned Wilson that such a concentration might lead to war. Apparently Wilson was aware of the risk he was running; when he left his cabinet he remarked "If there are any of you who still believe in prayer, I wish you would think seriously over this matter between now and our next meeting."

Huerta would be shown that Wilson's bluffing was over when firepower surrounded him. Yet Wilson did not want war. The United States naval commanders were told that the Administration wanted no hostilities. This, then, was an out-size bluff. Until Huerta fired the salute, the Navy would patrol Mexico and cut off needed supplies, which Huerta was purchasing in Germany.

Wilson and Bryan then wrote a soft note to Huerta. They appealed to his "military honor" to fire the salute. The agile Huerta suggested that the whole matter of the demands be submitted to the International Court of Arbitration at the Hague. Wilson remarked to visitors that this was "one of the humors of the situation." The Fleet would reach Tampico about April 22, and Wilson had to inform the country about the mounting crisis. He had decided that the salute must be fired, or else. Or else what? No detailed plans were made beyond that.

On Saturday, April 18, Wilson sent a last ultimatum to Huerta. The President gave him until noon Sunday to fire the salute or Wilson would lay the whole matter before Congress. At the very last minute, Huerta's Minister of Foreign Affairs—José López Portillo y Rojas—informed the American Chargé d'Affaires that Huerta would fire the salute if the United States would guarantee to return it immediately. The Chargé hurried this proposal off to Washington, where Wilson brushed it aside. The hour passed; no salute.

Bryan set about convening a joint session of Congress for Monday afternoon, April 20. The President was in West Virginia, writing his speech and a resolution giving him permission to use the armed forces against Huerta to secure his "recognition of the dignity of the United States." On his return, the President was jaunty, well-rested, and sanguine that his schemes were working well. He told reporters "I have no enthusiasm for war. I have enthusiasm for justice and the dignity of the United States, but not for war."

The cabinet meeting on Monday morning modified Wilson's plan. Wilson learned that his projected naval blockade had two serious loopholes: the interdiction of Mexican ports could not, under law of nations, affect third parties—German or British vessels could load or unload their cargoes of munitions at will. Secondly, Huerta was even at that moment receiving a ponderable supply of stores which might tide him over. On Sunday the steamer *Mexico* had unloaded a thousand cases of ammunition. Due soon was the German vessel *Ypiranga* bringing 200 machine guns and 15 million rounds of cartridges. The blockade scheme had to be revised.

The seizure of Veracruz was therefore at this meeting substituted for a naval demonstration off Tampico. The object was capture of Huerta's incoming munitions. The timing of the new operation had to be nice. The only way the Americans could prevent ammunition on the *Ypiranga* from passing into the Mexican president's hands was to seize it on the dock after it had been unloaded, but before it could get transshipped toward Mexico City. Thus at the end of the cabinet meeting on Monday morning all knew that there was going to be a landing at Veracruz. The time of it would be set by the arrival of the *Ypiranga*.

Next on Wilson's tight schedule that crowded day was a conference with Congressional leaders. As a show of bipartisanship in national crisis, Wilson called together the Republicans and Democrats on the House and Senate Foreign Relations and Affairs Committees and read them his speech and resolution. Henry Cabot Lodge, a powerful Republican, objected to both, but with seeming arrogance Wilson silenced him.

In his Congressional message on April 20, 1914 President Wilson rehearsed the three Mexican incidents and asserted that they would lead to an unwanted war if allowed to continue. Even if conflict should come, he stated, it would be only against "General Huerta and those who adhere to him," not against the Mexican people.

After reaffirming his intentions to respect the sovereignty and territorial integrity of Mexico he requested that Congress approve his use of armed force. There was little or no jingoistic talk in Congress, as in 1846. But Wilson's earlier handling of Lodge now bobbed up to plague him. By accident, the Republicans had a temporary majority on the Senate Foreign Relations Committee, which they used to embarrass and harass Wilson.

Lodge refused to allow passage of the resolution as drawn by Wilson. He pointed out that it lacked any references to loss of American life and property, and that the United States could not threaten by name a foreign person, however obnoxious; governments, yes; individuals, no. He wanted all references to Huerta cut out and loss of property and life inserted as the causes of intervention. All Wilson's and Bryan's cloakroom buttonholing could not get the unamended resolution through in time to authorize a landing on April 21, the date the *Ypiranga* was to arrive. When the normal party balances were restored it was passed April 23. But without his resolution, Wilson went ahead with his altered plans, the details of which occupied his attention now.

After his Congressional speech Wilson called a private conference. To advise him, the senior admirals and generals were present, as were Lind, Bryan, and Daniels. Certain technical difficulties had appeared. Mayo's units could not get from Tampico to Veracruz in time to help Fletcher, and the bulk of the fleet, now deflected toward the southern harbor, would not arrive until even later. There might be inadequate forces to take the port. Everyone agreed that it was to be taken, and that Admiral Fletcher would have to do the best he could. The civilians, including Wilson, were convinced that the Mexicans would not fight. When the definite arrival time was known, Washington would flash orders to Veracruz to set Admiral Fletcher in motion. Everyone went to bed for a while.

Later in the evening Bryan got word about the *Ypiranga*'s arrival. It would be 10:30 A.M., April 21. Wilson had Josephus Daniels (later Ambassador to Mexico) order the Navy to carry out the agreed scheme. About 8:30 A.M. on April 21 Admiral Fletcher, who had been alerted earlier, received the fateful orders: Take Veracruz. He immediately made arrangements with the Huertista commander to turn over to him unopposed the customhouse and docks. At 11:30 A.M. the United States Navy took the principal Mexican port.

An hour later the *Ypiranga* hove into port. All sorts of legal and international difficulties ensued about that ubiquitous Teutonic vessel. She was temporarily impounded and spent some time evacuating Americans. Finally, with the once important original munitions still in her hold, she docked at Puerto Mexico on May 26 and calmly unloaded them. It turned out that months before and all through the American military occupation of Veracruz, munitions had been reaching Huerta through this secondary port.

The actual taking of Veracruz on April 21 seemed to be moving like clockwork. During the afternoon, however, the Mexican civilian population, led by 200 Mexican naval cadets of the Veracruz Academy, opened lively fire on the few American Marines and sailors. Admiral Mayo withdrew them to his two battlewagons for the night and awaited the arrival of the rest of the fleet. Next day the enlarged force pulverized the Naval Academy and put an end to fighting by naval gunfire. The casualties of the occupation were 19 American dead, and 71 wounded; the Mexicans lost over 300, including some naval cadets.

When Wilson got news that fighting had actually occurred, with unexpected deaths involved, he was appalled and unnerved. He had not wanted trouble; it could lead to even more serious conflict. Both Huerta and Carranza immediately issued strong statements condemning the occupation and demanding the withdrawal of American personnel. Pancho Villa came to the favorable attention of Americans by stating that the American military forces could remain as long as they liked, just so they did not enter Constitutionalist territory.

In the United States, recruiting offices were jammed, but nobody quite knew whether the United States was at war with Mexico or not. This was the chief end product of moral imperialism. A national sigh of relief went up on April 24, 1914 when the Ambassador of Brazil and the Ministers of Argentina and Chile in Washington jointly offered their good offices to mediate the difficulties between the United States and Mexico. Wilson recovered his nerve, swapped Army occupation for the Navy in Veracruz, and accepted the Latin-American mediation offer. Huerta was still in power in Mexico City, more than a year after the vendetta had gotten under way.

2

LANSING-ISHII AGREEMENT

(1917)

Excellency:

I have the honor to communicate herein my understanding of the agreement reached by us in our recent conversations touching the questions of mutual interest to our Governments relating to the Republic of China.

In order to silence mischievous reports that have from time to time been circulated, it is believed by us that a public announcement once more of the desires and intentions shared by our two Governments with regard to China is advisable.

The Governments of the United States and Japan recognize that territorial propinquity creates special relations between countries, and, consequently, the Government of the United States recognizes that Japan has special interests in China, particularly in the part to which her possessions are contiguous.

The territorial sovereignty of China, nevertheless, remains unimpaired and the Government of the United States has every confidence in the repeated assurances of the Imperial Japanese Government that while geographical position gives Japan such special interests they have no desire to discriminate against the trade of other nations or to disregard the commercial rights heretofore granted by China in treaties with other powers.

The Governments of the United States and Japan deny that they have any purpose to infringe in any way the independence or territorial integrity of China, and they declare, furthermore, that they always adhere to the principle of the so-called "open door" or equal opportunity for commerce and industry in China.

Moreover, they mutually declare that they are opposed to the acquisition by any Government of any special rights or privileges that would affect the independence or territorial integrity of China or that would deny to the subjects or citizens of any country the full enjoyment of equal opportunity in the commerce and industry of China.

I shall be glad to have Your Excellency confirm this understanding of the agreement reached by us.

Robert Lansing

THE SECRET PROTOCOL

In the course of the conversations between the Japanese Special Ambassador and the Secretary of State of the United States which have led to the exchange of notes between them dated this day, declaring the policy of the two Governments with regard to China, the question of embodying the following clause in such declaration came up for discussion: "they (the Governments of Japan and the United States) will not take advantage of the present conditions to seek special rights or privileges in China which would abridge the rights of the subjects or citizens of other friendly states."

Upon careful examination of the question, it was agreed that the clause above quoted being superfluous in the relations of the two Governments and liable to create erroneous impressions in the minds of the public, should be eliminated from the declaration.

It was, however, well understood that the principle enunciated in the clause which was thus suppressed was in perfect accord with the declared policy of the two Governments in regard to China.

Robert Lansing
K. Ishii

3

THE LAST CRISIS
ERNEST R. MAY

No one knows or can know what went through Wilson's mind in those decisive days of March. He talked revealingly to no one. Such letters as he wrote were formal or perfunctory. During much of the time his superb analytical powers undoubtedly sought every possible alternative. He had by this time acquired considerable knowledge and experience in international politics. Few emotional attachments remained to blur the precision of his thought. Over a period of more than two years he had canvassed the subject of German-American relations with a wide range of advisers, especially with his shrewd and perceptive friend, House. It is true that he could not foresee what actually was to happen in 1919 and after. Nor could he foretell Brest-Litovsk, the offensives of 1918, and the expeditionary force of two million men. Otherwise, it can be assumed, he reviewed every consideration that any analyst has been able to imagine in restrospect.

The one clear alternative was that which Wilson had rejected before. He could surrender, asserting that American property losses would be the subjects of postwar claims. He could ask legislation in the spirit of the Gore and McLemore resolutions to prevent the loss of American life. There was no longer a compelling economic reason for resisting the German blockade. America had become so prosperous that she could afford to lose part of her trade with the Allies.

Reprinted by permission of the publishers from Ernest R. May, THE WORLD WAR AND AMERICAN ISOLATION, 1914–1917, Cambridge, Mass.: Harvard University Press, pp. 426–432, Copyright, 1959, by the President and Fellows of Harvard College. Footnotes omitted.

The unrestricted submarine campaign had seemed thus far to be relatively ineffective. Statistics published at the beginning of March indicated only slight increases in Allied tonnage losses.

Nor was it evident that acquiescence would injure the visible security interests of the United States. Despite the Zimmermann note and other warnings of German activity in Latin America, Wilson had not retracted his earlier assertion to House that no European power offered an immediate menace to the United States. A relatively long period of recovery would be necessary for Germany, he had said, even if she triumphed in Europe. And he had little or no reason to suspect that Germany would win, even if the United States tolerated the U-boat blockade. Page warned him, it is true, that the Allies were on their last legs, but Wilson had long made allowance for Page's excitable temper. Other reports from London, Paris, and even St. Petersburg exhaled confidence. No longer regarding the Allies as upholders of law and civilization, Wilson had said time and again that America's interest lay in a peace without victory. There was no reason for him to believe in March, 1917, that this interest precluded acquiescence in the recent German decree.

What did make it impossible was the fact that it would sacrifice America's prestige and moral influence. At the outset of the submarine controversy it had seemed apparent that America would not live up to her potential if she allowed her citizens to be denied the free right of travel. Partly to demonstrate that the United States was a power entitled to respect and deserving of influence, Wilson had taken the cautious gamble of resisting indiscriminate U-boat warfare. Each subsequent diplomatic victory had committed America's prestige more deeply. The submarine issue had also become the symbol of Wilson's willingness to stand up for the rule of law, for international justice, and, as he termed it, for the rights of humanity. If he now retreated he would, in effect, prove America incapable of exercising influence compatible with her population, resources, and ideals. He would demonstrate her Pharisaism, her inability to endure martyrdom for what she believed right. In view of his conviction that her own future turned upon her ability to prevent a recurrence of war, he simply could not accept the pacifist alternative.

Acquiescence was not, of course, the only alternative. Another was armed neutrality. American ships could be provided with guns. They could defend themselves against U-boats. The United States would thus be upholding her principles while waging only a very limited war. Professor Carlton J. H. Hayes of Columbia University had prepared a long and compelling memorandum outlining the virtues of this course. It would make clear that the United States opposed only Germany's illegal and immoral method of warfare. It would allow America to escape military involvement on the continent and leave her unentangled in the intricacies of Allied ambitions and European power rivalries. The President had read this memorandum before asking Congress for power to arm merchantmen. From his address at that time and from other comments, it is evident that this alternative had some attraction for him. While it is comparatively simple to infer his reasons for rejecting pacifism, it is rather harder to sense the rationale that led him away from limited belligerency.

One consideration undoubtedly was the practical difficulty of devising a suitable policy. The Navy Department sketched for him the alternative methods of carrying out an armed neutrality. One was for American ships to acknowledge the legal right of U-boats to conduct visit and search but to resist unlawful attacks. A second was for them to treat German submarines as hostile craft when encountered inside the war zone. A third was to treat U-boats as hostile craft wherever met and to attack them on sight. Each course presented obvious difficulties. One invited torpedoings; the second risked them; the third was not very different from a state of war.

Armed neutrality in any form involved a further danger of blurring the issues. American merchantmen might err in sinking submarines. Especially if the United States were to follow the third of the navy's three forms of armed neutrality, American captains were likely to act in excess of zeal. The result might easily be an American *Baralong* case, which the Germans might employ as a moral pretext for war. Armed neutrality would, in any case, allow Germany to choose her own time and occasion for opening hostilities.

Even so, Wilson could still have elected the alternative. He had always shown a disposition to postpone crises. It would not have been out of character for him to adopt a policy that threw the choice of peace or war back upon Berlin. The keys to his final decision probably lay first of all in his complete mistrust of Germany, secondly in his emphatic desire to preserve domestic unity, and thirdly in his conception of America's probable war effort.

He could no longer expect Germany to be deterred from any action by fear of war with the United States. Responses to the pressures applied during early February had indicated total indifference. Not only had Zimmermann asserted that there was no turning back, but a semiofficial newspaper (the Berlin *Lokal-Anzeiger*), quoted in the United States, had declared, "As to the neutrals—we can no longer be bothered by their opinions." In his message to Congress asking authority to arm ships, Wilson had referred to uncompromising statements by German officials and by the German press. The Zimmermann telegram itself had indicated no more than that Germany anticipated war. Wilson was more shocked apparently by the method of its dispatch. Zimmermann had sent the message to Bernstorff for forwarding, using State Department cable lines which had been opened for the sake of peace discussions. Coupled with Zimmermann's insouciant admission that the telegram was genuine, this revelation seemed to demonstrate that Germany no longer saw any advantage in keeping the peace. The *coup de grâce* for any lingering hope came in Bethmann Hollweg's address to the Reichstag, delivered on the day after Wilson requested power to arm merchantmen. According to the State Department's report of this speech, Bethmann spoke of America's "subjection to English power and control"; he declared that the severance of relations was meant neither to protect freedom of the seas nor to promote peace but only to help "starve Germany and increase bloodshed"; he ended by asserting, "now that our sincere desire to promote peace has met with nothing but ridicule at hands of our enemies there is no longer any retreat for us—nothing but 'Forward.'" It appeared from Wilson's perspective as if there were no longer a moderate party in Berlin. Whether the United States declared war or simply proclaimed an armed neutrality, Germany was likely in either case to treat her as an all-out enemy.

In view of this probability, Wilson undoubtedly foresaw difficulty in maintaining a mere armed neutrality. At the moment it seemed as if most of the country approved such a course. Many neutralists and some pacifists reluctantly accepted armed neutrality as an alternative to war. But chauvinism was visibly on the rise. The Zimmermann telegram and the sinking of the Cunard liner *Laconia*, with three Americans among the lost, had created a spreading excitement. The *Literary Digest* reported newspapers all over the country to be joining in clamor for war. The pacifists who filibustered against armed neutrality were widely denounced as traitors, and Tumulty advised the

President that these passions were not likely to cool. The President could also see, of course, the latent strength of pacifism. Bryan had thrown all his enormous energy into an outcry against war. Pacifist and socialist groups across the land joined him. But these forces remained for the moment inchoate and disorganized. The Zimmermann telegram and the *Laconia* sinking had shaken them. It was foreseeable, nevertheless, that a long period of armed neutrality would allow pacifists to regroup. Wilson had reason to believe that German agents were seeking to organize and finance them. Another intercepted German dispatch told of $50,000 to be spent in this cause. Future incidents would meanwhile strengthen and embitter the chauvinists. Other *Laconias* were certain to sink. Even as Wilson sat mediating in the White House, five American ships went down. Other disclosures like the Zimmermann telegram were also probable. There were suspicions, for example, of German activity in troubled Cuba. Armed neutrality was likely therefore to divide the country into irreconcilable groups.

From Wilson's standpoint such a division was dangerous to all his objects. He sought national unity for its own sake. He also sought it in order that the United States might influence the peace settlement. As the extremist factions grew, with erstwhile neutralists and nationalists swinging toward either pacifism or chauvinism, the inner strength of America would weaken. As it was, moreover, the extremist leaders differed with Wilson over the conditions of lasting peace. The winter had seen a queer alliance between pacifists like Bryan and Borah and chauvinists like Roosevelt and Lodge. They had joined in attacking the proposed League of Nations. If their respective followings should grow as a result of armed neutrality, the President might find it impossible either to exert significant influence over Europe's peacemakers or even to guide them by his own ideals.

If Wilson had foreseen the AEF of 1918 and the casualties of Chateau-Thierry and the Meuse-Argonne, he might still have chosen armed neutrality as a course that at least postponed full-scale war. His decision to reject this alternative probably grew in part out of a reasonable, if mistaken, estimate of what war would require. No statement by an Allied leader had indicated pressing requirements for manpower. Field Marshal Sir Douglas Haig had recently said, indeed, that he needed only ammunition and rolling stock to achieve victory in 1917. His prediction of early triumph had been reaffirmed

by General Brussilov, and the Russian revolution, so far from seem
ing to spell withdrawal from the war, was interpreted as an ever
which would strengthen her against Germany. The President knew
of course, of the War Department's plan for an expeditionary force
and when the Allies subsequently asked for men he readily complied
But 500,000 was the limit set by army planners, and most of these
were to be regular troops or volunteers. The draft, for which Wilso
called in his war message, was to replace these men at home station
He need not have been inwardly shaken by the thought of sendin
into the trenches men who went there willingly. He evidently con
ceived of America's war effort as designed primarily to reinforce th
Allies with arms, supplies, money, and naval craft.

The relatively small difference that he saw between armed neu
trality and war was vividly indicated in a letter written after he ha
decided on war. It was written, indeed, after he had composed h
stirring message to Congress. Answering a Progressive who advo
cated armed neutrality, Wilson asserted, "To defend our right on th
seas, we must fight submarines. . . . Apparently, to make even th
measures of defense legitimate we must obtain the status of bellige
ents." Expecting America to fight mainly with her factories and ship
Wilson chose war in preference to armed neutrality.

This is not to say that the President found the choice easy. N
matter how little American blood appeared in his imaginations, w
remained horrible to him. He had never ceased to express disgust fo
its barbarity and for the passions it aroused. He was well aware th
divisions into extremist factions would be avoided only at the price
uniting the country in animal hatred of a foreign enemy. He was n
at all sure that American institutions and ideals could emerge u
scarred. He was simply more sure that they could not survive if th
end of the war did not spell the end of all wars. The same dream
peace that had entered into all his diplomacy finally led him par
doxically to a decision for war.

WILSONIANISM AND LENINISM, THE IDEOLOGICAL CONFLICT

N. GORDON LEVIN, JR.

he world views of both Woodrow Wilson and Vladimir I. Lenin, ke those of most messianic political thinkers, were centered on a ominant faith or myth. At the core of Wilson's political creed was a onception of American exceptionalism and of the nation's chosen ission to enlighten mankind with the principles of its unique liberal eritage. In Lenin's case, the central myth concerned the imminent beration of mankind from liberalism, capitalism, and imperialism rough the means of a proletarian revolution led by a knowledgeable ocialist vanguard. From this basis, Leninist ideology would challenge ot only Wilson's ultimate goal of a capitalist-international system of ee trade and liberal order, but also the President's final decision to hieve this aim by fighting a liberal war against Germany in the terests of universalizing self-determination and democracy through- t Europe. In 1917, these two mutually exclusive visions of world story came directly into conflict when Lenin and Wilson both came, almost simultaneously, major historical actors.

BERAL AND REVOLUTIONARY SOCIALIST CRITIQUES F IMPERIALISM

'oodrow Wilson's vision of a liberal world order of free trade and ternational harmony did not oppose but rather complemented his

om *Woodrow Wilson and World Politics: America's Response to War and volution*, by N. Gordon Levin, Jr., pp. 13–18. Copyright © 1968 by Oxford Uni- rsity Press, Inc. Reprinted by permission. Footnotes omitted.

conception of the national interests of American capitalism. By the turn of the century it was clear to Wilson that the growth of the American economy, especially in heavy industry, meant that America would soon be competing for the markets of the world with the other major industrialized powers. The future President also correctly saw that the Spanish-American War and the subsequent annexation of the Philippines marked the realization by the nation that the next frontier to be conquered consisted of the fertile export market of Asia. Indeed this new frontier had to be conquered lest the United States burst with the goods its new industrial system was capable of creating. On the eve of his first presidential campaign, Wilson told the Virginia General Assembly that "we are making more manufactured goods than we can consume ourselves . . . and now, if we are not going to stifle economically, we have got to find our way out into the great international exchanges of the world."

A constant *leitmotif* in Wilson's speeches both before and during his campaign for the presidency in 1912 was the concern that recession and stagnation might overtake the American economy if exports were not drastically increased. Wilson also insisted that, in order to achieve the commercial expansion necessary for American prosperity it would be necessary to remove certain structural defects in the American economy. In this connection, he emphasized the inadequate credit facilities provided by American banking institutions for export expansion and also stressed his opinion that the merchant marine was inferior to those of America's competitors in international trade. Wilson also attacked the high protective tariff because, among other reasons, its rates brought retaliation against American goods by other countries. The essence of trade was reciprocity, and one could not sell unless one was also willing to buy. Wilson had no doubt that technological efficiency guaranteed American success in international commercial competition, and that, given a chance, "the skill of American workmen would dominate the markets of all the globe."

Wilson's Secretary of the Treasury, William G. McAdoo, was no less convinced than the President that American economic stability was dependent on the movement of surplus products into the main stream of foreign commerce. He championed, therefore, all Wilson's efforts to remedy the defects in American capitalism which were inhibiting our export expansion. In the same vein, McAdoo worked tirelessly throughout most of Wilson's first term for the passage of an act to create a government-supported merchant marine to prevent

oreign competitors from shutting the United States out of world mar-
:ets by discriminatory freight rates. McAdoo also understood that
eciprocity was basic to any effort to avoid depression by a policy of
xport expansion and that for this reason, among others, Wilsonian
fforts to lower the tariff were wise. Finally, McAdoo was fully aware
f the relationship of banking reform to the growth of America's com-
nercial role in the world. Writing in the summer of 1915, McAdoo
aid of the Federal Reserve Act that "this great piece of financial legis-
ation has put this country in position to become the dominant finan-
ial power of the world."

In this general area of commercial expansion, it is also significant
hat, under Wilson, Chairman Joseph E. Davies and Vice Chairman
:dward N. Hurley of the Federal Trade Commission conceived of the
ole of the FTC, in part, as one of coordinating joint government-
usiness efforts to make American capitalism rational, co-operative,
nd efficient. Davies and Hurley hoped thereby both to enhance the
tability of the American economy and to increase its competitive
otential in world trade. In late 1915, Davies proudly announced at
n exporters' convention that it was the purpose of the Federal Trade
:ommission to aid "in the development of the power and greatness
f this nation as an industrial, commercial and financial nation in the
vorld." In a similar vein, Secretary of State William Jennings Bryan
old the first National Foreign Trade Convention, meeting in Wash-
1gton in the spring of 1914, that the Wilson Administration was
earnestly desirous of increasing American foreign commerce and of
videning the field of American enterprise." Bryan also emphasized
hat the State Department would work to "obtain for Americans
quality of opportunity in the development of the resources of foreign
ountries and in the markets of the world."

It is little wonder that Wilson's speeches and letters in 1916
adiated pride in what his first Administration had done to promote
.merican trade abroad. Time and again Wilson stressed the aid given
y the Federal Reserve Act, the Federal Trade Commission, and the
:ommerce Department to American exporters, and called on the
ation's business leaders to rise to their global opportunities. It should
e noted, however, that the Wilsonian program of commercial expan-
ion did not go uncriticized domestically. On the Right, some Repub-
can and Progressive nationalist spokesmen, such as Theodore Roose-
elt, Albert Beveridge, George Perkins, and Henry Cabot Lodge, were
ot willing to see tariffs lowered as a means of increasing exports, and

they were not averse to having exports expanded by the alternate
method of international economic rivalry backed by naval preparedness. On the Left, socialists questioned the very concept of trade
expansion itself, arguing that there was no real surplus to export, but
only those goods which the lower classes were not able to consume
at existing price and income levels. Beyond the question of under-
consumption, socialists and some radical liberals also saw a danger of
navalism, imperialism, and war in any vigorous program of export
expansion. In the Center, however, the Wilsonian position implicitly
held, against both conservative and radical critics, that it was possible
to have economic expansion and yet to avoid such traditional imperialistic practices as protection, economic warfare, and navalism. Yet, in
order fully to understand how Wilson could ideologically fuse commercial expansionism with a form of anti-imperialism, it is now important to grasp that, for the President, export was the necessary
material aspect of a national mission to spread the values of American
liberalism abroad in the interests of world peace and international
liberal-capitalist order.

In essence, Wilson approached the question of America's export
trade from the perspective of the Puritan sense of "a calling." Like the
Puritans, who placed earthly vocations, or callings, in a larger context
of service to God and man, Wilson saw the enlargement of foreign
commerce in terms of a duty in the service of humanity. During the
early years of the war, and American neutrality, the President coupled
his exhortations to American businessmen of commercial expansion
with a messianic conception of the service which America was able to
provide to a suffering world whose productive facilities had been
upset by the struggle. "The war," he claimed, "has made it necessary
that the United States should mobilize its resources in the most effective way possible and make her credit and her usefulness good for the
service of the whole world." In this sense, the competitive advantage
in world trade which America possessed due to her technological and
productive efficiency was, for Wilson, not a threat to other nations
but rather a godsend. The peaceful triumph of America in the markets
of the world was, therefore, to be both a service and a lesson for
suffering humanity. In Wilson's terms:

> America has stood in the years past for that sort of political under-
> standing among men which would let every man feel that his rights
> were the same as those of another and as good as those of another,

and the mission of America in the field of the world's commerce is to be the same: that when an American comes into that competition he comes without any arms that would enable him to conquer by force, but only with those peaceful influences of intelligence, a desire to serve, a knowledge of what he is about, before which everything softens and yields, and renders itself subject. That is the mission of America, and my interest, so far as my small part in American affairs is concerned, is to lend every bit of intelligence I have to this interesting, this vital, this all-important matter of releasing the intelligence of America for the service of mankind.

The fusion which Wilson made here of America's economic and political missions reveals the roots of the President's combined vision of moral and material expansion. The commercial health of America was, for Wilson, the visible evidence of underlying political and moral strength. Having ideologically unified liberalism, capitalism, and missionary-nationalism, Wilson never doubted that "all the multitude of men who have developed the peaceful industries of America were planted under this free polity in order that they might look out upon the service of mankind and perform it." For the President, the extension of American trade around the world was inseparable from the export of American liberalism. In his eyes the national purpose was one of seeking "to enrich the commerce of our own states and of the world with the products of our mines, our farms, and our factories, with the creations of our thought and the fruits of our character." Toward the end of his first term, Wilson addressed a Salesmanship Congress in Detroit in words that speak volumes as to the unity of his world view of liberal-capitalist expansionism:

This, then, my friends, is the simple message that I bring you. Lift your eyes to the horizons of business; do not look too close at the little processes with which you are concerned, but let your thoughts and your imaginations run abroad throughout the whole world, and with the inspiration of the thought that you are Americans and are meant to carry liberty and justice and the principles of humanity wherever you go, go out and sell goods that will make the world more comfortable and more happy, and convert them to the principles of America.

5

THE VERSAILLES PEACE CONFERENCE

ARNO J. MAYER

The internal politics of the victor and defeated nations never ceased to infringe on the diplomatic labors of the Big Four. Throughout Europe and, to a lesser degree, in America, similar underlying conditions gave rise to unsettling and urgent political issues and pressures.

Soon after the exaltation over the Armistice subsided it became glaringly obvious that instead of settling major and divisive domestic issues, the war had actually exacerbated them. Especially now that a Socialist Revolution had swept Russia and threatened to sweep other countries, economic and social questions claimed first priority. Before the war, when the national capitalist economies were prosperous though unstable, the forces of order had remained adamant in the face of labor's insistent and organized agitation for the forty-eight-hour week, collective bargaining, welfare legislation, and tax reform. In 1919 reactionaries and conservatives threatened to become still more unyielding. In addition to denouncing even reformist labor and Socialist leaders for harboring Leninists projects, they claimed that the war had exhausted the exchequers and that the economies could not afford new overheads for social programs. They further stated that graduated income taxes would discourage innovative entrepreneurs from renewing and modernizing their plants, and that higher wages would impair the nation's competitive position in international trade.

On the other hand, labor and Socialist leaders were determined to cash in on the promises made to them when they accepted the political

From POLITICS AND DIPLOMACY OF PEACEMAKING, by Arno J. Mayer, pp. 559–564. Copyright © 1967 by Arno J. Mayer. Reprinted by permission of Alfred A. Knopf, Inc.

truce; there simply could be no question of returning to prewar conditions. They angrily refused to enter a second political truce, this one to be dictated by the harsh exigencies of recovery and reconstruction. Even the Social Patriots could not afford to advertise their moderation because they, too, were subject to radical pressures. The entire Left was energized by the example of Russia, the flood of new—and primarily young—recruits into the Socialist parties and trade unions, and the expansion of the franchise. At this same time the strains of reconversion gave a tangible stimulus to the impatience and clamor of labor: in the post-Armistice year the wage earners were hardest hit by the rising cost of living and by unemployment due to rapid demobilization, cancellation of war contracts, and shortages of raw materials. Not least important was the political isolation of organized labor and the Socialist parties, now that the specter of Bolshevism was frightening the radical bourgeoisie into the camp of the forces of order.

Because the Right dominated the legislative chambers as well as the press, the militants of the Left favored compensating for their Parliamentary weakness by having recourse to such extraparliamentary tactics as mass demonstrations, strikes, and, in the extreme, mutinies.

Especially in the victor nations the Right made effective use of its Parliamentary strength. Wilson was concerned about the opposition of Lodge rather than La Follette. He also realized that should Clemenceau or Lloyd George be overthrown, more intransigent premiers would replace them. In Italy, meanwhile, he hoped to use Bissolati and Turati to pressure Orlando into standing up to Sonnino and his supporters.

. At any rate, each of the Fig Four took time out to face his legislature at least once in efforts to quiet the seething right-wing rebellion; and not only Lloyd George but also Wilson, Clemenceau, and Orlando were each served with a summons signed by forbidding groups of defiant right-wing parliamentarians enjoining them to impose a harsh peace. Significantly, most of the same lawmakers who advocated a Carthaginian peace also were champions of the domestic *status quo;* only their reactionary and proto-fascist allies wanted domestic changes which were unacceptable to traditional conservatives. For the time being, however, conservative nationalists furtively welcomed the support of these jingoists in the battle for the stiff peace which they proposed to exploit in the interest of maintaining and consolidating the existing power structure. The campaign against the League Covenant in the U.S. Senate was designed permanently to arrest the New Freedom; the campaign for exorbitant reparations in Britain and France was calculated to obviate the need for tax and social reform; and the campaign for the annexation of Dalmatia in Italy was meant to help the Right explode the Socialist contention that Italian blood had been shed in vain.

With varying degrees of enthusiasm and disingenuousness the Big Four used the existence of these concerted right-wing pressures to justify selfish national demands: Wilson held out for the Monroe Doctrine rider, Lloyd George for astronomical indemnities, Clemenceau for a 15-year lease on the Saar, and Orlando for Fiume. Furthermore, the Russian policy of all four, but especially of Wilson and Lloyd George, was influenced by the anti-Bolshevik rampage of their right-wing critics.

The Socialists and trade unionists also made themselves heard and felt. Their Parliamentary leaders persistently raised questions, initiated debates, introduced resolutions, and moved votes of no confidence. However, such Parliamentary maneuvers invariably backfired; for these debates and votes merely dramatized their Parliamentary weakness, isolation, and impotence. Whereas La Follette, Wedgwood, Cachin, and Turati succeeded in registering their Wilsonian and reformist dissent, Lodge, Kennedy Jones, Franklin-Bouillon, and Salandra—supported by the jingoist fringe—moved in to marshal impressive votes for resolutions which either upheld the government or called on it to hold out for "twenty-four shillings to the pound" in peace negotiations and in vital domestic affairs.

Not that the Socialist representations were totally useless. By flaying the government and the Right in the hostile legislative halls the elected deputies not only publicized the Left-dissident cause but also slowed down the rise of the militant Socialist and labor leaders outside Parliament. Moreover, with regard to Allied intervention in the Russian Civil War this Parliamentary agitation had a decidedly restraining though not deterrent influence. Especially in Commons and in the *chambre* the dissenters exposed and dramatized the mutinies, warned of future military disobedience, protested the expense of the intervention, and castigated the Allies for making common cause with reaction in Russia as well as in the border states.

But even this Parliamentary critique of intervention would have been considerably less effective had it not been vigorously reinforced by extraparliamentary action. In fact, the deputies repeatedly and belatedly echoed the protests and exposés of the militant spokesmen of the parties, the unions, and the left-wing press. Without strikes and mass demonstrations and without lingering threats of coordinated direct action in the form of a general strike the Allied Governments and Parliaments would have expanded the intervention in Russia and would have refused the forty-eight-hour week. Presently, most of the leaders—in Parliament, in party councils, and in the unions—recognized that foreign and domestic policy could not be divorced from one another. They rightly estimated that substantive reforms were contingent on a Wilsonian peace and on the survival of the Russian Revolution. Should the superpatriots have their way at the Peace Conference and in Russia, they would use the political capital gained with this foreign policy triumph to get out of whatever reforms they had agreed to in the interest of maximum war production and under the duress of post-Armistice labor unrest.

Not surprisingly, therefore, the political overtones of the strikes of 1919 became increasingly pronounced. As of late March work stoppages—whether on the factory, municipal, regional, or national level —ceased to be narrowly or primarily industrial. In addition to demanding the forty-eight-hour week without a cut in take-home pay, the workers struck or threatened to strike for a Wilsonian peace, against intervention in Russia, and for basic structural changes. Eventually, by late May, the Allied Socialist and trade union leaders—and by no means only the Zimmerwaldians among them—decided that only a simultaneous general strike in Britain, France, and Italy could advance their political-*cum*-industrial cause. The abortive general strike of July 21–22, 1919, to protest the continuing intervention in Russia, was the outcome.

In their own countries the Big Four were more responsive to and intimidated by the Right than the Left. In viewing the defeated nations, however, they were worried about the danger of Bolshevik-type revolutions rather than about right-wing coups. In private even Clemenceau, Pichon, and Foch conceded that at this particular juncture in Central and Eastern Europe Bolshevism was a greater threat than Prussian militarism. Of course, as compared to Wilson and Lloyd George, they were much more resistant to blackmail: they calculated that without contact with Soviet Russia—which the *cordon sanitaire* precluded—the Spartacists could not take over; thus they were not easily frightened into giving either food or a lenient peace.

Still, when Károlyi turned over power to Béla Kun *all* the delegations were equally stunned and terrified. Whatever the ultimate diplomatic and military purposes of Colonel Vix's *démarche* may have been, neither Clemenceau nor Foch could have wished or anticipated this turn of events. Even though there were internal causes—political, economic, social, and military—for the Bolshevik ascendancy in Budapest, these were overshadowed by the external slights to Károlyi's liberal regime and to the Magyars' inflamed national arrogance. While the Big Four, *pour décourager les autres*, readily agreed to take every necessary measure first to isolate and then to crush Béla Kun, they continued to differ about the most effective way to prevent similar defiances elsewhere.

Until March 22 Allied realists considered Wilson unduly alarmist whenever he warned that the imposition of oppressive peace terms on the unstable governments and unsettled social and economic conditions of the defeated nations could produce catastrophic results. Hereafter such warnings could no longer be dismissed quite so lightly, particularly since the volcanic eruption in Hungary was followed by serious tremors elsewhere. There were authentic reports of an imminent collapse in Vienna; a Soviet-type republic was proclaimed in Bavaria; strikes broke out in the Ruhr, in Hamburg, and in Saxony; the sailors of the French squadron at Odessa mutinied, thus hastening the evacuation of this strategic Black Sea port; and the Red Army stayed Kolchak's advance and continued to push ahead in the Ukraine. To make matters worse, these worrisome developments in the defeated empires coincided with the upsurge of labor unrest in Britain, France, and Italy.

For the Wilsonian cause this convergence may have been fatal. At first it seemed that the President could only benefit from a renaissance of the Left in the Allied nations and from the panic which the Hungarian *coup de tête* produced in Paris. Certainly Lloyd George's Fontainebleau memorandum pointed in this direction. But the Right was quick to realize that leniency in Paris would merely encourage and fortify the Left in its direct-action campaign—that success would breed success.

Hence, the forced-draft campaign by the right-wing press, Parliamentary majorities, and satellite pressure groups to commit the three Allied Premiers to a Carthaginian peace was as much designed to contain the reformist Left at home as to root out the Revolution in

Russia and Hungary. The 300-odd Unionist members of Parliament not only challenged Lloyd George to keep his election promises with regard to indemnities and to streamline the operations against the Soviets; they were equally vocal in their insistence that the domestic demands of the miners, the T.U.C., and the Triple Alliance be rejected.

An additional consequence of this panic among the *traditional* Right was the encouragement of the *new* Right: in America the Red Hunt and the Centralia Massacre; in Britain the condoning of Brigadier General Page Croft and of the Amritsar Massacre; in France the shrill voice of the *Action Française;* in Italy the formal organization and the paramilitary sorties of Mussolini's Fascist anti-party party; and in Germany the ready reliance on the *Freikorps* to clean up the Ruhr and Bavaria, with Hitler an interested observer of the bloody liberation of Munich in early May 1919. Simultaneously, the intervention in Russia was capped with the recognition of Kolchak while General Mannerheim, Admiral Horthy, Dmowski, and Brătianu became increasingly welcome allies in the anti-Bolshevik freedom fight.

This uneven and uncoordinated drift toward conservatism, reaction, counterrevolution and proto-fascism resulted in the ruin of Wilsonianism and the erosion of moderate Socialism. Among Socialists and trade unionists, and notably among the young post-Armistice recruits, an apostasy of momentous dimensions and significance set in. It now appeared that Lenin's indictment of Wilson and Wilsonianism was not altogether without merit: however reluctantly, the President was one of the chief movers of the counterrevolutionary enterprise. Next to his role in the intervention and his consent to British, French, and Rumanian grabs, his ordering of the *George Washington* to Brest was at best a well-intentioned gesture. As for the Fiume appeal, he delayed it until after the cardinal British and French claims had been satisfied, thereby leaving the impression that he was trying to recover his virginity at Italy's expense. Furthermore, he did not return to his wartime and pre-Armistice diplomatic tactics until after the peak of the March-April crisis, in part for fear of excessively endangering the stability of the Allied Governments.

PART 3
REPUBLICAN
FOREIGN POLICY,
1921-1933

INTRODUCTION

For many years students of American history have debated the question: Was the United States isolationist in the 1920s? Some authors support the affirmative; others, who describe American policy as dynamic and expansionist, defend the negative. Regardless of the label attached to American foreign policy during the period from 1921 to 1933, the Republican administrations then in power eschewed as far as possible any direct political commitments outside the Western hemisphere (because the American people and Congress would not permit them) and concentrated on promoting the greatest possible scope for American trade and investment throughout the world. The American government had good reason for pursuing this goal, for the American response to wartime demands for goods had clearly demonstrated the enormous productive capacity of the United States. Furthermore, during the war America ceased to be a debtor nation and became the world's greatest reserve of capital. Consequently the United States in the 1920s found itself in need of markets for its goods and dollars.

Demand throughout the world for both these commodities was great, and to finance the purchase of goods and to make possible the use of dollars, American banks began making foreign loans. The Harding administration soon became aware, however, that many bankers were willing to lend money for projects even though such projects were not in the national interest or in keeping with the government's objectives; thus, in an effort to encourage loans only toward desirable ends, Washington devised a policy for the bankers' guidance. The government favored loans promoting trade and investment either directly by granting credits to be spent for goods in the United States, or indirectly by contributing to the economic and political stability of the borrowing country. The government's rationale for the indirect method rested on the theory that a nation torn by internal conflict and suffering from economic stagnation would be a bad customer. More specifically, the government frowned on advances for objectives harmful to American interests, the promotion or creation of monopolies, for example, or to countries which did not meet their obligations to the United States. Washington also discovered that the promise or refusal to grant a loan furnished excellent leverage in sticky negotiations.

In Latin America, of course, the United States had, since the days of Theodore Roosevelt, used loans as both carrot and stick in its efforts to foster stable governments, and from Taft's time had reinforced money with troops. The Republican administrations of this period continued to collect customs receipts in the Dominican Republic, Haiti, and Nicaragua. During this period American military contingents appeared off and on in Nicaragua, disappeared from the Dominican Republic, and were seemingly permanently ensconced in Haiti. During the 1920s central and municipal governments of Latin America contracted for a large number of loans from American banks, and the State Department blatantly used American capital as a vehicle for enforcing reforms in an effort to promote greater political stability.

Ever since the outbreak of the revolution in 1910, Mexico had confronted the United States with difficult problems. Furthermore, relations between the two countries were complicated by geographical propinquity, what with anti-Americanism prevalent among the Mexicans, and condescension toward Mexicans widespread in the United States. Diplomatic relations during this period were topsy-turvy: broken off in 1913, they were restored in 1917, only to be severed again in 1920 because of a revolution. Without American recognition Mexico found it difficult to get foreign capital. A big obstacle to recognition was the constitution of 1917, which embodied some socialist concepts, and which provoked the United States into regarding Mexico in much the same light as it did the Soviet government. Walter Scholes in Reading No. 1 describes how the State Department overrode American bankers' desire to lend money in order to make money; the Department insisted that Mexico not receive a loan until she agreed to certain specific conditions, including safeguards for American property.

With the onset of the depression, Latin American countries faced extremely difficult times. As the exchange of correspondence between Secretary of State Stimson and Moncada, the President of Nicaragua, suggests, the United States was not overly sensitive to the problems of underdeveloped nations plagued by political unrest and threatened by economic collapse. (Reading No. 2) Although both men agreed that a government's chief duty was to preserve law and order, they did not agree on the means to that end. Confronted by a fall in government revenues, the Nicaraguan President wanted to reduce the size of the national guard and cut back payments to American bankers, economies which would permit him to pay the army and civilian office holders and to proceed with the small public works projects under way. In this way he hoped to provide a certain amount of public employment and thus keep the Nicaraguans quiet. He also wished to concentrate his efforts on the more densely populated areas of the country. Except for a minor concession, Stimson rejected these suggestions. He insisted that the solution to Nicaragua's problems lay in building roads in the remote provinces, since, he argued, adequate means of communication would enable the army to control the bandits.

Although it offers a revealing insight into the American attitude toward underdeveloped countries, Stimson's Nicaraguan policy was of less concern to the State Department than the problem of formulating policies toward Europe. Since Europe played the greater role in America's economic life, the problems of Europe demanded more attention from the United States government than did the problems of Latin America. The key to European recovery after the war was Germany, and in the face of the Europeans' failure to solve that problem, the United States intervened. The resulting Dawes Plan (a sort of mini-Marshall Plan) brought economic and political stability to Germany by settling reparations payments and providing the Germans with a large loan. Carl P. Parrini in Reading No. 3 interprets United States relations with the European powers as a struggle to dominate the world market and the world economic community, and the Dawes Plan as reflecting a European concession of defeat. At the same time, the Europeans' great need for capital forced them, most importantly Great Britain, to retreat from their insistence on the closed door and to yield to American demands for the open door, especially in oil-producing regions. However—as Parrini argues in another chapter in his book—the United States did not live up to the obligations imposed by leadership; rather, it used its great power to develop its own national economic interests at the cost of a stable world economic community.

After World War I the powers faced two major problems in China. The old imperialist system, whereby the antagonisms mutually felt among the major powers prevented any one of them from becoming dominant, had been seriously impaired by the war. Russia and Germany no longer counted, whereas Japanese influence was greatly enhanced. Secondly, China was a nation divided in two: the disorganized national government of the war lords at Peking controlled only a fraction of the country, while the revolutionary government at Nanking, supported by Chinese liberals, controlled part of southern China. More important perhaps than either government was the strong tide of nationalism which began to sweep over China after the spring of 1919—a movement which demanded reforms. The reformers were antiforeign in that they wanted the powers to relinquish their rights in China and allow the Chinese to control the nation's destiny. On the other hand, aware of what Western technology had done for Japan, the reformers were eager to import the new ideas into China.

The United States desired order and stability in China too, and the Washington Conference in 1921–1922 signalled the Americans taking the lead in establishing a new basis of order in Asia. By means of the Washington Conference treaties, the United States tried to eliminate all vestiges of the imperialist system and to replace it with a new international code of conduct which all the powers at the Conference pledged themselves to observe (Reading No. 4). Although one of the chief objectives of United States policy was to curb Japanese expansion, initially the Japanese went along with the new code. The future success of the new arrangement depended on cooperation of the powers among themselves and with China, but since the Conference did not satisfy the national demands of the Chinese, they persisted in trying to break free of foreign control. When Chinese efforts appeared to be successfully challenging Japan's interests, the Japanese in 1931 disassociated itself from the new system, and forcibly moved into Manchuria and ultimately into China proper. The United States and Great Britain could not agree on a joint policy, and although each blamed the other for its hesitation to act, neither power was in fact willing actively to oppose Japan. China was thus left to face her enemy alone.

1

REACTION TO REVOLUTION: HUGHES' MEXICAN POLICY

WALTER V. SCHOLES

Although Mexico had won its political independence in the 1820's, almost a century later it was still—in fact if not in theory—a colonial dependency: the economic fief of foreign capitalists and the political fief of a local elite with whom the foreigners were allied. The revolution that began in 1910 and culminated in the constitution of 1917 expressed the Mexicans' determination to manage their own society, a process repeated by a few other underdeveloped nations after World War I and by many more after World War II. The constitution of 1917 marked out a new road: it deviated from capitalism toward a Mexican brand of socialism administered under a one-party system of government.

Mexico's revolution strained United States-Mexican relations because of the attacks on Americans and their property and the confiscatory implications of the new constitution. Since the Harding administration was no more willing than its predecessor to tolerate a move to the left on its own doorstep, it used every form of political and economic pressure on the Mexican government to check the radicalization of social and economic life and to insist on the legal rights of property as defined by the United States.

By 1915 Venustiano Carranza, who had proved himself the strongest of the generals, had pacified the country enough to win

From *Jahrbuch Fur Geschichte von Staat*, Wirtschaft und Gesellschaft Lateinamerikas, Band 6. Reprinted by permission. Footnotes omitted.

de facto recognition from the United States. Late the following year Carranza called a constitutional convention, and since he favored a gradualist solution to Mexico's problems while others demanded a more radical approach, the document promulgated in 1917 was a composite of both tendencies.

Four articles in particular embodied the demands of the radicals. Articles 3 and 130, reflecting the strong anti-clericalism in the country, were designed to curb the influence of the Catholic church. The first made primary education the sole responsibility of the government, and the second prohibited any political activity by the clergy. Article 123 guaranteed to labor certain conditions of employment which were very favorable by North American standards: the eight-hour day, a minimum wage, the right to organize and strike, and welfare benefits. Article 27 gave the government authority to expropriate large landed estates, for which it would compensate the owners, and distribute the acreage to the landless. It also vested in the nation direct ownership of all subsoil deposits including minerals and petroleum. Mexico was thereby reverting to the doctrine taken over from Spanish law that had been in force until the 1880's when individuals were permitted to acquire title to the subsoil. Although Carranza did little to implement these constitutional provisions, their inclusion in Mexico's fundamental law disturbed a great many Americans, who regarded them as atheistic and socialistic.

Although in later years Mexico's treatment of the Catholic church would arouse great indignation in the United States, in 1917 the most pressing question dealt with the rights to subsoil deposits. Was Article 27 retroactive and could it be applied to titles acquired before 1917? When the United States agreed to grant Carranza *de jure* recognition shortly after the constitution was promulgated, it apparently did so on the basis of Carranza's private promises that Article 27 would not affect the oil companies' rights. And although he did not in fact claim the subsoil for the nation, Carranza in 1917 and 1918 issued two decrees taxing the oil companies so stringently that the State Department suspected that he was trying to confiscate the fields in a retroactive policy of nationalization. In addition the 1918 decree was so worded as to imply that the companies owned only the surface of their land and seemed to concede to them merely a preference for concessions to work the subsoil.

While the United States was objecting vigorously to what it regarded as implementation of the constitution, Carranza was losing support at home for not making that document effective. In view of the temper of the people, this was a grave mistake. When he compounded his error by trying to pick his successor in 1920—the constitution forbade re-election—Alvaro Obregón led the revolt which ousted him from office. Obregón was then elected to the presidency, taking office on December 1, 1920.

For too long Mexicans had been exploited by their own and by foreigners. Now, in a groundswell of opinion that the President could ignore only at his own peril, they were demanding land and labor reforms—the constitution in action. If Obregón wanted to continue in office, he would have to make some concessions to both the rural and urban workers. By choosing to do so, he inevitably came into conflict with foreign governments especially the United States.

When Obregón sought American recognition, Wilson's Secretary of State, Bainbridge Colby, demanded that he pledge, in writing, to establish a mixed claims commission to judge the claims of foreigners whose property had been damaged during the revolution, not to enforce the retroactive provision of the 1917 constitution, and to recognize and service Mexico's foreign debt. Although Obregón readily gave oral assurances on all three points, he refused to put them on paper. The State Department would not accept this reply; Carranza too had made verbal promises.

When Hughes took over the State Department both the new appointees and the holdovers failed utterly to grasp what was involved in the Mexican revolution. The consensus was that the Mexicans were an inferior people who had been led astray by unscrupulous leaders. The State Department's representatives in Mexico made constant references to the "unruly agrarian and labor organizations and the rowdy elements generally," and indicated that "the reds have Mexico by the throat." North American leaders believed that granting land to the peasants would disrupt the entire economy because of the "innate indolence of the people." Undersecretary of State Henry Fletcher wrote to the President that the predominant elements in Mexico seemed bent on applying to property "the principles of present day Russia."

It was an unlikely prospect, therefore, that Washington under Harding would listen to the Mexicans any more sympathetically than it had under Wilson, which proved to be the case. As a matter of fact, Albert B. Fall boasted that Obregón would have to "sign on the dotted line." In an attempt to get Obregón to sign, Hughes proposed a Treaty of Amity and Commerce whose text included Colby's demands. In addition Articles 4–6, 8, and 10 guaranteed the open door by establishing complete equality of trading opportunity.

Although Presidents Harding and Obregón exchanged friendly letters through an intermediary and tried to explain to one another their respective positions, Obregón steadfastly refused to sign the treaty. Since he had privately agreed to the American position, he felt that the United States was questioning his word, as indeed it was. Furthermore, Mexican national pride would not tolerate making such concessions in writing to win recognition; for Obregón signing the treaty would be tantamount to political suicide. Recognition must come before signature.

In June 1921, during the treaty negotiations, Mexico substantially increased the export duties on oil. Although the government was in desperate need of money, the tax was more than a revenue measure: it was part of a design to take money from one set of capitalists (oilmen) as a guarantee to persuade another set of capitalists (bankers) to grant Mexico a loan. Claiming that the taxes were confiscatory and that few companies could ship oil except at a loss, most of the oil companies discontinued shipments in July.

When the American consul in Tampico, the port from which most of the oil had been exported, forecast probable disturbances in the city directed against Americans and American capital and advised precautionary measures, the Navy immediately ordered a warship to proceed to the port. The consul's fears proving groundless, the vessel was quickly withdrawn. Fletcher's remark to Dearing of the State Department that the Navy had gone off "half-cocked" seems to imply that the Navy acted without consulting the State Department.

In August, with the State Department's blessings, the oil companies sent representatives to Mexico City in an effort to reach some arrangement on the tax question. But when the companies consulted the Department on the advisability of discussing a loan with Mexican authorities, Fletcher made it clear that the Department strongly objected to lending the Mexicans any money until they accepted the American prerequisite for recognition, the Treaty of Amity and Commerce. Otherwise, Fletcher warned, nothing would restrain the Mexican government from levying new taxes whenever it needed money. In early September Mexico and the producers signed an agreement postponing the effective date of the June export tax increase until

December 25; until that date the companies could ship their oil tax free but would remain subject to a monthly production tax.

On August 30 the Mexican Supreme Court offered a ray of hope to the oil producers and the State Department. After considering an appeal by the Texas Oil Company, the court ruled that any company that had committed a "positive act" before 1917 to develop its oil holdings could continue to own the subsoil. Unfortunately the difficulty here was that a single ruling by the court did not establish a precedent; that required five consecutive favorable decisions.

Late in 1920 Mexico passed agrarian legislation to implement Article 27 of the constitution, giving the President authority to expropriate large land holdings and to distribute the land among the peasants. The United States accepted this principle provided as stated in the treaty proposed in 1921, that expropriation was resorted to only on proper grounds and not exercised without due process of law or the prompt payment of just compensation. Compensation became the issue and led to protracted wrangling between the two governments. Washington insisted that the central government of Mexico act as paymaster so that it would not have to deal with the various states. But the political climate in Mexico and the differences of opinion between the various state leaders and the national government made it impossible for the Obregón administration to assume the responsibility. Between February and June 1922 Hughes and the Mexican Minister of Foreign Affairs, Alberto J. Pani, exchanged notes without results. Mexico insisted that recognition precede a claims settlement on confiscated property; Hughes reversed the order of priority. And he wanted the agreement in writing because the word of the President of Mexico was no guarantee; both Carranza and Obregón had defaulted on their promises.

In June Hughes and Pani suspended their correspondence while awaiting the outcome of conversations in New York between the Mexican Minister of the Treasury, Adolfo de la Huerta, and the representatives of the banks and of the oil companies. William G. Teagle of Standard Oil of New Jersey, spokesman for the Petroleum Committee, and his counterpart for the International Committee of Bankers on Mexico, Thomas Lamont of J. P. Morgan and Company, kept each other fully informed on the talks. Although Hughes did not want it known, he kept in contact with all negotiations through Harold Walker of the Mexican Petroleum Company.

Lamont had tried earlier in Mexico City to persuade the government to make payments on its foreign indebtedness but had failed completely. Now, however, he and the Minister of the Treasury signed the Huerta-Lamont agreement by which the Mexican government recognized an indebtedness of over one billion pesos (about a half billion dollars) on account of bonds and notes issued largely prior to the Mexican revolution, including a half billion pesos in railroad indebtedness. Mexico also recognized interest arrearages of 400 million pesos, which it agreed to repay over a forty year period starting in 1928. Until that date Mexico would meet current interest partly in cash and partly in scrip paying three per cent; after 1928 payment would be in cash. To guarantee that it would pay, Mexico stipulated that between 1923 and 1927 it would turn over to the International Banking Committee all the oil export taxes, any railroad earnings, and the proceeds of a ten per cent tax on the railroads' gross receipts. In 1923 Mexico would pay a minimum of 30 million pesos in cash; each year thereafter the payment would increase five million pesos over the previous year.

To meet its external commitments and its domestic demands Mexico needed large sums of money and it was constantly trying to borrow abroad. On July 11, 1922, H. M. Branch, a Petroleum Committee representative, told Hughes that Mexico wanted the oil companies to advance $25,000,000 on petroleum taxes, the loan to be redeemed within at least five years. After pointing out that Obregón had not yet signed the Huerta-Lamont agreement, Hughes added that another arrangement worked out between de la Huerta and the oil men concerning future development of Mexico's oil fields was also awaiting Obregón's signature.

Besides these specific reasons for discouraging a loan, the Secretary referred to the uncertainties arising from future application of Article 27. It was true that the Supreme Court of Mexico had ruled favorably in the Texas Oil Company case, and apparently it had recently handed down the four additional decisions required to establish the precedent that Article 27 was not confiscatory or retroactive. Despite repeated efforts the Department had been unable to get copies of the recent cases, and in fact, it understood that they had not yet been officially published. Although Mexican officials had often stated publicly that congress would enact legislation explaining the terms of Article 27, no such law had been passed. In the absence of any executive, judicial, or legislative guarantees of American rights, the United States had proposed a Treaty of Amity and Commerce that included the necessary safeguards, but Mexico had not yet seen fit to negotiate a satisfactory accord.

In view of the Mexican attitude and also of the fact that the United States did not recognize Obregón, Hughes could not sanction a loan. He added, however, that if the petroleum companies wanted to give money to an unrecognized government, they were at liberty to do so. The Secretary had made his point: the oil companies did not pursue the matter. In late September 1922 Mexico approved the Lamont-Huerta agreement.

Hughes had spelled out his policy many times, and he reiterated it in Boston in October 1922. In the legalistic language of diplomacy he said that "When a nation has invited intercourse with other nations, has established laws under which investments have been lawfully made, contracts entered into and property rights acquired by citizens of other jurisdictions, it is an essential condition of international intercourse that international obligations shall be met and that there shall be no resort to confiscation and repudiation." In short, Hughes had two commandments for the Mexicans: thou shalt not expropriate property without immediate just compensation; thou shalt not deprive the oil companies of the subsoil under contracts granted before 1917. Although Hughes employed stern language, his position was moderate compared with that of the National Association for the Protection of American Rights in Mexico, which was demanding the annulment of Article 27 and all laws, decrees, and proceedings arising from it.

But despite the administration's hard line two events temporarily eased the strain in United States-Mexican relations. In February 1923 the American oil companies settled a tax dispute with the Mexican government by paying about 40 per cent of what the Mexicans claimed, around $6,750,000. Of greater importance was the Bucareli Conference held in Mexico City. Both Harding and Obregón had reacted favorably to the suggestion made by General James A. Ryan, a mutual friend, that they appoint representatives to engage in informal negotiations. Harding selected Charles Beecher Warren and John Barton Payne, and Obregón named Fernando González Roa and Ramón Ross. In May they began meeting in a building on Bucareli Avenue, which gave the conference its name.

Shortly after the delegates convened, Blair and Company consulted

Hughes about the advisability of lending the Mexican government $12,000,000 to help establish a bank of issue. The Secretary refused to discuss the matter, asserting that the State Department could not entertain the project of a loan to an unrecognized regime. He added petulantly that American citizens should support their government, not try to bolster regimes with which the United States was unable to enter into normal diplomatic relations. Late in July 1923, when the discussions in Mexico City had already made progress toward a settlement, Mortimer Schiff called on Hughes also to discuss a loan for a Mexican bank of issue. Since the Mexican government would probably not offer such favorable terms after winning American recognition, Schiff was anxious to conclude the deal at once. Hughes remained unswayed by these financial considerations. He told Schiff that he would best serve the United States' interests by delaying definite action until the negotiations with Mexico had ended. In other words, Mexico was to receive no encouragement until it had reached an agreement with the United States.

And by mid-August the conferees had worked out a compromise. The most important part of the undertaking—the agreements on compensation for expropriated property and oil rights—were included in what was termed an extra-official pact or gentleman's agreement. Although the wording of the text was imprecise, the Americans abandoned their demands that Mexico pay for expropriated lands in cash and agreed that part of the payment could be made in bonds. Any American citizen who felt unjustly treated could appeal to a special claims commission established under the agreement. In addition, a general claims commission would review all unsettled claims dating back to 1868. More important to the Americans was the Mexican government's pledge to respect and uphold the Supreme Court decisions on the doctrine of positive acts.

Convinced that the Bucareli Conference provided the guarantee of American rights that it had been demanding, the United States recognized the Obregón regime on August 31, 1923. The accommodation with the United States came at a fortuitous time for Obregón. When de la Huerta led a revolt against the government in December, the United States shipped arms to the national government while putting an embargo on military supplies to the revolutionists. Washington also facilitated the movement of Mexican troops by permitting them to cross American territory. Aided by these friendly acts, Obregón in the spring of 1924 was able to suppress the uprising. In the same year Obregón relinquished the presidency to Plutarco Calles who, by claiming that the gentleman's agreement did not commit his administration, revived the whole question of the petroleum companies' rights. This matter was not solved until 1927 when Mexico once again agreed to the position taken by the United States.

Many underdeveloped countries have learned a bitter lesson. As they try to win control of their own destinies, they need capital for economic development, which they can get only from the industrialized nations. The United States has always laid down conditions for loans, whether under the private loan system in the 1920's or the combined government-private loans later on. In many cases the concessions that an underdeveloped country has to make to the lender conflict with the demands of the masses and lead to an impossible domestic situation. In the 1920's Hughes, the State Department, and American economic leaders showed little or no grasp of the realities of the Mexican situation. Hughes would not alter his stand: no loans until the United States recognized Mexico; no recognition until Mexico conformed to North American standards. It is no wonder that Mexicans became even more anti-Yankee.

2

SECRETARY OF STATE STIMSON CALLS FOR LAW AND ORDER IN NICARAGUA, 1930

The Minister in Nicaragua (Hanna) to the Secretary of State

No. 222

MANAGUA, November 7, 1930.
[Received November 13.]

SIR: With reference to the Department's telegram No. 111 of October 31, 11 A.M., transmitting a message from the Secretary of State concerning the proposed reduction in the Guardia Nacional for delivery by this Legation to President Moncada and to the subsequent exchange of telegrams on this subject, I have the honor to enclose herewith a copy of the message as it was delivered to President Moncada.

I will not fail to keep the Department advised of developments in this important matter.

Respectfully yours,

MATTHEW E. HANNA

[Enclosure]
The Secretary of State to the President of Nicaragua (Moncada)

In conjunction with the Secretary of the Navy and other Navy officials I have most carefully considered the present situation in Nicaragua with a view to doing anything possible to be of help in the two acute

Reprinted from FOREIGN RELATIONS OF THE UNITED STATES, 1930, Vol. III, pp. 675–693. Footnotes omitted.

ituations now confronting Your Excellency's Government namely, he disturbances and brigandage in the border departments and the nancial and economic difficulties.

You will I feel sure readily agree with me that the primary duty of ny Government is to maintain law and order. Unless this is done no ;overnment can stand. The situation in Nueva Segovia, Jinotega and stelí is the big problem now facing the Nicaraguan Government. his situation must be met by the Nicaraguan Government and all ossible resources of the Government devoted to its solution. This is he first and paramount duty and obligation of the Government.

Nicaragua's present economic and financial problem is fully appre-iated by us. The whole world is passing through a period of great epression and practically all governments are suffering from a hrinkage of income. The question before Nicaragua is how can the uty of suppressing banditry and the maintenance of order elsewhere i the Republic be met by Nicaragua's resources.

After very careful consideration and deliberation on our part I feel iat the best suggestion that can be made at this time and which idicates the utmost that my Government can do in the matter is as)llows.

While all estimates indicate that the preservation of law and order nder existing conditions requires an effective and efficient Guardia f a minimum strength of 2,000 at an annual cost of $1,000,000 exclu-ve of maintenance of penal establishments, my Government would evertheless be willing in view of the present financial depression to)nsent to continue to cooperate in the Guardia at a less strength if id after an auxiliary force of the nature of a local police hereinafter ientioned has been created and has proved effective. In this connec-on I beg to refer to the penultimate paragraph of your letter of)ctober 3, 1930, to General McDougal in which you promise to itroduce into the next Congress a measure providing for contribution y the municipalities to the cost of maintenance of municipal police. uch a measure would appear to be fair and reasonable and would in self, if it proved effective in operation, materially decrease the cost f the Guardia to the National Government.

I am sure that as a military man you will appreciate fully, Mr. 'esident, how essential it is that funds be provided regularly and romptly for the maintenance of the Guardia. If troops are not regu-rly paid there is a possibility of mutiny and other disorders and this

Government cannot assume the responsibility for exposing its officer
to such danger more especially in the exposed and isolated section
of the disturbed departments. I feel that Your Excellency having thos
considerations in mind will readily agree with me that I am making a
perfectly reasonable request when I ask you to give explicit and irre
vocable instructions to the Collector General of Customs to segregat
during each month as a first charge on the customs revenues afte
paying the expenses of the collectorship and the service of the deb
sufficient funds so that he can pay directly to the Chief of the Guardi
on the first of each month the full amount necessary for the expense
during the ensuing month of the Guardia at a strength of 2,000 men
This amount to be reduced as and when the two Governments consen
to a reduction in the strength of the Guardia.

I contemplate that the reductions in the Guardia will be made fron
detachments stationed in the peaceful districts so that not only wi
there be no reduction in the Guardia forces operating in the band
infested area but even if possible that those forces may be augmente
by a greater concentration there of the Guardia forces. This woul
in a certain measure leave certain municipalities and areas withou
police protection and I contemplate that this deficiency should be sup
plied by the municipalities themselves through the establishment c
local police which will be a branch of the Guardia Nacional to b
known as the Guardia Municipal or some other appropriate title ind
cating that it constitutes an integral part of the Guardia Nacional.

Your Excellency will recall that at Tipitapa we agreed that one c
the outstanding needs of Nicaragua was a nonpartisan police force c
Guardia to be trained up by the United States Marines and whic
would be the sole military and police force in the country. I feel con
fident that you will concur with me that our view then was sound an
is still sound as regards the requirements of Nicaragua, both for mil
tary protection and for the preservation of law and order. The Guard
Municipal would be under Nicaraguan officers to carry on polic
duties in each locality; its officers and enlisted personnel would k
recruited by the Guardia Nacional and it would have the same rel.
tionship to the Guardia Nacional as has the local police recentl
created in Managua which is an integral part of the Guardia Nacion
but is paid for from municipal funds.

What I have outlined above covers merely the day to day hand
mouth necessity of preventing the spread of banditry in Nicaragu

It does not cure the cancer. To bring about a permanent betterment in conditions not only in the bandit infested area but throughout the Republic as a whole I feel very strongly, Mr. President, that you should divert all possible funds from other public works for road building in the affected area. I would suggest that $50,000 per month or as much thereof as may possibly be provided be set aside for this work. I realize that to do this may mean cutting down the public works in other localities and that this in itself may create in such localities a problem of law and order preservation for the Guardia. I feel that the retrenchment of public works should first be done in areas where there is the least likelihood of disturbances. The building of roads in the affected area will, by providing work for the inhabitants of these bandit ridden provinces, tend to stabilize men who might otherwise be tempted or driven into banditry. At the same time it will provide means for opening up this very sparsely settled area, making it possible to establish farms and other productive enterprises which will add to the general economic prosperity of the country and it will provide the means of communication necessary to patrol the country and hence keep it in a permanent state of law and order. This now seems to me to be the best and surest way of solving definitely the problem which has been acute in Nicaragua for three years and which is no nearer solution now than it was when you and I met at Tipitapa. This proposal I think opens the way for a definite solution of the problem and if you will carry it out will be one of the most statesmanlike acts of your administration and one for which I feel you will receive the gratitude and recognition of your country in years to come. I am not minimizing the necessity of development in the more densely settled portions of Nicaragua but this is something which I feel must be postponed until more prosperous times in order that the threat of banditry which is now upsetting the whole structure in Nicaragua may be removed.

I know it will be difficult to find funds for this work but the suggestion that occurs to me is that the profits from the operation of the Pacific Railway might very appropriately be used to this end. The construction of these roads will open up new territory and will act as feeders for the railroad; furthermore, the revenue from the railroad is a comparatively new source of revenue to the Government as most of the profits in the past when the railroad was hypothecated to the bankers as security for their advances was used in paying interest and amortization charges on these advances. Now that the railroad has reverted to the Government the profits from the railroad could most profitably be used in further productive enterprises. This Government will be glad to loan the services of its officers and engineers in supervising the road construction work and any Marine equipment such as trucks, et cetera, that may be available.

I have gone into this matter at great length with Your Excellency because after mature deliberation the above offers the best chance see for meeting the situation the seriousness of which is fully appreciated and in no wise minimized by me. Your Excellency will appreciate, however, that the preservation of law and order is as I have said the first obligation of a country. This Government would hesitate to continue to cooperate with the Guardia unless its expenses are met and even so it would feel that the work, money and effort expended would be wasted unless the fundamental problem of banditry is solved. I therefore feel that this Government is going as far as it can in a helpful attitude to Nicaragua in saying that it is willing to continue to cooperate with the Guardia eventually reduced as set forth above if first the arrangement as above outlined is made for the prompt and regular payment of the Guardia and secondly, if funds for road building in the disturbed sections are provided in order to solve this basic problem.

Orderly procedure requires that the reduction of the Guardia be made as indicated above and I sincerely hope that after considering this matter you will agree with me that the reduction cannot be made drastically by November 15th as contemplated in your recent letter to General McDougal. I therefore earnestly request you, Mr. President, to agree to modify that order in the manner outlined above or at least to hold it in abeyance pending the final solution of the present problem.

November 6, 1930.

3

THE UNITED STATES
AND EUROPE, 1916-1929
CARL P. PARRINI

From 1916 to 1923 the Europeans threw up every conceivable roadblock
to the seemingly new American plan to manage the world's economy.
In reality the American plan was to displace the faltering leader of the
previous century, Great Britain. One by one American leaders tore
down the obstacles to United States commercial leadership and the
Europeans—with Britain in the lead—fell back to new positions, until
in 1924 they surrendered.

The Allies agreed with the American contention that the European
economy had to be reconstructed if the great damage wrought to the
European social system by the war was to be repaired and Bolshevism
successfully repelled. They were unwilling, however, to pay the financial cost of eliminating the economic and political dangers. In all
essentials they wanted Germany and the United States to bear the
financial burden. Indeed, on May 22, 1919, Lloyd George went so far
as to suggest to Wilson that the Succession States to the Austrian
Empire be required to share in Austrian reparations obligations,
explaining that they should not "get their freedom without paying
for it." If in the British view the Czechs and Hungarians were legiti-
mately bound to pay for Austria's cocriminality with Germany in
launching the war, so much more so were the Germans liable for the
various costs of the war. Lord Cunliffe, former Governor of the Bank

From Carl P. Parrini, *Heir to Empire*, Pittsburgh, Pa.: University of Pittsburgh
Press, 1969, pp. 248–259. Reprinted by permission. Footnotes omitted.

of England, a man educated to the facts of international economic and thus aware of the commercial disaster implied in his own proposal, argued that the Germans could sustain an overall reparation bill of $120 billion and an annual amortization of $5 billion. Lloyd George admitted that such a bill could never be paid, but insisted nevertheless that such an obligation should be written into the Treaty with adjustment possible later. By supporting Cunliffe in such an unworkable proposal Lloyd George undoubtedly hoped to score points for the British argument that reparations and inter-Allied war debts were intimately linked and to bring pressure to bear upon the United States for mutual cancellation of war debts. This would of course place the ultimate cost of financing the war upon American taxpayers German reparations obligations were to be reduced in relation to the amount of Allied debts the American Treasury might cancel.

But despite the ex post facto popularity of the view among European and American academics that as chief commercial victor in the war the United States should have been willing to cancel Allied war debts as a condition of Allied agreement to a practical reparations bill for Germany, United States leaders could not reasonably have been expected to accept any such proposal. President Wilson and the succeeding Harding Administration believed that German investment seized by the Allies in Southern, Eastern, and Central Europe and in the Turkish Empire, as well as the preferential trading agreements they had imposed on the weaker nations, were more than sufficient repayment for the costs of the war. Cancellation of war debts would simply provide additional spoils for the Allies, with American taxpayers footing the bill. American leaders were willing to cancel part of the war debts if the Allies would agree to a reasonable reparations bill for Germany, and if they would dismantle preferential trading agreements among themselves. But the British and the continental Allies were not ready to make concessions until their own preferential and closed door methods failed at the end of 1923.

It would have been impossible in 1918 and 1919 for British leaders to accept the relatively equitable American peace proposal. Public opinion in Britain during the war had been charged in the direction of a harsh peace, and so the British supported the successful French demand that Germany be denied her prewar commercial treaty rights for five years (as previously resolved at the Paris Economic Conference of 1916), while the Allies would continue to force Ge

many to give them unconditional most-favored-nation treatment. A
Germany deprived of any sort of steady markets for five years would
give to the Allies time in which to gain a lead on Germany in world
markets. Even the threat of a Bolshevik Germany, which such commercial restrictions posed, failed to move British leaders to fix a definite payable reparations figure.

The apparently more selfish view of Europe did not, as so many
Americans assumed, reflect the innate superiority of the American
plan. The differing British and American programs reflected the
disparate and conflicting national interests of each society. Leaders
of the European nations, with Britain in the vanguard, believed sincerely that they could begin to view the world as a community only
after they had satisfied pressing demands of national interest which
they defined as keys to their continued existence as viable states.

The leaders of Europe had of necessity to define conditions of
stability in terms of their own experience. The Europeans lost material
and human resources to such an extent that in the case of Britain, for
example, the population was threatened with severely lowered living
standards. Britain's means of creating national wealth, foreign investments, export markets, and access to vital industrial raw materials at
low cost, and its ability to perform international services in the fields
of insurance, shipping, and finance were considerably diminished. At
the same time the ability of the United States to expand its wealth
had grown immensely—to a considerable extent at the expense of
Great Britain. The British believed fervently that before they could
cooperate with the United States in rebuilding a world market with a
system of trade, payments, and investment encouraging growth and
expansion—in other words, a world similar to the one that had existed
for most of the century prior to 1914—they had first to rebuild their
own system of expanding national wealth. Together with France in
Europe and the self-governing dominions around the world, they
hoped to accomplish this by means of preferential trading agreements
and tariff assimilation. Indeed, such policies reflected a hard-headed
assessment of national interest. But so too did the more objectively
generous American program reflect national interest.

The difference among the great powers over priorities to be observed in building a world community of interest were compounded
by the fact that for the first time in a century the fundamental
system of values shared by the nations of Europe and North America

were dangerously challenged by the Bolshevik Revolution and, to an alarming extent, by the Nationalist revolutionary movements of the Arab East, North Africa, and China. Unlike the participants in the liberal and democratic revolutions of the nineteenth century, who wanted merely to extend to themselves full rights in a system based on parliamentary democracy and free enterprise, and who believed the system itself to be equitable, the leaders of the revolts growing out of World War I sought to destroy the existing system.

To a very large extent the outbreak of the Bolshevik Revolution, causing the first breach in the international system evolved up to 1914, was the result of the interplay of two factors to which World War I gave rise: (1) economically, the outbreak of war destroyed the delicate network of commercial ties which constituted the world market, diminishing the amount of real wealth available to each contestant for purposes of waging war and sustaining the civil population; (2) politically, the consequence of this economic breakdown and the eroded living standards it implied resulted in a loss of faith in and respect for traditional hierarchies of political authority. To a greater or lesser degree all the European combatants suffered civil disaffection. But in Russia the ideological impact was so great that it tended to throw up political power to any element capable of seizing it. Lenin recognized this reality and took advantage of it to seize power in Russia. He also urged revolutionary leaders in other countries, imperfectly enjoying the fruits of the existing international division of labor, to follow Russia's example.

But it was the war which gave the Bolsheviks an audience for their appeal; in the absence of the destruction of capital, natural resources and human life flowing from the war, few people, even in the weakest national segments of the pre-1914 international economy, would have had probable cause for protesting the way in which the world market distributed income and concomitant privileges. President Wilson showed that he understood this when he argued at the Peace Conference that the "poison of Bolshevism" was a "protest against the way in which the world had worked," the antidote to which was in Wilson's view a "new world order."

But while the world would benefit from the American version of a "new world order," the United States as the managing element in the recreated world market would benefit most. The United States was to be the "engine" of the world economy, which would haul the world to prosperity. The United States was the only nation emerging from World War I with a surplus of capital available to develop at long term the world's resources and to finance the world's day-to-day merchandise trade. Before any new resources could be developed the products of previous investment had to be marketed. The links between Europe and Latin America, among other prewar commercial ties, had to be reopened. But in order for Europe to buy from and sell to Latin America on anything like its prewar scale, Europe had to be reconstructed—both vanquished and victor nations concurrently. Simple reconstruction of the victors would not suffice, because markets would continue to be too narrow.

During the period 1918 to 1922 American bankers made an effort to finance the orderly marketing of primary products in Latin America. The system of branch banks the Morgan and Rockefeller interests established in Latin America during these years were largely designed to funnel short-term capital on deposit in the United States banking system into financing Latin American merchandise trade. But by 1922 these efforts suffered dismal failure; many of the American branch banks sank into insolvency and suffered considerable losses. This proved to American bankers, and to some extent American manufacturers and political leaders, that without the reintegration of Germany into a world economy, markets would continue to be too narrow to absorb even existing production, much less encourage the investment of American capital in the development of additional resources.

Since American leaders thought of a recreated world market as the only long-run basis for social stability and economic expansion, they concentrated their efforts on forging weapons with which to force the Allies to dismantle preferential trading agreements affecting areas which had changed hands as a result of the war and the peace treaty and to allow Germany to reenter the world economy without excessive reparations obligations. The United States created tools to attain the former objective when it enacted into law the Webb-Pomerene Act in 1918, the Edge Act in 1919, and the Fordney-McCumber Tariff in 1922. The American weapon to obtain a workable place for Germany in the world economy consisted of its ability to refuse to lighten the burden of the war debts the Allies owed the United States, until they in turn eased Germany's burden.

The American effort was successful. By the fall of 1922 Britain found itself unable to sustain its own program without extensive

United States investment in Europe and the underdeveloped countries.
New negotiations began on the subject of German reparations, with
Britain showing a strong willingness to compromise on the issue. The
same was true on the issue of closed door administration of the mandates. By the time of the Lausanne Conference of 1922 the British
acknowledged that the closed door had failed; and so they accepted
the open door in the Near East. Shortly thereafter, during 1923,
British and American banking officials began to cooperate closely in
matters of international finance, a move symbolized on a grand scale
by discussion of a joint loan by Anglo-American bankers to the
German government to stabilize that country's currency. On the more
mundane scale British banking leaders agreed that the pound and the
dollar could both be used profitably in the day-to-day finance of world
trade.

In 1922 and 1923 the United States leaders also made some concessions in order to obtain British and French adherence to the projected world community. For example, they expressed some willingness to discuss the extent to which British and other Allied war debts
to the United States might be scaled down. Treasury Secretary
Andrew Mellon agreed with his predecessor, David F. Houston, who
argued that cancellation, "does not involve mutual sacrifices on the
part of the nations concerned. It simply involves a contribution
mainly by the United States." He agreed too that any adjustment of
war debts would have to "take into account advantages obtained by
such debtor countries under the treaty of peace." Such advantages of
course included seized German investments, "discriminatory advantages and exclusive concessions."

But under neither Harding nor Wilson was the United States
unreasonable. With the active assistance of Mellon and over the confused opposition of such a future New Deal statesman as Congress-
man Cordell Hull (Dem., Tenn.), the Harding and Coolidge Administrations reduced the war debts on the basis of ability to pay. This
kind of distinction meant, of course, that Britain as the great victor in
terms of commercial spoils, and the wealthiest in terms of per capita
income, would have to pay a much higher percentage of its original
war debt than Italy with its much lower per capita income and its
impoverished southern regions. Indeed, Mellon defended the extent
to which the United States had reduced the debt against Congressional attacks urging a more intensive collection on two essential

grounds: 1) the Allies should not have to pay that portion of their debts which they had actually spent in fighting World War I; 2) it was in the national interest of the United States to "think of the financial reorganization of Europe along the same general lines as the reorganization of some large industrial corporation heavily involved after some severe depression. We have become, whether we like it or not, the most important creditor of Europe. In this capacity we are like the general creditors of the embarrassed corporation. Our money is in and we want it out, but it is impossible to get more than the debtor can pay. If we insist on too difficult terms, we receive nothing. We must then settle upon such terms as will give our debtor reasonable opportunity to live and prosper."

Rightly or wrongly, Mellon believed that the United States had fixed a level of payments that Europe could sustain and that would not interfere with the reintegration of the world economy and the development of world markets upon which the ultimate prosperity of the world depended.

Once it was clear in 1923 that the European Allies were willing to allow Germany to reenter world markets on a relatively equal basis, American political leaders were willing to encourage American bankers to float, jointly with British bankers, a $200 million loan to a new German Central Bank. But American participation was conditioned on the agreement that these Dawes loans would take priority over reparations payments. Two problems remained. Some means had to be found to enable Germany to make fixed reparations payments, and some means had to be found or created to allow Germany to sell its exports in world markets. American leaders thought the Dawes Plan would create a mechanism to deal with reparations and, at the same time, create conditions for the long-run expansion of markets for German exports.

American leaders also regarded the Tariff Act of 1922 as a contribution to a reintegrated world economy and a world community of interest. During the debates and hearings in Congress on the Fordney-McCumber Bill the various special-interest groups had about arrived at a consensus that reciprocity, the exchange of mutual tariff-cutting concessions, was the best way for each interest and the collective majority to expand foreign markets for American goods. But such reciprocal negotiations led inevitably to special bargains and discrimination among nations. They encouraged preferential arrangements which would have tended to prevent the reformation of a true world market based on nondiscrimination. Without an integrated world market, world trade would expand at a relatively sluggish rate. The Administration had to muzzle the influence of special interests in the writing of the tariff. It did so; the Tariff Commission, together with the State and Commerce Departments, wrote the basic clauses of the Tariff Act of 1922 in such a way as to offer to foreign nations access to the huge American market on condition that they accept the unconditional most-favored-nation clause as the underlying basis of the network of world commercial agreements.

Once the United States and its former co-belligerents compromised on such basic issues as war debts, Germany's reparations bill, the open door, and an American tariff facilitating the unconditional most-favored-nation clause as the governing principle in the framing of commercial treaties, the United States was willing to open its formerly locked gates to American capital investment abroad. In that connection too, American leaders believed that they made a significant contribution to a world community of interest. Under Herbert Hoover's direction the United States attempted to frame a foreign investment policy which would (1) guide foreign investments into ventures expanding the production of real goods and services, therefore benefiting both the investors and the capital receiving nation and (2) prevent wasteful investment which might impoverish both foreign investors and the peoples of the investment-receiving countries.

Without a doubt American foreign economic policy from 1916 to 1929 was a continuum. Wilson and his Republican successors desired an economic community of interest which the United States would manage, with the Western Europeans and Japan acting as associates with full rights in the system. That was, in all essentials, what the United States in fact created from 1916 to 1929.

PART 4
THE ROAD
TO WAR

INTRODUCTION

When Franklin Delano Roosevelt was inaugurated in March 1933, the outlook for world peace and prosperity was bleak. Roosevelt's Secretary of State, Cordell Hull, came to office a convinced advocate of freer trade as a solution to the world's political and economic problems, in that it offered the best means for preserving peace. If all nations would cooperate in expanding world trade, the result, he declared, would be a world politically stable and economically healthy. Hull not unreasonably maintained that a people living in a society with full employment would be opposed to war. (Reading No. 1)

But Hull got little cooperation from the major powers. During the Great Depression internal economic dislocations led to a breakdown in world trade patterns, and in their efforts to mitigate the calamitous domestic effects of the depression, many nations began pursuing policies of economic nationalism: restriction of the home market as much as possible to domestic producers by high tariffs, appeals to patriotism, quotas, barter arrangements, and in the British Commonwealth, empire preference. Moreover, Hull desired a world system based on law, order, and trade, but there were leaders operating in the world with quite different objectives: Mussolini urged the Italians to recreate their heroic past, Hitler promised the Germans the *lebensraum* to which they were entitled; and Japanese leaders brushed aside counsels of moderation and proceeded to consolidate their gains in Manchuria.

Just as they were for many nations in Europe and Asia the thirties were a period of great divisiveness for the United States. The disillusionment and cynicism with which many Americans now looked back at World War I were sharpened and intensified by Congressional investigations which suggested that the American public had been duped into entering the war by the propaganda of foreign nations and the greed of American financiers. The isolationists were determined never again to fight other nations' battles; the internationalists were convinced that unless the United States joined the other democratic nations in restraining totalitarianism, this country would inevitably face the aggressor alone. Throughout the 1930s isolationist sentiment prevailed and resulted in the neutrality legislation of that period.

Although Roosevelt's New Deal measures had not solved the baffling problem of continued unemployment and the domestic economic situation still preoccupied most Americans, by late 1938 events abroad began to claim more of both the public's and the administration's attention. Even Secretary Hull had abandoned his earlier confidence in the curative properties of his trade program, and he gloomily admitted that "the world was racing hell-bent for destruction." National aggrandizement, turbulent political movements, and wrenching social change dominated the events of the decade. Japan had made further gains in China; Italy had conquered Ethiopia; Spain was flaming with civil war. More ominously, Germany had introduced conscription, remilitarized the Rhine and annexed Austria and part of Czechoslovakia. The question was not "if" but rather "when" war would start.

Uncertainty ended with Hitler's attack on Poland in September 1939. The second world war began when France and England declared war on Germany. After easily defeating the Poles, Hitler made no move for several months (the Phoney War), but in the spring of 1940 he launched a blitzkrieg to which Norway, the Low Countries, and France quickly succumbed.

At the low ebb of the war in 1940, Britain stood alone, and Prime Minister Winston Churchill explained to President Roosevelt his country's plight. Britain needed enormous amounts of planes, ships, arms, and goods but lacked the cash to pay for them. Although the neutrality legislation greatly circumscribed Roosevelt's freedom to act, he believed that England's survival was a vital American interest and decided that the United States had to find some way of removing the "silly, foolish, old dollar sign." He solved the problem by the novel idea of lending goods instead of dollars, and in early 1941 he presented his Lend Lease Bill to Congress. After two months of heated

Congressional and public debate, both houses approved the bill and the President signed it in March.

The practical effect of Lend Lease was to announce to the world that the British and Americans had joined a coalition against Hitler. After Hitler attacked the Soviet Union in June 1941, Russia too received aid under the Lend Lease law.

Since most members of the Roosevelt administration believed that Japan, through the Tripartite Pact, was working with Germany and Italy, they tried to find some method for checking the Japanese. One means availed upon (in the Summer of 1941) was the imposition of an embargo by the United States on such vital supplies as oil and steel. But the climax came on December 7 when the Japanese attacked Pearl Harbor and the United States actively entered World War II. In Reading No. 2 Robert A. Divine summarizes the American position in relation to Germany and Japan just before the attack on Pearl Harbor.

Although the United States concentrated most of its attention in foreign affairs on Europe and Asia during the prewar Roosevelt years, the administration also promoted the Good Neighbor program in an effort to improve relations with Latin America. Dick Steward, in Reading No. 3, however, shows that the United States drove hard bargains in its economic relations with the Latin American countries.

1

CRUSADE FOR
ECONOMIC SANITY
CORDELL HULL

While striving to prevent the political fabric of the world from being rent completely to bits, I kept hammering home the economic side of international relations as the major possibility for averting the catastrophe, and advocating rearmament for our defense in case the catastrophe came to pass. When 1937 arrived, the Trade Agreements Act had been in effect nearly three years. It had demonstrated its capacity to augment trade by lowering our own tariff barriers and inducing other nations to do likewise and by lessening discrimination in commerce. Our trade with the fourteen countries with whom we had negotiated agreements was markedly increasing. International groups such as the Pan American Conferences and the League of Nations recognized the reciprocal trade agreements on the most-favored-nation basis as the most practical method of curing the world's economic illness.

The Trade Agreements Act, about to expire June 12, 1937, now faced a major struggle as we sought legislation to renew it. The Act had formed one of the most controversial points of the Presidential campaign in 1936, and I could foresee that strong opposition would rise against it during the debate in Congress. Many Members would be for killing it entirely, others would seek to emasculate it.

Before I left for Buenos Aires we had begun at the State Department to prepare for the struggle. In talking it over with the President I found he favored making the bill permanent, instead of limiting it to

Reprinted with permission of The Macmillan Company from *Memoirs* by Cordell Hull, pp. 518–525, 576–577. Copyright 1948 by Cordell Hull.

three years as in the present Act. I also preferred the permanent idea, but seriously doubted our ability to pass it; hence I stood for the three-year limit, because I felt the bill thus would have a better chance to pass the House and Senate. The bill went up to the House as the President wanted it, but the House Ways and Means Committee inserted the three-year limitation, and it was introduced in that form.

I appeared before the House Committee on January 21, and presented a statement to the Senate Finance Committee on February 10, arguing for renewal of the Trade Agreements Act. To both committees I stressed the role that bettered economic conditions throughout the world could play in alleviating the political tension. "There is not the slightest doubt," I said to the Senate committee, "that our abandonment of the trade agreements program at this juncture would mean a resumption of international economic warfare which is now showing such marked signs of abatement. Renewed economic warfare would inevitably mean an intensification of the present-day political tension which is already pushing many nations in the direction of military conflict."

I pointed out that, if such a war came, even if we were not drawn into it, "we cannot avoid being hurt by the profound economic upheaval which must inevitably accompany a widespread military conflict anywhere in the world. There is, of course, only one sure way for us to be spared the damage wrought by war, and that is for war not to occur. There is no more dangerous cause of war than economic distress, and no more potent factor in creating such distress than stagnation and paralysis in the field of international commerce. In the years which lie immediately ahead, an adequate revival of international trade will be the most powerful single force for easing political tensions and averting the danger of war."

To the House committee I said: "No peace machinery, however perfectly constructed, can operate among nations which are economically at war rather than at peace with each other. . . . No nation is more ready to seek relief by the forcible acquisition of territory or is more easily stampeded into the hysteria of war than one whose population finds itself hopelessly mired in economic poverty and widespread privation."

The fight in both Houses was bitter. The Republicans generally united against the bill, and some Democrats, particularly from the cattle, wool, and copper states, joined them. Our opponents claimed that the trade agreements had let in a "flood" of imports, that it bound the hands of Congress, that nations with whom we did not have agreements got benefits without giving us any in return, and that we employed a "star chamber" system of negotiation. When the vote came, however, we obtained a considerable majority, 285 to 101 in the House and 58 to 24 in the Senate.

We now had three more years in which to spread the idea of freer trade throughout the world. But, with one war raging in Europe and a greater one preparing, there was every reason to doubt that we should have a fair trial.

With the greatest commercial nation of the world, Great Britain, we had as yet no trade agreement. I had been striving from the time of the London Economic Conference to convince the British Government that it should give up its ideas of preferential tariffs, which meant discrimination, and its policy of bilateral balancing agreements, which had the effect of causing discrimination and restricting trade. In numerous conversations with British Ambassador Sir Ronald Lindsay I sought to state and restate my economic principles so that he would convey them to his Government. It seemed to me that our trade agreements program could not be considered complete until the United Kingdom was inserted as the apex of the arch.

It seemed ironic to me that we should have so much difficulty getting Britain into our trade agreements system, because I had drawn heavily on the former policy of Britain herself in formulating our program. I had gone back to the British procedure before the Civil War, which was bilateral treatment coupled with the unconditional most-favored-nation policy. Once they had got it started, it spread like the waves of the ocean, two or three states coming in at a time. I had observed with interest that the British had built their great world structure of trade on this system, even though they abandoned it after the First World War.

I held a basic discussion of the whole trade question with Lindsay on January 22, 1936. Because of the importance of the conversation, I cabled a comprehensive memorandum on it to our diplomatic missions abroad. I said to the Ambassador I was not prepared to say what might happen to the world if this movement should break down through lack of support from important commercial nations, especially those greatly interested in international trade, as was Great Britain. I contrasted the broad policy of the United States in entering into trade agreements on the most-favored-nation basis with certain methods and policies in trade on the part of the British Government which I felt were seriously handicapping the prosecution of our international trade recovery program.

As an example of what I had in mind, I cited to Lindsay our trade agreement with Brazil. When it was signed, Brazil had a trade balance of $50,000,000 to her credit in this country. If we had adopted a narrow balancing agreement such as Britain, Germany, and other countries were negotiating, we would have insisted that this credit be applied to the purchase of American goods only, or toward the payment of Brazilian bonds owned by Americans. We did not take advantage of Brazil's credit, however, because we wanted to promote trade among all nations. Britain and other countries had benefited by this policy, because Brazil was thereby able to use the $50,000,000 credit to purchase goods from them as well as, or instead of, from us. I also pointed out that we had forgone sales of vast quantities of cotton to Germany rather than adopt a temporary, shortsighted trade practice.

I put it bluntly to Lindsay that a number of clearing arrangements reached by Britain with Argentina, Germany, Italy, and other countries were handicapping the efforts of this Government to carry forward its broad program with the favored-nation policy underlying it.

Lindsay argued that his Government's action was more or less natural because of the unfavorable balance of trade it had with some other countries.

The whole tendency in most of these clearinghouse cases, I replied, was to drive straight toward bilateral trading and to restrict and obstruct the sum total of world trade.

I then said his Government had suddenly had its attention attracted to an astonishing development in world affairs—Italy's ambitious military campaign in East Africa. It had to be admitted that if Italy's exports had approximated the pre-crisis volume, there was every likelihood that her armies would not today be involved in a campaign. Of course, Lindsay's Government could continue to proceed leisurely. But there was a real probability that other military forces would be on the march before this leisurely policy of restoring trade and employment had come to a head.

"The experience of Italy," I went on, "should be a warning to all our Governments alike. The most incomprehensible circumstance in the whole modern world is the dominating ability of individuals or one man to arouse the mental processes of the entire population of a country, as in Germany and Italy, to the point where overnight they insist upon being sent into the frontline trenches without delay. When people are employed and they and their families are reasonably comfortable and hence contented, they have no disposition to follow agitators and to enthrone dictators."

But the world, I pointed out, was producing and consuming substantially less than six, eight, or ten years ago, and there was ample room for a $20,000,000,000 increase in international trade and for immense investments that a hardheaded businessman would consider sound, both of which could provide employment for twelve to fourteen million persons. This action, I concluded, would probably mark the difference between war and peace in Europe in the not distant future.

I sent the President a copy of my memorandum on this conversation. On February 6 he sent me this note:

> You are splendid in what you said to the British Ambassador. Incidentally, I get it from a number of sources in England and Europe that your policy and mine, working toward the long-view program of general increase in trade, is beginning to get under their skins and that they are getting heartily sick of mere bilateral agreements. Keep up the good work.   F. D. R.

In the spring of 1936, I communicated frequently to the British Government my earnest request that they should issue a public statement that their commercial policy would follow the lines of our trade agreements. Those in authority in London, however, were not willing.

The British Ambassador went to Britain in the summer of 1936. While he was gone an event occurred that had prospects of assisting economic negotiations between Britain and the United States. In September and October, 1936, agreements were reached principally among the United States, Britain, and France, to stabilize the dollar, pound, and franc and base them externally on gold. The French franc was simultaneously devalued. These accords, we hoped, would remove one of the arguments so strenuously advanced at the London Economic Conference, that certain countries could not begin to consider eliminating trade barriers until they could take action on the basis of stabilized currencies.

British Ambassador Lindsay came back to see me October 22, 1936, for another basic talk, after having spent two and a half months in his own country. I said to Lindsay that a noted Britisher had recently told me that Great Britain had no particular objective in foreign policy just now except to arm heavily for defensive purposes and await a possible military explosion in central Europe within another year or two. I myself favored necessary rearmament of the democracies in view of the rearmament of the dictatorships; but I felt that we should also offer a positive program for cooperation—namely, our trade agreements.

Lindsay admitted that his Government did not have any alternative policy, at least deeply in mind.

I replied that the United States for some time had had a very definite policy in mind—namely, our program for world economic and peace rehabilitation.

Two things, I said, were as inevitable as fate within another two or three years. One was that if a great trading country like Great Britain and another great trading country like the United States became inert and undertook further self-containment alone, such countries as Japan, Germany, and Italy with their armies and navies would in two or three years dominate nearly every square foot of trade territory other than that under the immediate control of Great Britain and the United States. That would leave our two countries in an amazingly disadvantageous situation.

The second certainty, I continued, was that, if this course of further isolation of our two countries was pursued, the food and raw-material-producing countries would be driven to establish their own crude manufacturing plants to produce their manufactured necessities at double and treble prices. And the industrial countries would be desperately attempting to do their own farming at five to ten times the present cost of production. The world would then find itself in the most uneconomic condition it had been in within two hundred years.

I expressed my belief that people of both our countries were in the same boat as far as the dangerous future was concerned, and that we could not avoid leadership. I thought, however, that Britain should take the lead in Europe because the opposition sentiment in this country was far greater than it could possibly be in Britain.

I said I was keenly disappointed that the dominant statesmanship of Britain was only disposed to pursue the one course that contemplated a military explosion. We had to keep in mind that this static attitude of statesmen in Europe as to economic policy existed while Japanese militarism moved deeper into eastern Asia, Mussolini marched his armies into Ethiopia, and Germany marched into the Rhineland. And still worse experiences were ahead for inert governments like that of Britain.

If British statesmen declined to move forward at all in support of an alternative program of peace and trade restoration, I added, this fact would inevitably become known to every other country. This alternative movement, I concluded, must either go forward or perish.

At my request, James Clement Dunn, Chief of the Western European Division, summed up my views in a letter to Ambassador Bingham in London on October 27, 1936. Dunn, beginning at the bottom in the State Department, had attracted favorable attention constantly as he moved steadily upward. He was of particular aid to me and to the Department generally.

"The Secretary," he wrote, "has a very deep feeling that the responsible heads of the British Government, while initiating and organizing their rearmament program as a means of protecting England in case of an attack from the Continent, are definitely losing an opportunity to set forces in motion which would have a most helpful effect in preventing war through the adoption of a more liberal trade policy along the lines of that now advocated by this Government.

"He feels that it may be that war will come. It may be that war will come no matter what line of action is taken by the important nations of Europe within the near future, but the Secretary also feels, and feels very strongly, that a mere preparation for war is no way to prevent it, and no time should be lost in pressing forward the one possibility, even though it may be only a possibility, of avoiding war, that is, to reestablish sound and substantial trade upon a firm basis of equality of treatment and exchange of opportunities for trade to the greatest extent each nation can possibly contribute. In other words, the question which comes to the Secretary's mind, if he were to be told by British officials that they are rearming preparing to protect themselves for war would be, 'And what else are you doing with a view to working out an alternative program of international relations which will try to avert a war?' "

In January, 1937, Walter Runciman, president of the British Board of Trade, visited Washington, and had a long talk with me. While he tended to agree with my principles he emphasized the difficulties Britain would have in extricating herself from the Empire preferences agreements reached at Ottawa in 1932.

Runciman made a remark on the political situation which stuck out like an old stump in a field. He said Britain was waiting to see what Germany was going to do.

I jumped him. Apparently, I said, different groups were waiting to see what each was going to do. The result was that no movements along peaceful lines were now being even undertaken. Instead, most nations were arming to the teeth, ostensibly for self-defense.

I said I realized fully that the problems facing the nations of Europe were vastly more complicated than any immediately facing the nations of the Western Hemisphere. But until three years ago the twenty nations to the south of the United States were not speaking to us except as a matter of strained courtesy. If we had sat still as some of our good friends were now doing in different countries in Europe, waiting to see what the other nations might say or do, the nations of this hemisphere would not have been on speaking terms today.

Then I outlined a program to Runciman. My idea was that some important country in Europe—Great Britain, for instance—should take the lead in proclaiming a program of liberal economic relations, on a basis of world order under law. If a country like Britain did so, the Scandinavian countries would at once get behind it, as would the countries from Holland to Switzerland, some of the Balkans, possibly Poland, and certainly the twenty-two American nations.

"As a result," I went on, "nearly forty nations would be marching across the Western World proclaiming a broad, concrete basic program to restore international order and promote and preserve peace and the economic well-being of people everywhere. The tremendous economic and moral influence of all those nations would be exerted upon any country not disposed to join with them. Such a country could no longer question the good faith of any of the nations pursuing this peaceful program or its evident desire to establish fair and friendly relations.

"Consequently, all the important nations would, in all probability, join in such a broad, wholesome movement. If, for the time being, some nations should refuse to join, the nearly forty nations formulating and supporting such a program would, in any event, be doing the wisest and most profitable thing for themselves and the world."

My point was that the economic approach should be the spear point of the approach to peace. First, get all the commercial nations in agreement on liberalizing and increasing trade, removing trade restrictions and eliminating discrimination. And then, with nearly forty nations banded together on economic grounds, show recalcitrant nations like Germany and Italy the undoubted benefits of joining in the same movement.

If the Axis nations came in, the gate would be wide open for a discussion of political problems.

The United States had taken the lead in the trade agreements program, but I felt that Britain should take the lead in this concerted economic movement. This because she had been moving in the opposite direction, toward economic nationalism, and because her commercial relations with most of the nations of Europe were closer than those of other countries.

"If Great Britain," I said, "were to proclaim tomorrow her support and leadership in this program—as she could—it would literally thrill the world and especially the peace forces and the forces of law, order, morals, and religion everywhere."

Runciman listened attentively to my exposition, and occasionally nodded in the affirmative; but I was quite sure he was not with me as fully as I should have liked.

.   .   .

With Hitler in possession of Austria, with Japan spreading out over China, and with the war in Spain moving toward a climax, I delivered a fundamental speech on foreign policy on March 17, 1938, before the National Press Club in Washington, to state our position. The world was racing hell-bent toward destruction, and it was essential to show the extent of our concern and to make it clear that we had to be taken into account in world developments. The address was widely broadcast in the United States and the British Isles, along with translations in five other languages. The President went over the address and approved it in advance, writing on my copy:

C. H.
Grand!
F. D. R.

I stressed the necessity for our rearmament. "No policy," I said, "would prove more disastrous than for an important nation to fail to arm adequately when international lawlessness is on the rampage. It is my considered judgment that, in the present state of world affairs, to do less than is now proposed would lay our country open to unpredictable hazards. It would, moreover, seriously restrict our nation's ability to command, without purpose or occasion for resorting to arms, proper respect for its legitimate rights and interests, the surrender of which would constitute abandonment of the fundamental principles of justice and morality and peace among nations."

We did not have the slightest intention to police the world, I said, "but we equally have not the slightest intention of reversing a tradition of a century and a half by abandoning our deep concern for, and our advocacy of, the establishment everywhere of international order under law, based upon the well-recognized principles to which I have referred. It is our profound conviction that the most effective contribution which we, as a nation sincerely devoted to the cause of peace, can make—in the tragic conditions with which our people, in common with the rest of mankind, are confronted today—is to have this country respected throughout the world for integrity, justice, good will, strength, and unswerving loyalty to principles."

If we declined our responsibility to work for law, order, morality, and justice throughout the world, and withdrew within ourselves, the consequences would be disastrous. "Our security would be menaced," I said, "in proportion as other nations came to believe that, either through fear or through unwillingness, we did not intend to afford protection to our legitimate national interests abroad, but, on the contrary, intended to abandon them at the first sign of danger. Under such conditions the sphere of our international relationships—economic, cultural, intellectual, and other—would necessarily shrink and shrivel, until we would stand practically alone among the nations, a self-constituted hermit state." Thrown back upon our own resources, we should have to reorganize our entire social and economic structure. We should have less production, at higher costs; lower living standards; regimentation in every phase of life; economic distress to workers and farmers; and the dole on an ever increasing scale.

And should we really be avoiding war by these extreme measures? "Reason and experience definitely point to the contrary," I said. "We may seek to withdraw from participation in world affairs, but we cannot thereby withdraw from the world itself. Isolation is not a means to security; it is a fruitful source of insecurity."

I outlined what we would continue to do in carrying out our foreign policy; adhere fully to the fundamental principles underlying international order; urge universal observance of these principles; cooperate with other nations actuated by the same desires and pursuing the same objectives; safeguard our legitimate rights in every part of the world; while scrupulously respecting the rights of others, insist on their respecting our rights; strive, through our reciprocal trade program and other economic policies, to expand trade among nations; promote peace through economic security and prosperity; and participate in international technical conferences.

Further than this speech we could not go. The points I made would not please an isolationist determined to confine us to our own shores. They would not please an internationalist determined to commit us to alliances. But they represented a positive foreign policy under which we could exert our influence, as well as example, for peace, increase our strength, and render ourselves a factor that no aggressor could overlook in making his plans.

2

ACCEPTING THE CHALLENGE
ROBERT A. DIVINE

In September 1941 the Second World War entered its third year. The Axis powers were triumphant on all fronts. Germany controlled the major centers of population and industry in Europe. Her armies were moving deep within the Soviet Union, threatening Leningrad and Moscow and overrunning the fertile Ukraine and the industrial Donetz basin in the south. Stiffening Russian resistance denied Hitler the quick victory he confidently expected, but it appeared likely that he would complete his conquest of Russia by the spring of 1942. German submarines continued to take a heavy toll of English shipping in the North Atlantic, and Axis air power, striking from bases in Italy and Tunisia, closed the Mediterranean to the British, compelling them to supply their hard-pressed forces in Egypt by sending convoys around the Cape of Good Hope and up to the Red Sea. In the Far East, where Japan had been waging war since 1937, the outlook was no better. Japan controlled the entire coast of China and all her major cities. The occupation of Indo-China, completed in July, placed Japanese troops in a position to sweep over Southeast Asia and down into the Dutch East Indies. In this precarious world situation, America held the balance of power. If the United States continued to cling to its neutrality, the emergence of a New Order in Europe and Asia seemed assured.

The Roosevelt administration, aware of the importance of its decisions on the course of the war, focused on the problem of Japan in the late summer of 1941. The freezing order of July 26, designed

Reprinted from *The Reluctant Belligerent*, pp. 137–148, with permission of John Wiley and Sons, Inc., Publishers.

originally only as a dramatic warning, gradually developed into a full-scale embargo which ended all trade between the United States and Japan. Great Britain and her Dominions undertook parallel action, impounding Japanese assets and cutting off trade. In early August, the Dutch authorities in the Indies announced the cessation of exports, thereby completing the economic isolation of Japan. The results were disastrous for the Japanese, who depended on trade for many vital materials. Oil was the most crucial import; although Japan had carefully stockpiled petroleum products throughout the 1930's, at the time of the embargo she had less than two years' supply on hand. Oil was essential for the Japanese war effort; without gasoline the planes, tanks, and warships were useless. Japanese leaders each day witnessed the consumption of another 12,000 tons of petroleum. Either they must give in to the United States and abandon their ambitious plans of conquest, or they would have to stand and fight while they had the oil to do so. The endless round of negotiations between the two countries could no longer continue. "From now on the oil gauge and the clock stood side by side," commented Herbert Feis. "Each fall in the level brought the hour of decision closer."[1]

The Japanese Prime Minister, Prince Fumimaro Konoye, decided to undertake a bold step to break the deadlock. Realizing that Army and Navy leaders would insist on war rather than face surrender, Konoye proposed a personal meeting with President Roosevelt to seek a peaceful solution to the Japanese-American crisis. In Tokyo Konoye won the grudging consent of the military to pursue this plan, but only with the understanding that if Roosevelt refused to accept Japanese dominance in Asia, the Prime Minister would "be prepared to assume leadership in the war against America."[2] On August 8 Ambassador Nomura met with Cordell Hull, who had returned to Washington from White Sulphur Springs, to explore the issues separating their two countries. When Nomura suggested that the heads of government meet, possibly in Hawaii, Hull dismissed the proposal, stating that such a meeting would be impossible until Japan gave specific evidence of abandoning her aggressive policies in the Far East.

Undiscouraged, Nomura raised the idea again when he was called to the White House on August 17 to receive the warning that Roosevelt and Churchill had discussed at the Atlantic Conference. The

[1] *The Road to Pearl Harbor* (Princeton, 1950), p. 244.
[2] *Ibid.*, p. 253.

President read two statements to the Japanese Ambassador, but they did not constitute the severe warning Churchill had wanted, and when the President had finished, Nomura again brought up the idea of a summit conference between Roosevelt and Konoye. The President was evidently intrigued with the idea, and although he made no commitment, he suggested that such a meeting might take place in Juneau, Alaska in mid-October.

The next day the Japanese Foreign Minister, Admiral Teijiro Toyoda, held a two-and-a-half hour conference with Ambassador Grew in Tokyo. Toyoda pleaded for a meeting between Roosevelt and Konoye, claiming that Japan did not want war, and that Konoye was breaking all precedent in proposing to leave his country to carry on negotiations. "This determination of Prince Konoye," Grew reported Toyoda as saying, "is nothing but the expression of his strongest desire to save the civilization of the world from ruin as well as to maintain peace in the Pacific by making every effort in his power. . . ." Toyoda's sincerity impressed Grew, and in a separate cable to the State Department, the Ambassador urged that the proposed meeting be given "very prayerful consideration." Grew felt it presented an opportunity to break through the "apparently insurmountable obstacles to peace" in the Far East.[3]

Worried by the lack of response from Washington, Prince Konoye a week later sent a personal message to the President. Reiterating his desire to avoid war between the United States and Japan, which he feared would lead to "the collapse of world civilization," Konoye stated his conviction that the poor relationship between the two countries was due to a serious lack of understanding that could be remedied only by an agreement between the heads of the two governments. In an accompanying document, submitted to Roosevelt by Nomura on August 28, the Konoye government gave its terms. Japan had occupied Indo-China in order to "accelerate the settlement of the China Incident" and intended to withdraw her forces as soon as the war in China could be ended. The note stated that Japan did not intend to use her position in Indo-China as a springboard to invade Southeast Asia. "In a word," the note pledged, "the Japanese Government has no intention of using, without provocation, military forces against any neighboring nation."[4]

[3] *Foreign Relations: Japan, 1931–1941*, II, 563, 565.
[4] *Ibid.*, pp. 572, 574–75.

Cordell Hull did not believe the Japanese. Although President Roosevelt again indicated that he was receptive to the idea, Hull feared a trap and began to throw his considerable influence against the proposed meeting. When Nomura met with Hull on the evening of August 28 and began discussing detailed arrangements, Hull brought him up short by insisting that Japan would have to agree to nullify the Tripartite Pact and withdraw her troops from China before any conference between Konoye and Roosevelt could be held. Nomura indicated that the Tripartite Pact was not a major obstacle, but when he said that Japan could not easily compromise her interests in China, Hull made it unmistakably clear that "the China question was one of the pivotal questions underlying relations between the United States and Japan."[5] A week later, on September 3, President Roosevelt handed Nomura a note declaring that Japan would have to agree in advance to American principles of territorial integrity, commercial equality, and observance of the *status quo* in the Pacific. This note in effect ended any possibility of a summit conference. The United States was demanding that Japan give up her New Order in Asia as a precondition to meeting, while Konoye had promised the military leaders in Japan he would use the conference to secure American approval of Japanese dominance in the Far East.

Even before Roosevelt's discouraging note of September 3 reached Tokyo, the Japanese Army and Navy leaders had decided to invade the Dutch East Indies before the end of the year to secure desperately needed oil. The Army general staff insisted that the war preparations would have to be put in motion by October; if diplomacy failed to restore normal trade with the United States by that time, war would follow.

On September 3 Konoye accepted this proposed timetable, still hopeful that he could negotiate a peaceful agreement with the United States. Three days later an Imperial Conference made the fateful decision "to proceed with war preparations so that they be completed approximately toward the end of October." Meanwhile, Japan would seek to have England and the United States agree to her "demands." "If, by the early part of October," the conference agreed, "there is still no prospect of being able to attain our demands, we shall immediately decide to open hostilities against the United States, Great Britain, and the Netherlands."[6] Japan was determined to carry out her

---

[5] *Ibid.*, p. 578.
[6] Robert J. C. Butow, *Tojo and the Coming of the War* (Princeton, 1961), p. 250.

program in the Far East, by diplomacy if possible, by war if necessary.

Throughout September Nomura attempted to secure Hull's agreement to the Japanese demands in the Far East. Peace was possible, the Japanese envoy argued, if only the United States would end its economic sanctions, stop its aid to Chiang Kai-shek, and permit Japan to liquidate the war in China. Although American military leaders pleaded with the administration to avoid a showdown in the Far East until American strength in the Pacific could be increased, Hull and Roosevelt agreed that the United States could not buy time by selling out China. On October 2 Hull replied to Japan. In a long note he reviewed the negotiations between the two countries and the major point at issue. No meeting between Roosevelt and Konoye could be held, Hull asserted, until Japan gave a "clear-cut manifestation" of her intention to withdraw her troops from China and Indo-China.[7] This rigid statement of American policy ended the last chance for diplomatic accommodation between Japan and the United States in 1941. Hull was asking Japan to give up all her hard-won gains of the past decade—Manchuria, China, Indo-China—as well as the prospects for acquiring control of all Southeast Asia, in return for American trade and friendship. The price was too high. Konoye had exhausted his allotted time for diplomacy; on October 16 his government fell from power, and General Hideki Tojo, leader of the army expansionists, formed a new cabinet pledged to fulfill Japan's destiny in Asia.

Historians have ever since asked whether a conference between Konoye and Roosevelt could have averted war. The consensus is that it would have failed. The two nations were on a collision course, and neither leader could compromise the vital interests of his country. Konoye could not forego Japan's New Order in Asia merely to placate the United States. Any such surrender would have been repudiated by the Japanese military leaders and would have cost Konoye his position and probably his life. Nor could Roosevelt permit Japan to subjugate China and dominate the Far East. Yet a more flexible and realistic American policy might have delayed a showdown with Japan. By meeting with Konoye and seeking a temporary *modus vivendi*, Roosevelt could have gained the time that American military leaders felt was essential to strengthen the defenses of the Philippines, Hawaii, and other American outposts in the Pacific. By standing

[7] *Foreign Relations: Japan, 1931–1941*, II, 660.

firmly on principle, Roosevelt and Hull missed an opportunity to postpone the inevitable clash with Japan.

In the Atlantic as in the Far East, the United States moved inexorably toward war in the fall of 1941. The submarine menace eased somewhat in July and August following the American occupation of Iceland. Nine eastbound British convoys carried over 4 million tons of supplies across the North Atlantic during the summer, and not a single ship was lost. But in September the U-boats again found their targets. On September 8 twelve German submarines attacked a slow British convoy south of Iceland and over a three-day span sank 15 merchant ships. Britain had badly overtaxed her limited destroyer strength in escorting the heavy run of summer convoys, and the strain on ships and crews was reaching a critical point. Supply shipments to Russia, which had to go around the German-occupied coast of Norway to Murmansk, added a new and very heavy burden that Britain could not handle alone. Unless the United States Navy shared the escort duty, Great Britain would lose the battle of the Atlantic by default.

Roosevelt, fully aware of the British plight, had promised at the Atlantic Conference that American naval units would escort convoys of British ships as far as Iceland. Yet despite this pledge, he held back, uncertain how he would justify such a policy to the American people. On September 1 Admiral Ernest King drew up an elaborate operation plan for convey duty by the Atlantic fleet, but still Roosevelt hesitated. Then on September 4 Germany provided the pretext the President was seeking. The American destroyer *Greer*, carrying passengers and mail to Iceland, was attacked by a German submarine in the North Atlantic. The submarine fired two torpedoes; both missed the *Greer*, which responded with depth charges that also missed. Later reports revealed that the *Greer* had been trailing the submarine for over three hours in cooperation with a British patrol plane which dropped four depth charges on the U-boat. The submarine commander, far from being guilty of an unprovoked assault, had turned in desperation on his pursuer in an effort to escape destruction.

President Roosevelt, however, did not wait to ascertain the full story of the *Greer* episode. At a press conference on September 5 he called the attack deliberate. Later that day he met with Secretary of State Hull and Harry Hopkins and decided to institute the long-delayed convoys by the American Navy. He asked Hull to prepare a draft of a speech he would deliver to the American people about this momentous decision. When Hull cautiously sent in a weak statement, Hopkins and Judge Sam Rosenman, the President's chief speech writer, prepared a much stronger draft, which Roosevelt strengthened even more. On September 10 Roosevelt read the speech to Secretaries Hull, Knox and Stimson, who warmly endorsed it, and the next day he went over it with a bipartisan group of Congressional leaders.

Roosevelt delivered his address, one of the boldest speeches of his long career, to a nationwide radio audience on September 11. In blunt, biting phrases, he accused Germany of piracy in the *Greer* incident and called U-boats "the rattlesnakes of the Atlantic." Germany, he warned the nation, was seeking to secure control of the seas as a prelude to conquest of the Western Hemisphere. "This attack on the *Greer* was no localized military operation in the North Atlantic," declared Roosevelt. "This was one determined step towards creating a permanent world system based on force, terror, and murder." Therefore, the President continued, American ships would no longer wait to be attacked, implying, but not clearly stating, a new policy of shoot-on-sight for American destroyers. Then, in unambiguous language, he announced the beginning of American convoys: ". . . our patrolling vessels and planes will protect all merchant ships—not only American ships but ships of any flag—engaged in commerce in our defensive waters." "From now on," he concluded," if German or Italian vessels of war enter the waters the protection of which is necessary for American defense they do so at their own peril."[8]

This "shoot-on-sight" speech, as it has been deceptively labeled by many historians, marked a decisive step toward war. Ever since the passage of the Lend-Lease Act in March, Winston Churchill, along with many of the President's own advisers, had been urging Roosevelt to insure the delivery of supplies by authorizing the United States Navy to undertake escort duty. Repeatedly, the President had given in to this pressure only to reverse himself on the grounds that the American people were not yet ready to face the risk of war involved in convoying. Now he had committed himself publicly.

Yet Roosevelt's boldness was misleading. Even in taking a momentous step, he acted deviously, seizing on a questionable incident and

[8] Department of State, *Peace and War: United States Foreign Policy, 1931–1941* (Washington, 1943), pp. 741–42, 743.

portraying it as a simple case of aggression, which it clearly was not. Roosevelt evidently still believed that he could not be honest with the American people. The public opinion polls, however, indicate that he seriously overestimated the strength of isolationism. Surveys in September showed that nearly 80% of the people opposed participation in the war; but such results were to be expected—rarely do people respond positively to a simple query about entering a major conflict. In early October, when George Gallup asked the more realistic question, Do you think it more important to defeat Hitler than to stay out of the war?, over 70% answered that it was better to insure defeat of Hitler. The American people wanted to stay at peace, but not at the cost of a German victory. Thus, to the President's relief, they responded enthusiastically to his convoy decision, taking in stride its risk of war. Indeed, the public reaction was so favorable that Roosevelt could have begun convoys months earlier with solid public support.

On September 16, five days after the President's speech, the first American-escorted convoy left the Canadian port of Halifax for the hazardous voyage across the Atlantic. Five United States Navy destroyers relieved the initial Canadian escort vessels south of Newfoundland on September 17. For a week fifty merchant ships lumbered through the Atlantic while the destroyers patrolled for submarines. On September 25, some five hundred miles south of Iceland, the American escort transferred the convoy to British units without incident. Roosevelt's estimate that Hitler wanted to avoid a showdown with the United States while he was engaged in the Russian campaign proved to be correct. When news of the President's September 11 speech reached Berlin, Admiral Raeder had prepared a long memorandum for Hitler setting forth the reasons why Germany would have to begin attacking American ships. The Nazi leader agreed with the arguments, but he insisted that submarine commanders must take care "to avoid any incidents in the war on merchant shipping before about the middle of October."[9] For the time being, at least, Germany would refrain from challenging the American Navy in the North Atlantic.

The next problem confronting Roosevelt was the prohibition on arming American merchant vessels and the ban on their entry into war zones contained in the 1939 Neutrality Act. With American cargo

[9] Hans L. Trefousse, *Germany and American Neutrality, 1939–1941* (New York, 1951), pp. 120–21.

ships now traveling to Iceland to supply the American garrison there, it was essential that they be permitted to carry deck guns for protection against surface attacks by German submarines. In addition, if the United States was fully committed to the policy of insuring the delivery of lend-lease supplies to Britain, it would be very helpful to have American ships carry these goods across the Atlantic and thus relieve the over-burdened British merchant marine. When Roosevelt's advisers had pressed this question on him in July, he had consulted with Congressional leaders, and their negative reaction had caused him to defer the issue. Encouraged by the favorable response to his convoy speech, the President decided to ask for revision of the Neutrality Act. Yet again he acted with indirection. On October 9 Roosevelt asked Congress to repeal only Section VI of the Act, which prohibited the arming of merchant ships, a step he knew most Congressmen favored. Then, in less specific terms, he urged Congress to "give earnest and early attention" to other phases of the Neutrality Act. With studied vagueness, he suggested that Congress reconsider "keeping our ships out of the ports of our own friends," but he never specifically asked for repeal of the combat zone provisions of the Neutrality Act of 1939.[10]

The House of Representatives considered the President's ambiguous requests in late October. Fearful of defeat by the isolationists, Congressional leaders restricted the legislation to repeal of Section VI, and thus the issue was confined to arming American merchant ships. As the debate reached its climax, news arrived that a German submarine had torpedoed an American destroyer, the *Kearney*, while it was attempting to beat off a wolfpack raid on a British convoy. The *Kearney* managed to limp back into Iceland, and the next day the House voted to arm American merchant ships by the impressive margin of 259 to 138. In the tally Democratic Representatives backed the administration overwhelmingly, while three out of every four Republicans voted no.

The attack on the *Kearney* and the vote in the House led to public demands that the Senate repeal the entire Neutrality Act. The administration, however, remained cautious, and finally decided to ask only that the Senate expand the legislation to strike out the ban on Amer-

---

[10] Samuel Rosenman, ed., *The Public Papers and Addresses of Franklin D. Roosevelt* (13 vols.; New York, 1938–1950), X, 409.

ican ships entering combat zones. Even this request caused a bitter debate in the Senate. The sinking of the American destroyer *Reuben James* with the loss of 115 lives on October 31 intensified the isolationist opposition, and lent support to the America First charge that Roosevelt was "asking Congress to issue an engraved drowning license to American seamen."[11] If Britain needed American ships, suggested the administration's opponents, why not give them to her under lend-lease and thus avoid risking American lives on the high seas? However, on November 7, the Senate voted 50 to 37 to permit the administration to arm American merchant ships and send them into the war zone. The bill was then referred back to the House, which concurred in the combat zone provision by 18 votes, 212 to 194.

The narrow margin by which Congress revised the Neutrality Act in November 1941 seemed to confirm Roosevelt's caution. Yet the vote did not reflect the attitude of the American people. Many Congressmen voted against the administration to protest what they considered lax labor policies that were hampering the defense effort. Other Representatives and Senators, aware that the public favored revision, felt compelled to vote against a measure that might soon lead to a war which the people had repeatedly said they did not want to enter. Unable to reconcile the conflicting public desire to do everything possible to speed the defeat of Hitler yet remain at peace, these Congressmen decided to play it safe. Given the failure of the President to deal forthrightly with this contradiction in the public mood, their vote is understandable.

Despite the closeness of the vote, the meaning of the Congressional action was clear. The United States had finally abandoned the major portions of neutrality legislation adopted in the prewar years. The only meaningful restrictions left in force were the ban on American travel on belligerent ships and the prohibition on loans, which had long since been circumvented by the Lend-Lease Act. All that remained then was a hollow shell which stood as a monument to the naive belief of the American people in the mid-1930's that they could find safety behind a legislative barricade when the world went to war. As long as it lasted intact, the Neutrality Act had served its purpose of keeping the nation out of war. But in the interval the American people had been taught by events overseas that the security of the

[11] Wayne S. Cole, *America First* (Madison, Wis., 1953), p. 163.

nation, not avoidance of hostilities, was the true goal of American foreign policy.

The revision of the Neutrality Act, together with the even more important convoy decision, brought American policy in the Atlantic in line with the stand taken in Asia. In both regions the United States had exhausted the techniques of peaceful diplomacy and had challenged the Axis powers to a showdown. Just as Japan had to face the issue of peace or war over the freezing order of July 26, so Nazi Germany had to decide whether to accept the provocative American policy in the North Atlantic. In essence, Roosevelt surrendered the decision for war to Tojo and Hitler. It was now only a question of who would strike first.

3

IT ACTUALLY COSTS
US NOTHING
DICK STEWARD

The New Deal did not represent the United States' first attempt to negotiate trade agreements incorporating the unconditional most-favored-nation clause. In 1931 the State Department described United States commercial policy as seeking to give equal commercial treatment to all nations and to secure for itself unconditional most-favored-nation treatment through the negotiation of such agreements. In this way the United States sought to prevent sudden discrimination against American trade. The impetus behind these policy decisions can be found in the 1919 Tariff Committee Report which suggested that America had reached the stage of financial and industrial maturity to merit reversal of her traditional commercial policy. In 1923 the Harding administration implemented these recommendations by the incorporation of unconditional most-favored-nation treatment. However, the Fordney-McCumber Tariff and the 1930 Hawley-Smoot Tariff effectively cancelled out any ensuing benefits. Section 338 of the Tariff Act of 1930 authorized prohibitive duty rates on many import commodities thereby making the unconditional most-favored-nation clause "exceedingly embarrassing in practice." The State Department suspended further negotiations.

With the advent of the New Deal, the State Department took up the cudgels for liberal trade. The Department also found whole-hearted support from business groups such as the National Foreign

From "In Search of Markets: The New Deal, Latin America, and Reciprocal Trade," Ph.D. diss., University of Missouri, 1969, pp. 34–46. Reprinted by permission. Footnotes omitted.

Trade Council and other organizations interested in the promotion of American export trade. The New Deal's first attempt to negotiate a reciprocity treaty focused on the Republics of Latin America and in particular Colombia. As early as April 1933 the State Department began plans to obtain "the maximum possible advantage for American commerce" through a trade agreement with Colombia. Probably the major factor which influenced the State Department in beginning its negotiations with Colombia was the strong bargaining position of the United States relative to the Colombian economy. In July 1933, a 79 page memorandum prepared by the Bureau of Foreign and Domestic Commerce entitled "Factors Affecting United States-Colombian Trade" reached the State Department. The memo stated that the United States purchased over 80 percent of Colombia's exports, while over 40 percent of Colombia's imports came from the United States.

The implications of the report suggested that the United States was in a position to drive a hard bargain with the Colombians (a fact which the State Department tactfully exploited). United States exports to Colombia in 1933 totaled only $14,600,000, while Colombian exports to the United States both dutiable and free equaled $47,600,000. The United States balance of payments in 1933 (exclusive of receipts by the United States on direct investments) with Colombia stood at a minus $30,000,000. Moreover, Colombia's economic position continued to deteriorate with each year of the depression, due primarily to the fall in coffee prices. Since 92 percent of her coffee exports (which accounted for nearly 60 percent of total export trade) found a duty free market in the United States, a suspension of Colombia's coffee from the American free list would precipitate complete economic chaos. The prospects of such a cataclysm augured no ray of encouragement for United States-Colombian relations. The Colombia coffee industry consisted of a large and politically powerful number of independent producers heavily dependent on mortgage and commercial banks to continue operations. The possibility of the imposition of import duties by the United States on coffee (a commodity with a very elastic price demand) enhanced the likelihood of the drying up of badly needed foreign loans. Colombia's absence of a well-defined system of financing coffee production was matched only by her poor transportation facilities for the transport of coffee to the world markets. The need, therefore, for economic overhead investment capital further increased Colombia's dependence on the United States.

The Colombian Government in 1931 took complete control of foreign exchange operations, although she did not discriminate against the United States in the exchange allocation. The Colombian Congress in the same year enacted a higher customs tariff in order to conserve dwindling gold reserves and protect infant industry. Duties on wheat, barley, cereals, rice, lard, fresh and canned fruits, cement, paper, cotton, silk, and woolen products all handicapped American trade to Colombia. American exports also felt the squeeze due to customs surcharges, excise, municipal taxes, and discrimination in transportation services. The shippers suffered because of difficulty in obtaining dollar remittances for export products shipped to Colombia. The Bureau's report traced the decline in dollar value of Colombian exports from $130,520,000 in 1928 to only $67,067,000 in 1932, and hearkened this phenomena to the fall in Colombian coffee prices, which accounted for a large percentage of the volume of Colombia's exports. Although Colombian coffee was both milder and of higher quality than her nearest competitor, Brazil, the price differential continued to slip due to the American consumer's shift to cheaper products. The trade figures for the year 1929 through 1933 bear witness to the export debacle. In 1929 Colombia exported to the United States, duty free, $103,100,000 worth of products. In 1930 the figure slipped to $96,500,000, but by 1933 Colombia's duty free exports to the United States plummeted to a meager $42,200,000. Although America's direct investments in the production of Colombian coffee was slight, the indirect results of the fall in coffee prices adversely affected American interests. Approximately 70 percent of the purchasing, marketing, and distributing of the Colombian coffee crop was controlled by the United States.

Most areas of American export business were quick to realize the importance of the United States market to the Colombian economy. Walter S. Brewster, President of the Textile Export Association of the United States, compared Colombia's dependence on the United States to Argentina's reliance on Great Britain and intimated that America follow the British-Argentine example incorporated in the Roca-Runciman Agreement. The National Foreign Trade Council lamented the shrinkage of American export trade *vis à vis* foreign competition and hoped to see the trend reversed. The American Council of Foreign-Bondholders also voiced admonitions that Colombia's federal, departmental, and municipal debts could not be met without an increase in

United States-Colombian trade. Congressmen throughout the early New Deal years also stressed the necessity for the United States to turn away from the markets of Europe and Asia and concentrate on Latin America. The United States, remarked Senator Robert Reynolds of North Carolina, cannot compete in the Orient against the Japanese and, therefore, must make Latin America an American market.

In taking advantage of Latin America's lack of export diversification, the State Department carefully analyzed the economies of each Latin American state and pointed to the vulnerabilities inherent in a one-crop economy. What coffee was to Colombia and Brazil, nitrate was to Chile, sugar to Cuba, and meat to Argentina and Uruguay. Armed with a plethora of vital statistics, the New Deal moved cautiously into the arena of world commerce. The story of the New Deal's first attempt at trade negotiations formally began during the London Economic Conference. At this time the passage of the Trade Agreements Act of June 12, 1934, appeared highly improbable. On the initiation of Franklin Delano Roosevelt, the State Department contacted several states concerning the possibility of Tariff Legislation. Assistant Secretary of State Jefferson Caffery referred to the trade schemes as "a well thought out program" limited to Brazil, Argentina, and Colombia. The agreements were to be bi-lateral in nature, incorporating the unconditional most-favored-nation clause and a reciprocal reduction of tariff barriers, and subject to approval by the United States Senate. The United States signed only one such reciprocal trade treaty before the passage of the Trade Agreements Act, and this with the Republic of Colombia. The story of these negotiations provided an important chapter into the philosophy and methods used by the State Department in the ensuing years.

Formal discussions with Colombia began in July 1933. President Enrique Olaya Herrera's initial attempt to have the discussions conducted at Bogatá received an unwelcomed response by the State Department which contended that Washington must be the center for all future negotiations. Olaya did not press the matter. In August 1933 he appointed Francisco Plata and Arturo Hernández to assist the Colombian ambassador, Fabio Lozano, in the coming negotiations. Washington's position on the trade agreements involved an examination of all principal items of trade between the United States and Colombia, with tariff reductions on most American products in return for United States pledges that Colombian exports (a large percentage of which came to the United States duty free) would remain on the free list. But Washington's concessions held forth very little in the way of positive benefits for Colombia. As one State Department memorandum put it, tariff concessions to Colombia "actually costs us nothing."

The Olaya Government, therefore, encountered a difficult problem. Washington gave little concrete assurance that freer trade held forth in the prospect of increased commerce for all the Americas. In fact, many Colombians suspected the American reciprocal trade program simply provided a rhetorical camouflage in which to disguise the aspirations of economic nationalists. Yet the consequences of commercial retaliation by the United States spelled the total collapse of the Colombian economy. Faced with mounting American pressure, Olaya's alternatives narrowed appreciably. To save her principal export market Colombia might well have been forced to make sacrifices in domestic industry or delay the discussions as long as possible, calculated on the premise that the United States would never resort to unilateral imposition of import duties. The United States had carefully phrased its dispatches in order to refrain from just such threats. But to run the gambit of commercial peril in order to save incipient manufacturing interests no doubt poised a grave risk for the Bogotá Government.

In late August Allan Dawson, the American chargé in Bogotá, reported the suspicion prevalent among Colombians toward a trade agreement. Singled out by the United States as the first nation to open reciprocal trade negotiations amounted to a rather dubious honor. Fear of possible United States duties on Colombian coffee and the abolition of Colombian exchange restrictions created a most unpropitious environment for discussion. *El Tiempo, El Espectador*, and *Mundo Al Día* echoed the cacophony emanating from both industrial and agricultural circles in Colombia. The Colombian Agricultural Society and The Third National Agricultural Congress reflected the view that Colombia's agriculture must not be sacrificed to meet the demands of the United States. The National Federation of Industrialists voiced the same protectionist demands for their products. The State Department, however, pressed forward, confident that comprehensive tariff reductions on both agricultural and manufactured products were possible. American pressure forced Olaya to a point of compromise. The Colombian President submitted "that the United

States was trying to drive a hard bargain" and agreed to a series of tariff reductions on manufactured imports. In a communiqué to Hull in August 1933, Dawson substantiated the fact that the Colombian manufacturing class, in a show of strength *vis à vis* the coffee interests, would be swept aside. Olaya, however, remained adamant against any duty reductions on foodstuffs, especially wheat, rice, flour, crackers, and biscuits. Clearly, Colombian agricultural interests predominated. Olaya also intimated that Congressional authority enabling him to establish a system of maximum and minimum tariffs might be the most efficacious way to grant tariff concessions to the United States. In this way the reciprocal trade agreement might be put into effect without ratification by Congress.

Colombia, however, remained skeptical toward the reciprocity program. On August 22 the United States handed the Colombians a draft proposal which requested substantial industrial and agricultural concessions by the Olaya government. Colombia countered by a sharp reminder that American trade statistics did not convey "true reality" since the greater portion of profit from the sale of Colombian coffee, bananas, and petroleum went to United States citizens and companies. The following week Lozano continued the *démarche* by impressing upon the United States the importance of custom duties as the principal source of income for Colombia. The minister further proclaimed that Colombia would not sacrifice agricultural interests or essential industries to United States markets. With these points reaffirmed, the ambassador submitted a counterdraft of the Reciprocal Trade Agreement.

Bogotá also remained especially cool toward the United States position on the unconditional most-favored-nation clause. The acceptance of the clause, argued the Colombians, might produce unforeseen effects on Colombia's exports and would necessitate the renegotiation of existing trade treaties. Colombian officials offered an alternative solution which incorporated tariff reductions on exports from nations purchasing a certain amount of Colombian products. A memorandum by the Treaty Division of the Department of State on October 3 refused to countenance any deviation from unconditional most-favored-nation status since the conditional clause offered no guarantee of equality of treatment. It afforded American exporters no assurance that Colombia "will not lower still further the reductions made in the agreement on their behalf, or reduce other products which may compete with theirs, and fail to accord to them corresponding reductions." The unconditional most-favored-nation clause was viewed as the legal embodiment of the principle of equality of treatment. The memorandum likewise insisted that Colombia must grant the United States substantial tariff reductions on agricultural products. In return, the United States might possibly broaden the scope of import reductions on Colombian products.

Further trade difficulties included the Colombian proposal allowing municipalities and departments to have taxing power over imported articles. Colombia also wanted assurances that green coffee would not be subject to anti-dumping laws in the United States and further suggested that no restrictions be put on the volume of imports from one nation to the other (a move designed to strike squarely at NRA and AAA import regulations). The United States, however, proposed to limit the provision against prohibitions only on those specified articles in the schedules.

Colombia also insisted upon a larger oil quota from the United States since she produced the third largest volume of petroleum in Latin America. But her production capabilities suffered from the limited capacity of the pipelines to serve the oil fields. An increased oil quota might, therefore, serve as an incentive for attracting foreign investment capital to the country. American oil interests in Colombia likewise sponsored the idea. The State Department, however, opposed Bogotá's importunities due in large part to the fact that Colombia did not represent the principal supplier of oil imports. Any oil concession granted to Colombia in a trade agreement and extended unconditionally to all nations increased the danger of adverse political and economic criticism at home. The position of both nations appeared explicit and firm. The danger of an impasse measurably increased.

As a possible catalyst for trade discussions, a statement by Budget Director Lewis Douglas in early October 1933 proposed a five cent per pound tax on imported coffee. Obviously distressed, Lozano urged United States reconsideration. On October 26 Assistant Secretary of State Jefferson Caffery handed the American redraft to the Colombian Minister. Douglas' veiled threat no doubt helped to speed up the trade discussions. In early December the United States and Colombia reached a final agreement.

The first agreement signed with Colombia on December 15, 1933, required Congressional legislation in order to give it effect. The minimum term of the agreement was put at two years. The United States agreed not to impose import duties, excise taxes, or prohibitions on a list of nine duty-free products set forth in Schedule Two. These products included roasted and unroasted coffee, root of ipecac, bananas, emeralds, gutta balata, platinum, reptile skins, tagua nuts and tamarinds. American anti-dumping laws excluded coffee. Colombia gave the United States concessions on 150 items of which half received customs reductions and the remainder assured of tariff treatment no less favorable than that enjoyed in 1933. American agricultural exports enjoyed limited reductions on hog lard, prepared cereals, potatoes, canned vegetables, fruits, milk, and hides. Each nation granted national treatment in regard to transportation charges. Both nations granted unconditional most-favored-nation status, a victory for United States commercial policy. Washington and Bogotá also reached the compromise position that all United States articles were to be exempted from state and municipal taxes other than those in force at the time of the agreement. The imposition of future taxes on import commodities could not exceed the maximum taxes in effect at the time of the agreement. These provisions only affected interstate commerce in the United States and, therefore, did not seriously curtail America's freedom of action. Roosevelt also insisted that tariff concessions to Colombia did not affect American territorial possessions such as Puerto Rico, the Virgin Islands, and Hawaii. The President reacted to the draft treaty with Colombia by giving it "an enthusiastic endorsement." A circular issued by the Colombian Minister of Finance said in part, "That the proposed treaty . . . does not mar any national industries of importance nor any branch of agriculture."

The final settlement appears in retrospect heavily weighted toward the American side. Edwin Wilson, of the Division of Latin American Affairs, remarked to Caffery that Congressional ratification of both a Colombian and Brazilian treaty should be easy to obtain since the United States made few if any substantial concessions. For extra insurance against the possibility of violent reaction in Colombia, the text of the trade agreement was withheld until May 1934.

PART 5
WORLD WAR II
DIPLOMACY,
1941-1945

INTRODUCTION

The most important objective of American diplomacy during the war years was to keep the Grand Alliance intact despite the mutual distrust among its members. The antipathy that had characterized their relations since 1917 heightened the normal difficulties of wartime cooperation, and the heated exchanges over Poland and Italy and the timing of the second front reflected—and probably increased—the long-standing mistrust between Russia and the West. That the powers nonetheless cooperated surprisingly well as long as they faced a common enemy can be attributed in part to American and British awareness that the Soviet Union carried the brunt of the fighting from 1941 to the spring of 1944. But as the end of the war approached and the conflicting peace-time objectives of the Big Three emerged more clearly, the alliance began to deteriorate.

Most accounts of World War II diplomacy have concentrated on strategy, summit meetings, and statesmen. In Reading No. 1 Herbert Feis follows the traditional pattern, describing the conversations in Washington between American political leaders and Sir Anthony Eden, the British Foreign Secretary, in March 1943. Although the invasion of Europe was more than a year away, Anglo-American statesmen were already considering the future of Europe, the desirability of some sort of world organization, and the major points of friction with Russia. It is interesting to compare the opinions expressed at these informal talks with the decisions made by Roosevelt, Churchill, and Stalin at Yalta in 1945. (Reading No. 2)

In one sense the Washington conversations were unrealistic, for as Feis notes, Eden and the American officials made no attempt to coordinate military strategy with desired political ends; in fact, they spent relatively little time even discussing how military developments might affect the postwar political settlement. Later, in the conquest of Germany, General Dwight Eisenhower deployed his troops chiefly on the basis of strategic necessity rather than on considerations of political consequences. He concentrated on the military defeat of Germany while paying little heed to the political advantage that might follow as a consequence of the position of his troops at the end of the fighting.

After a successful military operation in North Africa, the Americans and the British moved into Italy, and they worked out a pragmatic solution to the basic political problem facing the coalition resulting from military activity; namely, how to deal with the conquered nations. Italy was the first major belligerent to surrender to Allied troops, and there the United States and Great Britain set the pattern that would prevail in later conquests; although they kept the Soviet Union well informed about the negotiations, the British and Americans would not tolerate Soviet interference in the administration of Italy. Henceforth, whichever power's army occupied a defeated country that power would control it—the Four Power administration of Berlin being the one exception to this practice.

In Reading No. 3 Gabriel Kolko emphasizes the economic aspects of World War II diplomacy, which during the conflict were as significant as the military and political developments and which in the postwar world were probably more important. In contrast to the political objectives—which were disputed within the administration and were not clearly formulated—the economic objectives, being deep-rooted principles of American foreign policy, were soon well defined and generally accepted. Hull had never abandoned his belief that the economic nationalism of the 1930s had been largely responsible for the war; if history were not to repeat itself, the postwar world economy must be governed by the principle of freer trade.

Although its main concern was the support and, later, reconstruction of Europe, the Roosevelt administration did not ignore the then underdeveloped countries, which have figured prominently in the diplomacy of the postwar era. Throughout the war President Roosevelt had shown his distaste for colonial empires, and shortly before his death he expressed his views on the future of colonies and the "brown people". (Reading No. 4) Roosevelt had hoped to place France's colony of Indochina under a United Nations' trusteeship, but in 1945 he approved its return to France.

1

SIR ANTHONY EDEN IN WASHINGTON, MARCH 1943

HERBERT FEIS

The American government had been inclined to put off discussion of the political issues to be met when and as the Axis nations were defeated. It wished them to stay behind the armies, but they could not be kept there. They crept forward; as they had when the Anglo-Soviet treaty of alliance was being made, and as soon as Allied troops landed in North Africa. They came in for attention whenever, in fact, British and Soviet diplomats looked at any part of the European land area between them. They appeared on the horizon whenever military planners mapped campaigns in the Pacific and Far East.

So the American government was compelled to heed and discuss them sooner than it wished. The worst of the military perils having passed, the British government began to look ahead. It wanted to do so in company with the American government since our assent would be necessary to any major decision. Thus in March, Eden travelled to Washington.

In reflecting upon Eden's talks with American officials we should bear in mind that at this time both Roosevelt and Churchill thought it would be possible to get along with the Soviet Union after the war. Roosevelt had not allowed himself to be harried out of this opinion, either by the overbearing ways of the Russians or by the warnings of those who thought otherwise. And this was one of the periods in

Selections from Herbert Feis, *Churchill-Roosevelt-Stalin: The War They Waged and the Peace They Sought* (copyright © 1957 by Princeton University Press; Princeton Paperback, 1966): pp. 119–125. Omission of footnotes. Reprinted by permission of Princeton University Press.

which Churchill was also hopeful about the future of relationships with the Soviet Union. He had been openly saying so, as, for example, in his talk with the President of Turkey some six weeks before, aimed to get that country to enter the war. Churchill minimized the need to fear how the Soviet Union would act at the end of the war, saying that he had seen Molotov and Stalin and his impression was ". . . that both desired a peaceful and friendly association with the United Kingdom and the United States." He had stressed the fact that although he could not see twenty years ahead, Britain, nevertheless, had a twenty-year treaty with the Soviet Union.

Both Hull and Eden at this time were similarly hopeful about being able to live and work satisfactorily with the Soviet Union after the war.

The most important of Eden's talks (March 12th-30th) were in the White House with Roosevelt and Harry Hopkins, Welles being the liaison with the State Department. Once or twice Hull was present. But he received Eden separately in his office.

There, to tell first of his part in the consultations, Hull used his chance mainly to try to bring the British government into line on a few matters close to his heart. After reviewing his grievances against de Gaulle to the verge of being querulous, he besought Eden to assert the power of the British government to compel that Frenchman to be more pliant. He also tried to persuade the British Foreign Minister to go along with measures which he had in mind for converting colonies into "trusteeships" on the way to independence. His aim in this field was to place all dependent peoples under international supervision; colonial relationships were to be allowed to continue, subject however to inspection by international agencies which would be authorized to publish all pertinent facts regarding their administration. This was one of the two great transformations which Hull sought to bring about as an outcome of the war—the other being the formation of a universal collective security system.

The numerous talks in the White House touched many subjects in a lively though inconclusive way. In brief the main ones were:

1. Concerning the Form of the Permanent Organization for Peace and Security. During the year that had elapsed since he had expounded them to Molotov, the President's conceptions in this field had evolved, probably due to the tuition of State Department committees guided by

Hull and Davis. In his talks with Eden he visualized three connected parts within the new organization which was to be world-wide; a general assembly in which all nations were to have a place; an advisory council of representatives of the great powers and some six to eight other countries; and an executive council made up of the United States, Great Britain, the Soviet Union, and China, to which he hoped the advisory council would entrust pretty wide powers. In essence as expressed by the President, ". . . finally, that the real decisions should be made by the United States, Great Britain, Russia, and China, who would be the powers for many years to come that would have to police the world."

Eden said that his government was thinking along similar lines. But he doubted whether it would be possible or practicable to entrust so great authority to an executive group of the Great Powers alone. And he, as had been Molotov before him, was skeptical as to whether China ought to be treated as one of them. About this time Churchill was publicly showing favorable interest in a variant scheme of international organization—one which visualized regional bodies, a council of Europe, and a council of Asia under the world institution. This confused the discussions in Washington somewhat.

Roosevelt tried out on Eden another idea for assuring that the new organization would be able to prevent aggression. He suggested that it should secure and keep permanent control over strategic points and bases ("strong points") in different parts of the world. Some of these might be in Germany or Japan or Italy. Others might be located in other countries. As examples of the latter he mentioned Bizerte in Tunis, Dakar in French West Africa, and the harbor of Formosa. All of these, his idea seems to have been, should be formally under collective direction, but each was to have been garrisoned by the forces of some one member to whom the assignment was given. It is hard to tell from the talks just what Roosevelt had in mind on this point—whether he conceived that these garrisons would all be part of one international armed military force or separate national units provided by the "Four Policemen."

In any case, as will be seen, this improvisation did not weather well. Even if it had been judged desirable and practicable, one very hard fact would have stood in the way of its realization; the strategic points in mind could have been detached from national control only by compulsion.

2. Some Prospective Soviet Territorial Claims. The President asked Eden whether he thought there was anything in the view that the Soviet government was determined to dominate the whole of Europe by armed force or propaganda. Eden answered that he did not believe so. But in any case he thought it wise to cultivate Soviet confidence and friendship—to pave the way toward cooperation and avoid rigid Soviet hostility. That, he added, was not always easy to do since the Soviet government was difficult and so very mistrustful. Some further light on Eden's thought is cast by a comment he made in the course of another talk about the future of Germany. As recorded by Hopkins, "Eden said he believed one of the reasons Stalin wanted a second front in Europe was political; that if Germany collapsed, he had no desire, in Germany, to take full responsibility for what would happen in Germany and the rest of Europe, and he believed it was a fixed matter of Russian foreign policy to have both British and U.S. troops heavily in Europe when the collapse comes."

Eden summed up for Roosevelt what he thought Soviet territorial demands would be. He could be definite since Maisky, the Soviet Ambassador in London, had called on him just before he left for Washington and had described freely what the Soviet government wanted.

a. The Baltic States. Eden thought that the Soviet government would insist on absorbing these, and that it would reject the proposal which Roosevelt thought ought to be made—that a second plebiscite should be held in these countries before any such action was taken. Roosevelt remarked that we might have to agree to this absorption but, if so, it ought to be used as a bargaining counter with Russia.

b. Poland. Eden thought that the Soviet government would claim for itself some of the territory that had been part of Poland in 1939— possibly up to the Curzon Line. He observed, however, that the extent of Soviet claims in this region might depend somewhat on the way in which it regarded the group who might be controlling Poland at the time of the peace conference.

The discussion also touched, though only loosely, on Poland's western frontiers. The President and Eden agreed that Poland might have East Prussia after the war. Eden thought the Russians would agree to that, but were not yet ready to say so to the Polish government in London. Stalin also was disposed, he thought, to change the Silesian frontier in favor of Poland. With these accessions in the west,

Poland would have a satisfactory living space, and Stalin, Eden thought, wanted Poland to be strong.

In general, in his talks with Eden, the President's comments on frontier questions were reserved. But he did remark, apropos of the pretensions of the Polish government in London, that the big powers would have to decide what Poland should have, and that he did not intend to bargain with the Poles or other small countries at the peace conference.

This comment was stimulated by Eden's account of how assertive the Polish government-in-exile was being; how utterly unreal in its notions of the place and power of Poland after the war; and how stubborn in its wish to keep the eastern frontiers which it had between the two world wars. Eden thought that the Soviet government would not insist on having a Communist government in Poland, but he was sure that it would demand that any and all future Polish governments be representative of the popular will. Therefore it would not be disposed to allow the existing exiled group in London to retain power, though not unfriendly to some of its individual members.

This whole patch of discussion with Eden about Polish matters was tinged with worry as to what Russia might do. But no special ways were seen to guard against a possible bad outcome.

c. Bessarabia. The President agreed with Eden that the Soviets were entitled to regain this province—on the Romanian frontier—as it had been Russian throughout most of its history.

d. Finland. The President and Eden agreed that the Soviets would insist on the boundary line that had been drawn at the end of its war with Finland in March 1940. They both thought this reasonable. But Eden forecast that the Soviet government would also demand Hangoe as necessary for the security and defense of Petrograd. They both also seemed to think that it would be hard to dispute this claim since the war had shown how dangerously exposed the city was to capture.

e. Yugoslavia. The President thought it would be absurd to force the Croats and the Serbs to continue to live together as a nation. But Eden thought otherwise; he felt that they could and should live together.

f. Czechoslovakia, Romania, Bulgaria, Turkey, and Greece. The President and Eden agreed that the future determination of the frontiers of these countries should not cause serious trouble.

g. Austria and Hungary. The President and Eden agreed that these should be established as independent states. Austria was presumably to regain its former frontiers. Eden thought Stalin would want to punish Hungary and have it yield territory to Romania.

h. Germany. The President seems to have left it mainly to Welles and Hull to talk with Eden about the future of Germany. Eden told Welles that the thoughts of his government, and his own thoughts in particular, were turning toward dismemberment. It would of course be best, he added, if this came about spontaneously. Welles, saying that he was talking for himself alone, thought nothing short of partition would end the German menace. He sketched four steps—including the transfer of East Prussia, the separation of Prussia, and the formation, out of the rest of Germany, of two or three other independent states. But Hull, talking with Eden that same day, said that he had not made up his mind whether anything of the sort should be done. The talk recorded agreement that it would be well for the world if Germany were partitioned, but did not decide whether partition ought, if necessary, to be imposed by force. Obviously the subject would have to wait upon consultation with the Russians.

i. China. The President and Hull told Eden they were sorry that Churchill, in a speech which he had made the day before, had not mentioned China as among the great powers. The President said that he thought that since China might be of use in policing Japan, he wanted to strengthen it in every possible way. But Eden said he was doubtful whether China could stabilize itself and thought it might have to go through a revolution after the war. Moreover, he remarked, "he did not much like the idea of the Chinese running up and down the Pacific."

j. Other Far Eastern Questions. The President suggested that Manchuria and Formosa be returned to China; that Indochina be placed in trusteeship; that Korea also be put under a trusteeship to be directed jointly by China, the United States, and one or two other powers; and that the Japanese mandated islands be internationalized. The inconclusive discussion that followed left Roosevelt free to develop them later on, as he did in the momentous Cairo Declaration—which pronounced the end of the Japanese Empire.

All early talks about postwar arrangements, such as these with Eden, had to be a forced exercise in imagination, a drill guided by surmise about facts that only the future would define. This is one reason why the record of these discussions leaves the impression that they were conducted in a vacuum. But there was, I think another reason as well. The contingencies of war were not allowed to complicate the exchange of opinions of what ought to be done after the war was won. Not enough heed was paid to the way in which military developments could affect political possibilities. Only once, at dinner on the 14th, did the talk straggle onto this subject. As recorded by Hopkins, "We then discussed at some length, the political effect of our troops being in Italy as against France at the time of the collapse of Germany and, while both Eden and the President thought it would not be as advantageous, it was far better than not being there (on the Continent) at all." No one suggested that military strategy be adjusted to serve the political purposes and settlements in mind.

Roosevelt was trying to fight a coalition war without coalition politics, lest these hinder the conduct of the war. The State Department was intently engaged in studying the politics of peace. Hull was content not to be called on so soon to deal with the barbed issues in this field of moving events.

As soon as the talks with Eden were over (on March 31st) Hull summarized for Litvinov what had been said. In doing so he stressed that Eden had shared our desire to work with Russia after the war, and the opinion that the Americans, Russians, and British must together try to restrain agitation and troublemakers in their own as well as other countries. He also took pains to tell of the formula which had been explained to the British about the policy toward "dependent peoples," based on our hope of seeing a general forward movement around the world relating to an awakening of these peoples. On the same day the State Department sent a similar account of the Eden talks to Ambassador Standley for Molotov. This more definitely called attention to the fact that no attempt had been made to formulate agreements or decisions. Molotov did not say whether or not he believed this statement. It will be seen how anxious Roosevelt and Hull continued to be right up to the end of the war to give the Russians no ground for believing we were in a secret combination with the British, or in a separate camp with them.

2

YALTA CONFERENCE

Protocol of Proceedings

PROTOCOL OF THE PROCEEDINGS OF THE CRIMEA CONFERENCE

The Crimea Conference of the Heads of the Governments of the United States of America, the United Kingdom, and the Union of Soviet Socialist Republics which took place from February 4th to 11th came to the following conclusions.

I World Organisation

It was decided:

1. that a United Nations Conference on the proposed world organization should be summoned for Wednesday, 25th April, 1945, and should be held in the United States of America.
2. the Nations to be invited to this Conference should be:
    (*a*) the United Nations as they existed on the 8th February, 1945 and
    (*b*) such of the Associated Nations as have declared war on the common enemy by 1st March, 1945. (For this purpose by the term "Associated Nation" was meant the eight Associated Nations and Turkey.) When the Conference on World Organisation is held, the delegates of the United Kingdom and United States of America will support a proposal to admit to original membership two Soviet Socialist Republics, i. e. the Ukraine and White Russia.
3. that the United States Government on behalf of the Three Powers should consult the Government of China and the French Provisional Government in regard to the decisions taken at the present Conference concerning the proposed World Organisation.

4.   that the text of the invitation to be issued to all the nations which would take part in the United Nations Conference should be as follows:

INVITATION

"The Government of the United States of America, on behalf of itself and of the Governments of the United Kingdom, the Union of Soviet Socialist Republics, and the Republic of China and of the Provisional Government of the French Republic, invite the Government of _____ to send representatives to a Conference of the United Nations to be held on 25th April, 1945, or soon thereafter, at San Francisco in the United States of America to prepare a Charter for a General International Organisation for the maintenance of international peace and security.

"The above named governments suggest that the Conference consider as affording a basis for such a Charter the Proposals for the Establishment of a General International Organisation, which were made public last October as a result of the Dumbarton Oaks Conference, and which have now been supplemented by the following provisions for Section C of Chapter VI:

" 'C. *Voting*

'1. Each member of the Security Council should have one vote.

'2. Decisions of the Security Council on procedural matters should be made by an affirmative vote of seven members.

'3. Decisions of the Security Council on all other matters should be made by an affirmative vote of seven members including the concurring votes of the permanent members; provided that, in decisions under Chapter VIII, Section A and under the second sentence of paragraph 1 of Chapter VIII, Section C, a party to a dispute should abstain from voting'.

"Further information as to arrangements will be transmitted subsequently.

"In the event that the Government of _____ desires in advance of the Conference to present views or comments concerning the proposals, the Government of the United States of America will be pleased to transmit such views and comments to the other participating Governments".

TERRITORIAL TRUSTEESHIP

It was agreed that the five Nations which will have permanent seats on the Security Council should consult each other prior to the United Nations Conference on the question of territorial trusteeship.

The acceptance of this recommendation is subject to its being made clear that territorial trusteeship will only apply to (a) existing mandates of the League of Nations; (b) territories detached from the enemy as a result of the present war; (c) any other territory which might voluntarily be placed under trusteeship; and (d) no discussion of actual territories is contemplated at the forthcoming United Nations Conference or in the preliminary consultations, and it will be a matter for subsequent agreement which territories within the above categories will be placed under trusteeship.

II Declaration on Liberated Europe

The following declaration has been approved:

"The Premier of the Union of Soviet Socialist Republics, the Prime Minister of the United Kingdom and the President of the United States of America have consulted with each other in the common interests of the peoples of their countries and those of liberated Europe. They jointly declare their mutual agreement to concert during the temporary period of instability in liberated Europe the policies of their three governments in assisting the peoples liberated from the domination of Nazi Germany and the peoples of the former Axis satellite states of Europe to solve by democratic means their pressing political and economic problems.

"The establishment of order in Europe and the re-building of national economic life must be achieved by processes which will enable the liberated peoples to destroy the last vestiges of Nazism and Fascism and to create democratic institutions of their own choice. This is a principle of the Atlantic Charter—the right of all peoples to choose the form of government under which they will live—the restoration of sovereign rights and self-government to those peoples who have been forcibly deprived of them by the aggressor nations.

"To foster the conditions in which the liberated peoples may exercise these rights, the three governments will jointly assist the people in any European liberated state or former Axis satellite state in Europe where in their judgment conditions require (a) to establish conditions of internal peace; (b) to carry out emergency measures for the relief of distressed peoples; (c) to form interim governmental authorities broadly representative of all democratic elements in the population and pledged to the earliest possible establishment through free elections of governments responsive to the will of the people; and (d) to facilitate where necessary the holding of such elections.

"The three governments will consult the other United Nations and provisional authorities or other governments in Europe when matters of direct interest to them are under consideration.

"When, in the opinion of the three governments, conditions in any European liberated state or any former Axis satellite state in Europe make such action necessary, they will immediately consult together on the measures necessary to discharge the joint responsibilities set forth in this declaration.

"By this declaration we reaffirm our faith in the principles of the Atlantic Charter, our pledge in the Declaration by the United Nations, and our determination to build in co-operation with other peace-loving nations world order under law, dedicated to peace, security, freedom and general well-being of all mankind.

"In issuing this declaration, the Three Powers express the hope that the Provisional Government of the French Republic may be associated with them in the procedure suggested."

III Dismemberment of Germany

It was agreed that Article 12 (a) of the Surrender Terms for Germany should be amended to read as follows:

"The United Kingdom, the United States of America and the Union of Soviet Socialist Republics shall possess supreme authority with respect to Germany. In the exercise of such authority they will take such steps, including the complete disarmament, demilitarisation and the dismemberment of Germany as they deem requisite for future peace and security."

The study of the procedure for the dismemberment of Germany was referred to a Committee, consisting of Mr. Eden (Chairman), Mr.

Winant and Mr. Gousev. This body would consider the desirability of associating with it a French representative.

IV   Zone of Occupation for the French and Control Council for Germany
It was agreed that a zone in Germany, to be occupied by the French Forces, should be allocated to France. This zone would be formed out of the British and American zones and its extent would be settled by the British and Americans in consultation with the French Provisional Government.

It was also agreed that the French Provisional Government should be invited to become a member of the Allied Control Council for Germany.

V   Reparation
The following protocol has been approved:
1. Germany must pay in kind for the losses caused by her to the Allied nations in the course of the war. Reparations are to be received in the first instance by those countries which have borne the main burden of the war, have suffered the heaviest losses and have organised victory over the enemy.
2. Reparation in kind is to be exacted from Germany in three following forms:

   (*a*) Removals within 2 years from the surrender of Germany or the cessation of organised resistance from the national wealth of Germany located on the territory of Germany herself as well as outside her territory (equipment, machine-tools, ships, rolling stock, German investments abroad, shares of industrial, transport and other enterprises in Germany etc.), these removals to be carried out chiefly for purpose of destroying the war potential of Germany.

   (*b*) Annual deliveries of goods from current production for a period to be fixed.

   (*c*) Use of German labour.

3. For the working out on the above principles of a detailed plan for exaction of reparation from Germany an Allied Reparation Commission will be set up in Moscow. It will consist of three representatives—one from the Union of Soviet Socialist Republics, one from the United Kingdom and one from the United States of America.

4. With regard to the fixing of the total sum of the reparation as well as the distribution of it among the countries which suffered from the German aggression the Soviet and American delegations agreed as follows:

> "The Moscow Reparation Commission should take in its initial studies as a basis for discussion the suggestion of the Soviet Government that the total sum of the reparation in accordance with the points (a) and (b) of the paragraph 2 should be 20 billion dollars and that 50% of it should go to the Union of Soviet Socialist Republics."

The British delegation was of the opinion that pending consideration of the reparation question by the Moscow Reparation Commission no figures of reparation should be mentioned.

The above Soviet-American proposal has been passed to the Moscow Reparation Commission as one of the proposals to be considered by the Commission.

VI   Major War Criminals
The Conference agreed that the question of the major war criminals should be the subject of enquiry by the three Foreign Secretaries for report in due course after the close of the Conference.

VII   Poland
The following Declaration on Poland was agreed by the Conference:

> "A new situation has been created in Poland as a result of her complete liberation by the Red Army. This calls for the establishment of a Polish Provisional Government which can be more broadly based than was possible before the recent liberation of the Western part of Poland. The Provisional Government which is now functioning in Poland should therefore be reorganised on a broader democratic basis with the inclusion of democratic leaders from Poland itself and from Poles abroad. This new Government should then be called the Polish Provisional Government of National Unity.
> "M. Molotov, Mr. Harriman and Sir A. Clark Kerr are authorised as a commission to consult in the first instance in Moscow with members of the present Provisional Government and with other Polish democratic leaders from within Poland and from abroad, with a view to the reorganisation of the present Government along the above

lines. This Polish Provisional Government of National Unity shall be pledged to the holding of free and unfettered elections as soon as possible on the basis of universal suffrage and secret ballot. In these elections all democratic and anti-Nazi parties shall have the right to take part and to put forward candidates.

"When a Polish Provisional Government of National Unity has been properly formed in conformity with the above, the Government of the U. S. S. R., which now maintains diplomatic relations with the present Provisional Government of Poland, and the Government of the United Kingdom and the Government of the U. S. A. will establish diplomatic relations with the new Polish Provisional Government of National Unity, and will exchange Ambassadors by whose reports the respective Governments will be kept informed about the situation in Poland.

"The three Heads of Government consider that the Eastern frontier of Poland should follow the Curzon Line with digressions from it in some regions of five to eight kilometres in favour of Poland. They recognise that Poland must receive substantial accessions of territory in the North and West. They feel that the opinion of the new Polish Provisional Government of National Unity should be sought in due course on the extent of these accessions and that the final delimitation of the Western frontier of Poland should thereafter await the Peace Conference."

VIII   Yugoslavia

It was agreed to recommend to Marshal Tito and to Dr. Subasic:

(*a*) that the Tito-Subasic Agreement should immediately be put into effect and a new Government formed on the basis of the Agreement.

(*b*) that as soon as the new Government has been formed it should declare:

(i) that the Anti-Fascist Assembly of National Liberation (AUNOJ) will be extended to include members of the last Yugoslav Skupstina who have not compromised themselves by collaboration with the enemy, thus forming a body to be known as a temporary Parliament and

(ii) that legislative acts passed by the Anti-Fascist Assembly of National Liberation (AUNOJ) will be subject to subsequent ratification by a Constituent Assembly;

and that this statement should be published in the communique of the Conference.

IX Italo-Yugoslav Frontier
Italo-Austria Frontier
Notes on these subjects were put in by the British delegation and the American and Soviet delegations agreed to consider them and give their views later.

X. Yugoslav-Bulgarian Relations
There was an exchange of views between the Foreign Secretaries on the question of the desirability of a Yugoslav-Bulgarian pact of alliance. The question at issue was whether a state still under an armistice regime could be allowed to enter into a treaty with another state. Mr. Eden suggested that the Bulgarian and Yugoslav Governments should be informed that this could not be approved. Mr. Stettinius suggested that the British and American Ambassadors should discuss the matter further with M. Molotov in Moscow. M. Molotov agreed with the proposal of Mr. Stettinius.

XI South Eastern Europe
The British Delegation put in notes for the consideration of their colleagues on the following subjects:

   (a) the Control Commission in Bulgaria
   (b) Greek claims upon Bulgaria, more particularly with reference to reparations
   (c) Oil equipment in Roumania.

XII Iran
Mr. Eden, Mr. Stettinius and M. Molotov exchanged views on the situation in Iran. It was agreed that this matter should be pursued through the diplomatic channel.

XIII Meetings of the Three Foreign Secretaries
The Conference agreed that permanent machinery should be set up for consultation between the three Foreign Secretaries; they should meet as often as necessary, probably about every three or four months.

These meetings will be held in rotation in the three capitals, the first meeting being held in London.

XIV The Montreux Convention and the Straits
It was agreed that at the next meeting of the three Foreign Secretaries to be held in London, they should consider proposals which it was understood the Soviet Government would put forward in relation to the Montreux Convention and report to their Governments. The Turkish Government should be informed at the appropriate moment.

The foregoing Protocol was approved and signed by the three Foreign Secretaries at the Crimean Conference, February 11, 1945.

E R Stettinius, Jr

B. Mojotob. [Molotov]

Anthony Eden

Protocol on German Reparation

PROTOCOL ON THE TALKS BETWEEN THE HEADS OF THE THREE GOVERNMENTS AT THE CRIMEAN CONFERENCE ON THE QUESTION OF THE GERMAN REPARATION IN KIND

The Heads of the three governments agreed as follows:
1. Germany must pay in kind for the losses caused by her to the Allied nations in the course of the war. Reparation are to be received in the first instance by those countries which have borne the main burden of the war, have suffered the heaviest losses and have organised victory over the enemy.
2. Reparation in kind are to be exacted from Germany in three following forms:
    (*a*) Removals within 2 years fom the surrender of Germany or the cessation of organised resistance from the national wealth of Germany located on the territory of Germany herself as well as outside her territory (equipment, machine-tools, ships, rolling stock, German investments abroad, shares of industrial, transport and other enterprises in Germany etc.), these removals to be carried out chiefly for purpose of destroying the war potential of Germany.

(*b*) Annual deliveries of goods from current production for a period to be fixed.

(*c*) Use of German labour.

3. For the working out on the above principles of a detailed plan for exaction of reparation from Germany an Allied Reparation Commission will be set up in Moscow. It will consist of three representatives—one from the Union of Soviet Socialist Republics, one from the United Kingdom and one from the United States of America.

4. With regard to the fixing of the total sum of the reparation as well as the distribution of it among the countries which suffered from the German aggression the Soviet and American delegations agreed as follows:

"The Moscow Reparations Commission should take in its initial studies as a basis for discussion the suggestion of the Soviet Government that the total sum of the reparation in accordance with the points (*a*) and (*b*) of the paragraph 2 should be 20 billion dollars and that 50% of it should go to the Union of Soviet Socialist Republics."

The British delegation was of the opinion that pending consideration of the reparation question by the Moscow Reparation Commission no figures of reparation should be mentioned.

The above Soviet-American proposal has been passed to the Moscow Reparation Commission as one of the proposals to be considered by the Commission.

WINSTON S. CHURCHILL
FRANKLIN D ROOSEVELT
И. Стајин [STALIN]

FEBRUARY 11, 1945.

Agreement Regarding Entry of the Soviet Union Into the War Against Japan

AGREEMENT

The leaders of the three Great Powers—the Soviet Union, the United States of America and Great Britain—have agreed that in two or three months after Germany has surrendered and the war in Europe has terminated the Soviet Union shall enter into the war against Japan on the side of the Allies on condition that:

1. The *status quo* in Outer-Mongolia (The Mongolian People's Republic) shall be preserved;
2. The former rights of Russia violated by the treacherous attack of Japan in 1904 shall be restored, viz:

    (*a*) the southern part of Sakhalin as well as all the islands adjacent to it shall be returned to the Soviet Union,

    (*b*) the commercial port of Dairen shall be internationalized, the preeminent interests of the Soviet Union in this port being safeguarded and the lease of Port Arthur as a naval base of the USSR restored,

    (*c*) the Chinese-Eastern Railroad and the South-Manchurian Railroad which provides an outlet to Dairen shall be jointly operated by the establishment of a joint Soviet-Chinese Company it being understood that the preeminent interests of the Soviet Union shall be safeguarded and that China shall retain full sovereignty in Manchuria;

3. The Kuril islands shall be handed over to the Soviet Union.

It is understood, that the agreement concerning Outer-Mongolia and the ports and railroads referred to above will require concurrence of Generalissimo Chiang Kai-Shek. The President will take measures in order to obtain this concurrence on advice from Marshal Stalin.

The Heads of the three Great Powers have agreed that these claims of the Soviet Union shall be unquestionably fulfilled after Japan has been defeated.

For its part the Soviet Union expresses its readiness to conclude with the National Government of China a pact of friendship and alliance between the USSR and China in order to render assistance to China with its armed forces for the purpose of liberating China from the Japanese yoke.

И. Стаʌин [STALIN]
FRANKLIN D ROOSEVELT
WINSTON S. CHURCHILL

FEBRUARY 11, 1945.

3
PLANNING FOR PEACE
GABRIEL KOLKO

What kind of peace and world order did the leaders of the United States hope to attain after the war, and what type of world did they expect would emerge from the chaos and disintegration of the period? What did the Americans believe they were fighting for, and what were their peace aims?

There were two crucial aspects to American objectives. The first critical ingredient was economic—clear, explicit, and well outlined from 1943 onward. Indeed Washington's definition of its economic peace aims were by the inception of the war deeply established principles of American foreign policy, inherited almost completely from the world view of Woodrow Wilson. On the political level American objectives until Yalta were impressionistic and improvised with experience, but after February 1945 the policy-makers defined a firm American position on political peace aims. If Roosevelt and his advisers could disagree on political objectives and assumptions for the postwar period, though ultimately hammer out a unified position, there was strikingly little dispute over matters pertaining to the contemplated role of the United States in the world economy.

The Atlantic Charter Roosevelt and Churchill issued in August 1941 was the only statement of American peace aims with any pretense of formally indicating the objectives of the Anglo-American alliance and the alternatives it posed to fascism. The charter was a remarkably obtuse document referring to no territorial aggrandizement or changes

From THE POLITICS OF WAR, by Gabriel Kolko pp. 242–252. Copyright © 1968 by Gabriel Kolko. Reprinted by permission of Random House, Inc.

without the consent of the people concerned; self-determination; free access of all states to economic opportunities, trade, and raw materials; freedom of the seas; disarmament; and "freedom from fear and want." One could make the broadest interpretation of its political meaning, for the charter said little concerning the procedures to implement its sweeping goals, save in the area of economic policy, where it was indeed quite clear. Roosevelt's public statements on war and peace aims in subsequent years were hardly more than vague homilies—"a decent peace and a durable peace" as he told Congress in January 1943—and the effective thinking on such matters was covert and subdued, and ultimately armies and diplomats meeting together at Moscow, Casablanca, or Teheran would hammer out such questions, at least on an abstract level.[1] Certainly the United States had not been isolationist during the interwar period, and it based its refusal to enter the League of Nations as much on its unwillingness to subordinate American power to a league in which the weak and strong alike were equals as on any other consideration. Everyone in Washington during the interwar years acknowledged American global interests, economic and strategic, and only the relative priority they assigned to this interest, as opposed to domestic problems, varied. American power existed, and the issue was less the basic role of the United States in the world than the conditions under which it would employ its power. When its interests were threatened, the United States had not hesitated to defend them, via diplomacy, occasional forays into Latin American nations, and finally entry into the massive global war. There was no chance whatsoever that the United States would isolate itself after the war, for that had been a physical impossibility for three decades. The question, rather, was what type of world strategy it would pursue.

Reflecting primarily on the lessons of World War I the United States began to plan for the peace in 1941 and by 1943 had a fairly coherent formulation of objectives—highly explicit in the economic field and less precise as to the political instrumentalities required—which it shaped into a well-articulated world view in the two years preceding Yalta. That the impact of the war would not be apocalyptic nor result in chaos and the radical transformation of the political and economic world system was the chief, if unspoken, axiom of American planning. Without this sanguine estimate rational plans for the attainment of

---

[1] Holborn, *War and Peace Aims*, 192.

functional goals would have been impossible. Even when the United States devoted increasing energy and time to restraining the pressures and disintegration the war in Europe and Asia created, it never expected that the operational basis of its planning would have to assume inevitable, widespread revolution in the world, revolution that might radically subvert the foundations of American policy. That realization, at least in part, came after the war ended, for during the war itself the obvious problems emerging from the breakdown of the Old Order seemed soluble—with patience, economic resources, and determination —to the men in Washington.

The basic responsibility for American political and economic planning for the peace befell the Department of State, which is to say Cordell Hull of Tennessee. Hull, Secretary of State longer than any other man in American history, was strong-willed and of firm convictions. That Hull was a minor figure under Roosevelt is a myth without basis in fact. It was Roosevelt's wont to take advice from many sources, even when contradictory and inept, and he often excluded Hull from the first round of such deliberations, even occasionally not informing him of their very existence. In the long run, however, Hull and the State Department made their full weight felt in subsequent discussions of foreign policy, and they more often than not prevailed by the time issues of policy were finally resolved. Due in part to the ultimate consensus on essential premises that everyone in Washington shared, disagreements were invariably over only means and tactics. Hull could often exploit this by lining up other powerful advisers behind his policies. Also Hull's tenacious manners created personal difficulties between himself and Sumner Welles, his Under Secretary, that undermined the influence of both. But by the fall of 1944, after Welles's departure, no one could doubt the State Department's active role in the definition and conduct of American foreign policy. And throughout the war Hull shared the basic responsibility for the formulation of economic peace aims, on which everyone in Washington agreed in principle, and of political objectives, on which there was more dispute and therefore many counterpressures to Hull's advice.

Hull was a disciple of Woodrow Wilson and the Wilsonian world view, which expressed in its essentials the foundations of American foreign policy. He recalled in his memoirs:

> But toward 1916 I embraced the philosophy I carried throughout my twelve years as Secretary of State. . . . From then on, to me, unham-

pered trade dovetailed with peace; high tariffs, trade barriers, and unfair economic competition, with war. Though realizing that many other factors were involved, I reasoned that, if we could get a freer flow of trade—freer in the sense of fewer discriminations and obstructions—so that one country would not be deadly jealous of another and the living standards of all countries might rise, thereby eliminating the economic dissatisfaction that breeds war, we might have a reasonable chance for lasting peace.

This theme was critical to United States policy, and Hull followed it with a literalness which gradually permeated all phases of American foreign policy. "It is the collapse of the world structure, the development of isolated economies," Hull declared in 1935, "that has let loose the fear which now grips every nation, and which threatens the peace of the world." This economic interpretation of the fascist challenge to the more conventional capitalist states led Hull later to write, "I kept hammering home the economic side of international relations as the major possibility for averting the catastrophe," and during 1938 he saw Nazi expansion as a simple German desire for raw materials, resources that would be available "if the German Government decides to change its course and adopt our liberal commercial policy. . . ." Even when it became painfully obvious that Germany would not pursue this advice, in 1940, as Hull envisioned the postwar world, "I believed . . . that the trade agreements program should be retained intact to serve as a cornerstone around which the nations could rebuild their commerce on liberal lines when the war ended."[2] In the last analysis the solution to the world's political problems could be found in a rationally ordered world economy, and this guiding assumption colored United States response to specific problems in Europe, Asia, and Latin America continuously during World War II and thereafter. Even when they could not create the ideal world system the model of it existed as a beacon toward which the Americans would attempt to strive.

There was an inflexibility in Hull's determined views that oriented his response to all specific political proposals and often led him to disagree with his peers in Washington, and most especially with Great Britain. But by the time Edward R. Stettinius replaced him at the end of November 1944, he had essentially defined American economic and political peace aims, and Stettinius, who was the son of a J. P. Morgan

Hull, *Memoirs*, 81, 391, 518, 594, 746.

partner and himself a former vice-president of General Motors and president of United States Steel, was not inclined to alter this course. Roosevelt chose the affable, handsome, and always smiling Stettinius because his colorless past—"a curious blend of businessman and world social reformer," as one contemporary put it—had left him with fewer powerful enemies than James F. Byrnes, Hull's first choice as his successor.[3] Stettinius was an expert on internal administration within the State Department, and his major policy interest was in the creation of a United Nations organization which Hull and the rest of Washington had already outlined for him. During the crucial 209 days Stettinius spent in office, Joseph Grew served as Acting Secretary of State for 110 of them.

TOWARD A RECONSTRUCTED WORLD ECONOMY

The impact of the prewar world depression and the experience of the 1930's profoundly colored United States planning of its postwar peace aims. Hull unsuccessfully attempted to cope with that upheaval, and he and the other leaders in Washington were determined to undo its still pervasive consequences to the world economy, and perhaps above all, to prevent its recurrence. For this reason the United States did not simply wish to repair the prewar world economy, but to reconstruct i anew. There was a remarkable unanimity in Washington on this objective, and it was by far the most extensively discussed peace aim, surpassing any other in the level of planning and thought given to it. While the United States faltered for a time in regard to its postwar political objectives, it entered and left the war with a remarkably consistent and sophisticated set of economic peace aims.

The world depression had been cataclysmic, and if ultimately a consequence of the collapse of the European political order that World War I engendered, it nevertheless accelerated the emergence of fascism and Nazism and the new war. Hull for his part took an economic interpretation of the origins of World War II and saw the need to uproot their exacerbating potentialities in the postwar era. The breakdown of the world economy, to which the United States contributed so heavily in its high-tariff Fordney-McCumber Act of 1929 and

[3] Richard L. Walker, *E. R. Stettinius, Jr.* (New York, 1965), 10.

refusal to commit itself to making a success of the London Economic Conference of 1933, affected the United States more than any other nation, for employment and industrial and economic activity declined more precipitously and for a longer time in the United States than in any other industrialized nation. American exports abroad, which had been $5.4 billion in 1929, declined to $2.1 billion in 1933 and $3.1 billion in 1938. American direct investments overseas stagnated and declined slightly during the decade. With the depression came the creation of exclusive trading blocs, the largest of which centered about the British sterling area, which progressively excluded American goods and threatened to tie up critical raw materials essential to a mineral-deficient American economy. This division of the world into increasingly self-sufficient blocs as much as any consequence of the world depression greatly alarmed the Americans.

Western European exports as a percentage of their national products declined sharply from 1929, and in the case of England from 15 percent in 1928 to 8 percent in 1938. Even more important was the fact that more and more of this lower volume of exports stayed within the sterling bloc or was bartered in bilateral exchange agreements that minimized the role of gold and dollars in world trade. By 1938 the sterling bloc accounted for one-third of world trade, depending less and less on United States imports and more on the products of other sterling-based economies.

To a very large extent such trade restrictions increasingly tied down essential imports in primary products—foodstuffs, agricultural raw materials, and minerals—that the United States had to have for a balanced industrial economy, and future growth. The exports of such primary products from the nonindustrial, usually colonial, economies grew by almost one-tenth in the decade after 1928, while exports from the industrialized nations dropped 15 percent. But since these nonindustrialized nations suffered the worst decline in the prices received for their goods, the depression compelled them more than any others to confine their foreign trade to barter, the sterling bloc, and various restrictions which increasingly excluded the United States from the global economy.[4]

[4] U. S. Congress, Joint Committee on the Economic Report, *Hearings, Foreign Economic Policy.* 84:1. November, 1955. (Washington, 1955), 518; General Agreement on Tariffs and Trade [GATT], *Trends in International Trade: A Report by a Panel of Experts* (Geneva, 1958), 20–22.

Despite its own high-tariff policy and the existence of over a hundred legalized export-trade and price-fixing associations authorized by the Webb-Pomerene Act of 1918, the United States throughout the 1920's strenuously fought international price fixing and output-restriction agreements that discriminated against American industrial consumers, especially in tin, rubber, and potash. The depression only accelerated the formation of such restrictive agreements and outright cartels, until 40 to 50 percent of the total world trade prior to the war was subject to some degree of their control. Dozens of the largest American corporations entered into comprehensive agreements with their powerful equivalents in Europe to stabilize world prices and restrict the output of literally hundreds of essential products, and to divide up marketing areas in a manner that ended competition among the industrial nations in numerous fields. Concomitant with such stabilizing agreements was stagnation in the world economy, especially its industrialized sector, and the retardation of America's recovery from the depression.[5]

Hull watched this development of a divided world economy with its exchange controls and barter arrangements and he vainly attempted to reverse the deep, if not primary, American responsibility for its development. The Trade Agreements Act of June 1934, which allowed for as much as a 50 percent tariff reduction for a reciprocating nation, was his sole victory throughout this period, but it hardly altered the much more fundamental trend toward economic autarchy, much less the collapse of American exports and investment abroad. Since Roosevelt's preference for emphasis on national economic recovery largely insulated from the problems of the world economy had not proven successful in restoring full employment, by the outbreak of the war Hull could embark on a redefinition of America's role in the world economy with a remarkable degree of support for his views, for events appeared to vindicate his belief that the collapse of the international economy had brought on the war.

The United States therefore planned for the peace on the basis of the experience of the depression and its relations with the United Kingdom on the economic plane. Given the critical importance of the

---

[5] Edward S. Mason, *Controlling World Trade: Cartels and Commodity Agreements* (New York, 1946), 26; Gabriel Kolko, "American Business and Germany, 1930–41," *Western Political Quarterly*, XV (1962), 713–28.

sterling bloc, it seemed that the resolution of the problem meant winning England to the American viewpoint. . . . Yet it had to formulate larger assumptions and attitudes apart from the problem of England and the sterling bloc, and these revealed the foundations of American policy and the outlines of the new world the United States hoped to create out of the rubble of the war.

In May 1941 Hull publicly enunciated the "few and simple" "main principles" of American foreign economic policy, principles that the United States did not essentially alter throughout the war. Indeed what is remarkable about this statement is not that the principles were precise, but that they were open to free interpretation if the circumstances required. "Extreme nationalism" could not be expressed "in excessive trade restrictions" after the war. "Non-discrimination in international commercial relations must be the rule," and "Raw material supplies must be available to all nations without discrimination," including the careful limitation of commodity agreements affecting the consumer nations, such as the United States. Lastly, in regard to the reconstruction of world finance, "The institutions and arrangements of international finance must be so set up that they lend aid to the essential enterprises and the continuous development of all countries, and permit the payment through processes of trade consonant with the welfare of all countries."[6] For the next four years United States planners merely moved from the general to the specific in defining the instrumentalities for implementing this constant set of principles.

The British avoided comment on these public statements of American peace aims, but since they desperately needed American intervention in the war they attempted to meet American pressures to endorse these goals by issuing the minimum and vaguest possible words. In the summer of 1941, while the British were negotiating in Washington for the American Lend-Lease aid that they required for survival, John Maynard Keynes frightened top officials of the State Department by hinting that the postwar era might compel Britain to resort to far more stringent and discriminatory trade control to save its depleted financial resources. As a result, Welles, Hull, and other American officials determined to obtain British endorsement of their sharpened economic peace aims as the price of American support during the war, thus compelling the Americans to define these aims

[6] DS, *Postwar Foreign Policy*, 46.

even more explicitly. When Roosevelt arranged to meet Churchill off Newfoundland during mid-August 1941, Welles and other American leaders accompanying him came prepared to extract British support for what in effect was Hullian and official doctrine. This in fact became one of the stickiest and most unpleasant aspects of the conference, for the British, aware of American plans, came with their own vague and innocuous proposals for "a fair and equitable distribution of essential produce" which committed them to very little and infuriated the Americans. Welles immediately pointed out to Roosevelt that such pieties would alter nothing, least of all in the sterling bloc, and he offered his own amendment, categorically calling for "the elimination of any discrimination" and "access on equal terms to the markets and to the raw materials" of the world.[7] Churchill immediately rejected the proposal, indicating that a stroke of his pen could not eliminate the Ottawa Agreement on which the sterling bloc was based, nor were the members likely to alter it in any event. To Welles this was bitter medicine, and he recalls telling Roosevelt and Hopkins "that if the British and United States governments could not agree to do everything within their power to further after the termination of the war, a restoration of free and liberal trade policies, they might as well throw in the sponge and realize that one of the greatest factors in creating the present tragic situation in the world was going to be permitted to continue unchecked in the postwar world. . . ." When Roosevelt and his aides confronted Churchill with such reasoning he could only cynically recall "the British experience in adhering to Free Trade for eighty years in the face of ever-mounting American tariffs. . . . All we got in reciprocation was successive doses of American protection."[8]

Roosevelt and Hopkins shared the Hullian view, but during the Atlantic Conference they did not appreciate the argumentative and divisive problems the issue posed, and they were willing to accept a loftier and less legal-sounding compromise and depend on other occasions under way in Washington at the very time in conjunction with the Lend-Lease negotiations to cover the specifics. The compromise was the famous Article IV of the Atlantic Charter, the most carefully

---

[7] Hickman, *European Recovery Program*, 66–67. See also Richard N. Gardner, *Sterling-Dollar Diplomacy: Anglo-American Collaboration in the Reconstruction of Multilateral Trade* (Oxford, 1956), 41–42.

[8] Gardner, *Sterling-Dollar Diplomacy*, 45.

discussed of the entire document: ". . . they will endeavor," the statement read, "with due respect for their existing obligations, to further the enjoyment by all States, great and small, victor or vanquished, of access, on equal terms, to the trade and to the raw materials of the world which are needed for their economic prosperity."

The United States could not afford, however, to compromise on the essential principle of breaking down the sterling bloc, for that was the key to the reconstruction of the world economy after the defeat of the Axis. All concerned themselves with the issue, not only the State Department, whose well-supported Commercial Policy Division carried on the most sophisticated planning on the subject, but the Treasury and Commerce departments as well. Hull was "keenly disappointed" with Article IV, and Washington made sure that they included a more precise statement in the Master Lend-Lease Agreement with Britain that they ultimately signed on February 23, 1942.[9]

The British would not agree to Article VII of the Lend-Lease proposal embodying American economic aims, and both sides haggled over the matter until February. This was the only article of the Lend-Lease Agreement the British would not accept in essentially the form the Americans suggested, and they made it plain that they had no intention of giving up the imperial trade preference system to pay a debt. Hull, with the support of Washington, stood firm and when Churchill came to the United States in January 1942 he again argued for American flexibility. The final text was broad enough to convince both sides that they had won their points, but in fact it merely opened the door to future controversies.

> In the final determination of the benefits to be provided to the United States of America by the United Kingdom for aid furnished under the Act of Congress of March 11, 1941, the terms and conditions thereof shall be such as not to burden commerce between the two countries, but to promote mutually advantageous economic relations between them and the betterment of world-wide economic relations. To that end, they shall include provision for agreed action by the United States of America and the United Kingdom, open to participation by all the other countries of like mind directed to the expansion, by appropriate international and domestic measures, of production, em-

[9] Hull, *Memoirs*, 975–76.

ployment, and the exchange and consumption of goods, which are the material foundation of the liberty and welfare of all peoples; to the elimination of all forms of discriminatory treatment in international commerce, and to the reduction of tariffs, and other trade barriers; and, in general, to the attainment of all the economic objectives set forth in the [Atlantic Charter]. . . .[10]

To the British, who immediately hedged on the meaning of the agreement, it meant little more than immediate aid without massive postwar debts to complicate their economic position. To Hull it was "a long step toward the fulfillment, after the war, of the economic principles for which I had been fighting for half a century."[11] The United States insisted that other nations signing Lend-Lease agreements endorse provisos exactly or nearly identical to Article VII of the British agreement.

There were so many other reiterations of such general statements of economic objectives that it would be uselessly tiring to cite more than a few. More to the point were the specific proposals that permit one to see how the United States hoped to apply such principles, what they would mean in practice for America and for the rest of the world, and the assumptions they revealed as to the nature of international conflict and peace. In brief, it was not merely a question of what the United States was willing to advocate for others, but what it was willing to do itself to implement freer world trade, the breakdown of which the United States greatly aided through its own interwar policies. For if the program was merely for other nations to fulfill without specific guarantees from the United States that it would go at least as far, the policy would be nothing more than a lever with which to open the markets and resources of the world to American exploitation.

What is most interesting about the more general American economic statements after 1942 is not their content, but the relative importance attached to their release. When Hull in July 1942 decided to make his first major public address since October 1941 to discuss United States war aims, and to give the press advance notice of its special impor-

[10] U.S. House, Special Committee on Post-War Economic Policy and Planning, *Hearings, Post-War Economic Policy and Planning.* 78:2, 79:1 (Washington, 1945), 1073.

[11] Hull, *Memoirs,* 1153. See also Gardner, *Sterling-Dollar Diplomacy,* chap. IV; E. F. Penrose, *Economic Planning for the Peace* (Princeton, 1953), chap. II.

tance, he was again specific only on economic matters. Welles, Henry Wallace, the very uninfluential Vice-President, Stimson, Hopkins, Roosevelt, and of course Hull again and again, privately and publicly, stressed this economic theme. The future required American leadership in the world economy, "the opposite of economic nationalism," or a new internationalism which many American allies feared was synonymous with American hegemony over the world economy. To the colonial nations Hull's often repeated words conveyed undertones of a new colonialism: "Through international investment, capital must be made available for the sound development of latent natural resources and productive capacity in relatively undeveloped areas." And the supreme role of the United States in this global undertaking struck many Allies as potentially damaging to their interests: "Leadership toward a new system of international relationships in trade and other economic affairs will devolve very largely upon the United States because of our great economic strength. We should assume this leadership, and the responsibility that goes with it, primarily for reasons of pure national self-interest."[12] Exactly this realistic theme aroused anxiety among the Allies.

The major allies of the United States heard about these problems often, for Hull never lost an opportunity to expound American postwar economic projects at various international conferences. At the Moscow Foreign Ministers' Conference he proposed that the Allies accept American doctrines and open systematic discussions for their implementation. The failure of the Entente during World War I to develop common economic peace aims especially obsessed Hull and Stimson, and they repeatedly cited the analogy. For, as Stimson typically commented after the Moscow Conference, "while these political arrangements are good, they haven't any grasp apparently of the underlying need of proper economic arrangements to make the peace stick."[13] Both Stimson and Frank Knox, Secretary of the Navy, felt such compacts were especially critical, for other than England, future American relations with the Allies in the postwar period would have to be limited "mainly to economic agreements in respect to (a) sound

[12] Holborn, *War and Peace Aims*, 277, 280. See also *ibid.*, 199, 235–39, 276, 280; Hull, *Memoirs*, 1177–78.
[13] Stimson Diary, October 28, 1943, HLS Mss. See also Hull, *Memoirs* 1303–04.

money; and (b) the prohibition of tariff obstacles."[14] The importance of this concept cannot be overemphasized.

Well before it formulated a coherent policy on political goals or the United Nations, therefore, the United States had reduced its postwar economic objectives to a precise form. The British too devoted much time and energy to this topic, and of course posed the largest single problem insofar as the implementation of United States policy was concerned. In Washington, however, the State Department and Henry Morgenthau's Treasury Department assumed the major responsibilities for postwar economic planning, with the Commerce and Agriculture departments also contributing specific reports and recommendations. This profusion of activity meant that the United States would have an elaborately constructed policy covering all phases of the world economy, for while it is true that on a personal and organizational level the Treasury and State departments were on especially cool terms, their practical functions were entirely complementary and essential to each other. The Treasury Department concerned itself with the reform of the international financial system, State with trade and raw materials policies; reform in one field was impossible without the other and all understood and accepted this fact. Both worked within the same set of assumptions, reflected in Hull's statements, and their cool personal relations did not detract from their parallel functions. Both defined American foreign economic policy in its larger sense for the war period, and it was of no special significance that Britain gave first consideration to the Treasury Department's rather than the State Department's proposals at the beginning of 1943.

The motives for advocating a reconstructed world economy were not at all deductive, based on the abstract premises of some logical theory, but reflected Washington's specific understanding of the problems that would confront the American economy after the war. The Department of Commerce in its first studies, published in 1943, pointed to the vastly increased industrial capacity that the economy would have to deal with during the period of transition to peace, and similar reports, many confidential, by other economic agencies followed. The War Production Board in April 1944 calculated that the termination of the war with Germany alone would free almost immediately five and one-half to six million workers, only two million being soldiers from a

14 Stimson Diary, September 7, 1943, HLS Mss.

military force five times that size. They predicted peace with Germany would release some $27 billion worth of annual industrial capacity by fall 1945, at which time they still expected to be at war with Japan.[15] By spring 1944 the United States government financed three-quarters of the $20 billion in new industrial plant constructed during the war until that time, in addition to contracting for the construction of 2,700 Liberty ships to carry goods abroad. It was not merely a question of foreign trade, but how much they would need to maintain a reasonable level of employment, and the means by which they might obtain it. The State Department's "Special Committee on the Relaxation of Trade Barriers" in its interim report of December 1943 stated as its first "basic objective" that "A great expansion in the volume of international trade after the war will be essential to the attainment of full and effective employment in the United States and elsewhere, to the preservation of private enterprise, and the success of an international security system to prevent future wars."[16]

In this context the American economic war aim was to save capitalism at home and abroad.

[15] Penrose, *Economic Planning for the Peace*, 39–40; Gardner, *Sterling-Dollar Diplomacy*, 72–76; Hickman, *European Recovery Program*, 78–80; War Production Board, Bureau of Planning and Statistics, "War Production and Civilian Output After Victory in Europe." Part I, April 24, 1944 (Washington, 1944), 7, 9, 27, EAL Mss, box 11.

[16] DS, *Postwar Foreign Policy*, 622. See also War Production Board, "War Production and Civilian Output," *passim*, EAL Mss; House Committee on Post-War Economic Policy, *Post-War Economic Policy*, 622.

4

ROOSEVELT'S VIEWS
ON COLONIES AND
"BROWN PEOPLE"

*Memorandum of Conversation, by the Adviser on Caribbean Affairs
(Taussig)*

[WASHINGTON,] March 15, 1945.

The President opened the conversation with a reference to the Yalta Conference, saying that he had had a successful time. He then said, apparently referring to our last meeting at luncheon, "I liked Stanley".[1] He thought that Stanley was more liberal on colonial policy than Churchill. He then asked me if Stanley was going to San Francisco. I said I did not know. The President said he hoped he would. I told him that, although Stanley was hard-boiled, I felt there was a genuine streak of liberalism in him, and that under his leadership, the British would make some substantial changes in their whole colonial policy. I told the President of the £120,000,000 appropriation that Parliament had made for Colonial Development over the next ten years, and gave him some little detail of the debate in Parliament (February 7, 1945).

TRUSTEESHIP

I outlined to the President the discussion on the above subject between the General Staffs and the State Department as it had developed in the Committee on Dependent Area Aspects of International Organiza-

---

[1] Col. Oliver Stanley, British Secretary of State for the Colonies, who had lunched with the President and Mr. Taussig on January 16.

From FOREIGN RELATIONS, 1945, Vol. I, pp. 121–124.

tions. I outlined the agreement that had been reached on the general category of strategic areas, and told the President that the military had indicated that they would interpret strategic areas as an entire area— for instance, all of the Japanese islands, north of the Equator, that might come under the administration of the United States. I told him that under their interpretation, the entire group of islands irrespective of whether they were fortified or not would be exempt from substantially all of the international agreements pertaining to civilian populations; that the military had been unwilling to agree to divide strategic areas into two categories—closed areas and open areas.

The President said that he would favor these two categories and that the open areas should be subject to international agreements. He said that if the military wanted, at a later date due to change in strategy, to make all or part of the open area a closed area, it should be provided that this could be done with the approval of the Security Council.

The President then asked me, "What is the Navy's attitude in regard to territories? Are they trying to grab everything?" I replied that they did not seem to have much confidence in civilian controls. The President then asked me how I accounted for their attitude.

I said that I thought that the military had no confidence in the proposed United Nations Organization. The President replied that he thought that was so. I told the President of the letter that Admiral Willson showed me addressed to the Secretary of the Navy, referring to the need of sending representatives to San Francisco in order to protect themselves against "the international welfare boys". The President then said that neither the Army nor the Navy had any business administering the civilian government of territories; that they had no competence to do this.

I then referred to the Cole Bill which would turn over the administration of all our territories to the Navy. The President said that he had not been informed about this bill, and appeared to be interested.

I told the President about the conversations I had been having with the Under Secretary of the Interior, Abe Fortas, regarding the possibility of the United States, at an auspicious time, volunteering to have our own territories report to the Organization, and also to respond to requests from the Organization for specific information. The President said he would approve of this and that it might provide a useful trading point at San Francisco.

ARABIA

The President said that one of the most important goals we must have in mind for the post-war world is to increase the purchasing power of great masses of people who now have a negligible purchasing power. He said a case in point was Arabia.

He spoke of his meeting with Ibn Saud. The President said that he had told Ibn Saud that essentially he, the President, was a business-man; that he had been the head of a big insurance company—the Maryland Casualty; that as a businessman he would be very much interested in Arabia. He told Ibn Saud that he knew considerable of the history of Arabia and had always been interested in that country; that Arabia needed irrigation projects; that it had plenty of water about sixty feet below the surface; that it had oil; that, using their own oil for fuel as operating pumps, they could develop an irrigation system in Arabia. He said that he told the King that if he, the President, were in the pump business, he would regard Arabia as a great potential market, and that the development of irrigation projects would increase the productivity of the land and considerably increase the purchasing power of the country which would be of great benefit to the world.

CARIBBEAN BASES

I told the President of my recent trip to the Caribbean bases with General Brett, and outlined in brief to him the substance of my report to the State Department. The President reacted to the report by saying, "We must keep the bases active and leave no room for doubt that we are there to stay."

THE PEOPLES OF EAST ASIA

The President said he was concerned about the brown people in the East. He said that there are 1,100,000,000 brown people. In many Eastern countries, they are ruled by a handful of whites and they resent it. Our goal must be to help them achieve independence—1,100,000,000 potential enemies are dangerous. He said he included the 450,000,000 Chinese in that. He then added, Churchill doesn't understand this.

INDO-CHINA AND NEW CALEDONIA

The President said he thought we might have some difficulties with France in the matter of colonies. I said that I thought that was quite probable and it was also probable the British would use France as a "stalking horse".

I asked the President if he had changed his ideas on French Indo-China as he had expressed them to us at the luncheon with Stanley. He said no he had not changed his ideas; that French Indo-China and New Caledonia should be taken from France and put under a trusteeship. The President hesitated a moment and then said—well if we can get the proper pledge from France to assume for herself the obligations of a trustee, then I would agree to France retaining these colonies with the proviso that independence was the ultimate goal. I asked the President if he would settle for self-government. He said no. I asked him if he would settle for dominion status. He said no—it must be independence. He said that is to be the policy and you can quote me in the State Department.

CHARLES TAUSSIG

PART 6
TRUMAN AND
THE COLD WAR

INTRODUCTION

Western Europe and the United States had fought World War II in the belief that democracy, individual freedom, and capitalism could not coexist with the Axis dictatorships, yet victory brought no relief from the threat of dictatorial domination. During the war American leaders were inclined to overlook Soviet intransigence on many issues, bearing in mind the great sacrifices that were made by Russia in the fight against Hitler. But the prospect of peace and the need to defend America's national interests in the postwar world brought a less tolerant attitude that led to a reevaluation of policy. Even before President Roosevelt's death in April 1945, Soviet maneuvering in Eastern Europe and particularly in Poland had aroused great fear of Russian intentions; despite Stalin's commitments at Yalta, Western statesmen were aware that he did not think much of democratic societies. Not that many people believed Russia wanted another war; indeed, with approximately 20 million dead she seemed scarcely able to afford further bloodletting.

As viewed from the West, the greatest threat posed by Russia was not by conquest but rather by subversion. The European nations, whose social fabric had been badly frayed in the prewar and war years and whose Communist parties were active and influential, seemed especially vulnerable to such tactics. Between 1945 and 1953 the Truman administration defined and practiced a foreign policy designed essentially to curb Russian expansion; indeed that policy's basic concept still dominates American relations with the rest of the world: containment of Communism and expansion of American capitalism. The diplomatic exchanges, threats and counter-threats, actions and reactions that characterized these years of acrimonious dueling between the United States and the Soviet Union have come to be known as the Cold War.

Among the first to question the assumptions of the American-Russian war policy and to offer suggestions for a change was Averill Harriman, the American ambassador in Moscow. (Reading No. 1) Firmly convinced that the Russians were pursuing a policy designed strictly to promote their own selfish interests, Harriman urged the use of American economic power to thwart Soviet designs. Unless Americans were prepared to live in a world in which Soviet influence predominated, he warned, the United States would have to help the nations of Western Europe rehabilitate themselves financially, since a sound economic system was the best defense against Communist penetration. Furthermore, Harriman wanted the United States to settle its political differences with the other Allies, for if they felt that they could depend on the United States economically and politically, they would probably be willing to follow the American lead in policy.

On one point Harriman was firm and insistent, stressing it both in his dispatches from Moscow and at his meetings with State Department officials and President Truman after President Roosevelt's death. The Russians regarded the Americans' considerate and generous attitude toward them as a sign of weakness, and consequently they flouted American wishes and refused to cooperate in the ventures in which the United States was interested. The only way to regain their respect and restore some chance for future cooperation was to stand firm against their demands and to make them pay with political concessions for economic aid.

Even though the Soviet Union and the Western governments met from April to June 1945 in San Francisco to set up the United Nations and even though the Big Three in August at Potsdam reached several agreements concerning the future control of Germany, East-West tension continued unabated throughout Truman's presidency. Neither the Soviet Union nor the West would make concessions, and interminable meetings of the foreign ministers could find no solution to problems rooted not only in deep mutual suspicion but also in genuine conflicts of interests. Russia seemed intent on taking over some of Italy's former colonies in North Africa, maintaining her grip on Eastern Europe, establishing some control over the Dardanelles, and creating unrest in Western Europe. The United States refused the

Russian request to share in the occupation of Japan, rejected an appeal by Russia for a loan, and tried by various devices to loosen the Russians' hold on Eastern Europe.

Perhaps the issue that most disillusioned Washington about the possibility of American-Russian cooperation in the postwar world and did the most to arouse suspicion of Soviet intentions was the Polish question. At Yalta the United States and Great Britain thought that they had extracted a promise from the Russians that free elections would be held in Poland. When they were not held, the West believed that the Soviet Union had nullified the Yalta accords with regard to Poland. In an effort to reestablish relations with Poland, the United States offered the Polish government a loan to help rebuild the country, coupled with the proviso that it must agree to Article VII of the Lend-Lease agreements. Acceptance would have meant Poland's return to the Western European–American economic sphere, since Poland would have had to adopt an open door trade policy and thus would have greatly reduced her chances of developing her own industry. The Poles rejected the loan.

The question of a loan to Russia herself to facilitate postwar reconstruction had been discussed within the administration for some time. Some historians have argued that American relations with the Russians would have improved had the United States acceded to their requests, as it did to Britain's, for a large loan. However, the Harriman faction in the State Department was predominant and no loan was made to Russia.

From the end of 1945 until early 1947 the stalemate continued, as Western leaders, recalling that appeasement and disarmament had failed to insure peace in the 1930s, became determined not to repeat the mistakes of the past. But as of 1947 neither side had adopted a rigid stance, and until Britain requested American aid to save Greece, some sort of arrangement between the two blocs to coexist in peace if not in amity still seemed possible. Britain could anticipate American aid to Greece since she knew that the United States was vitally interested in the eastern Meditteranean. Moreover, Greece had been allotted to the British by a settlement between Stalin and Churchill. Greece was so torn by civil war that the British had neither the economic nor the military reserves to cope with the problem. The hope for coexistence faded when the United States responded to Britain's appeal by proclaiming the Truman Doctrine, which promised aid to

Greece and Turkey and included an open ended commitment to defend "free peoples" *everywhere*. As Walter LeFeber points out in Reading No. 2, the Truman Doctrine was regarded as a check to an anticipated Russian movement through Greece and Turkey into the underdeveloped areas of Asia and Africa. The Marshall Plan, which evolved naturally from the Truman Doctrine, reoriented policy to focus on Europe and the rebuilding of Germany as another check to the Soviet Union. Introducing the Marshall Plan represented Washington's final attempt to rely chiefly on economic power to restrain the Soviet influence and expansion. After the Czech crisis and the beginning of the Berlin blockade in 1948, the United States began to emphasize the military aspect of containment rather than the economic, and in the spring of 1949 the American government signed the North Atlantic Treaty Alliance (NATO).

Did the policy of containment achieve its objective? Many authors have theorized that the policy was in fact so successful that the Communists, frustrated in Europe, sought after greater rewards in Asia, where their activities ultimately issued in the Korean War. These observers also find the Korean War responsible for a major change in the strategy on which the containment policy had heretofore been based. No longer would the American government think in terms only of total, atomic war; it would also be prepared to engage in limited "brushfire" conflicts. In Reading No. 3, however, Ambrose argues to the contrary: that containment had not checkmated Russia in Europe, since the United States lacked the military power—atomic or conventional—to enforce that policy if Russia began moving troops toward the west. He suggests that the war in Korea resulted from independent action by the North Koreans and that the Truman administration used the conflict to extend the policy of containment to Asia and to convince the American people that they had to rearm to thwart the advance of international communism.

Recently historians have hotly debated the assigning of blame for the Cold War, and their writings fall roughly into three categories. Conventional interpreters accept the Establishment view that Russia caused the Cold War; the radicals place the responsibility on the West and especially on the United States; and the moderate revisionists find that both sides contributed. In Reading No. 4 Pachter summarizes and criticizes these theories.

1

AMBASSADOR HARRIMAN'S VIEWS OF THE SOVIET UNION AND ADVICE TO THE STATE DEPARTMENT

THE AMBASSADOR IN THE SOVIET UNION (HARRIMAN) TO THE SECRETARY OF STATE

Moscow, April 4, 1945—8 p. m.
[Received 10:22 p m.]

1038. I fully agree with the Department's views expressed in 768, April 1, 11 p. m. [*a. m.*], regarding the British proposal for tripartite conversations in Moscow on relief supplies for Europe. Aside from the practical reasons given in the Department's cable indicating that these tripartite conversations would overlap other established commissions I feel that we have now ample proof that the Soviet Government would use such conversations to promote only their own welfare and political objectives. As we would approach the conversations from the humanitarian aspect we would start at an insuperable disadvantage. Should our own study of these problems together with British develop specific matters on which we wished to obtain Soviet cooperation I believe we should then approach the Soviet Government through one of the established commissions or through diplomatic channels in order to attempt to persuade or induce the Soviets to cooperate. I refer to such things as the general problem of feeding Germany, since I understand that the Russians will occupy the food surplus areas of Germany whereas the British and we will occupy some food deficit areas. Another case might be the stimulation of production and the direction of

From FOREIGN RELATIONS, 1945, Vol. V, pp. 817–824 (footnotes omitted), 839–846 (some footnotes omitted).

the distribution of oil in Rumania. In this case I still believe that we should insist upon the establishment now of the tripartite committee of experts in Rumania as has been suggested by the Department and also in Hungary. I can see no reason why we should not inform the Soviet Government that until they show willingness to cooperate along these lines we will be forced to give less attention to Soviet protocol requests for petroleum products. Pressure of this kind is the only way we can hope to obtain even partial Soviet cooperation.

Turning to the matter of policy, we now have ample proof that the Soviet Government views all matters from the standpoint of their own selfish interests. They have publicized to their own political advantage the difficult food situation in areas liberated by our troops such as in France, Belgium and Italy, comparing it with the allegedly satisfactory conditions in areas which the Red Army has liberated. They have kept our newspaper correspondents under strict censorship to prevent the facts becoming known. They have sent token shipments to Poland of Lend-Lease items or those similar thereto in order to give the appearance of generosity on the part of the Soviet Union. The Communist Party or its associates everywhere are using economic difficulties in areas under our responsibilities to promote Soviet concepts and policies and to undermine the influence of the western Allies.

In my War Department message of March 31 to the Protocol Committee in answer to the War Department message the Department refers to, which evidently crossed the Department's cable to which I am now replying, I suggested in the first paragraph "that minimum requirements of our western Allies be given first consideration". I feel I should expand the reasons for this suggestion and if the Soviet Government had shown any willingness to deal with economic questions on their merits without political considerations, as we approach them, I would feel that we should make every effort to concert our plans with those of the Soviet Government. On the other hand our hopes in this direction have proved to be futile. Unless we and the British now adopt an independent line the people of the areas under our responsibility will suffer and the chances of Soviet domination in Europe will be enhanced. I thus regretfully come to the conclusion that we should be guided as a matter of principle by the policy of taking care of our western Allies and other areas under our responsibility first, allocating to Russia what may be left. I am in no sense suggesting that this policy should have as its objective the development of a political bloc or a sphere of influence by the British or ourselves, but that we should, through such economic aid as we can give to our western Allies, including Greece as well as Italy, reestablish a reasonable life for the people of these countries who have the same general outlook as we have on life and the development of the world. The Soviet Union and the minority governments that the Soviets are forcing on the people of eastern Europe have an entirely different objective. We must clearly recognize that the Soviet program is the establishment of totalitarianism, ending personal liberty and democracy as we know and respect it. In addition the Soviet Government is attempting to penetrate through the Communist parties supported by it the countries of western Europe with the hope of expanding Soviet influence in the internal and external affairs of these countries.

Since we under no circumstances are prepared to involve ourselves in the internal political affairs of other countries by such methods, our only hope of supporting the peoples of these countries who resent totalitarian minority dictatorships is to assist them to attain economic stability as soon as possible. Lack of sufficient food and employment are fertile grounds for the subtle false promises of Communist agents.

The Soviet Government will end this war with the largest gold reserve of any country except the United States, will have large quantities of Lend-Lease material and equipment not used or worn out in the war with which to assist their reconstruction, will ruthlessly strip the enemy countries they have occupied of everything they can move, will control the foreign trade of countries under their domination as far as practicable to the benefit of the Soviet Union, will use political and economic pressure on other countries including South America to force trade arrangements to their own advantage and at the same time they will demand from us every form of aid and assistance which they think they can get from us while using our assistance to promote their political aims to our disadvantage in other parts of the world.

I recognize that it may be thought that much of this has no relationship to the question raised by the Department's message. On the other hand, I am stating it in order to justify my final recommendation, namely that the Soviet Government's selfish attitude must, in my opinion, force us if we are to protect American vital interests to adopt a more positive policy of using our economic influence to further our broad political ideals. Unless we are ready to live in a world dominated largely by Soviet influence, we must use our economic power to assist those countries that are naturally friendly to our concepts in so far as we can possibly do so. The only hope of stopping Soviet penetration is the development of sound economic conditions in these countries. I therefore recommend that we face the realities of the situation and orient our foreign economic policy accordingly. Our policy toward the Soviet Union should, of course, continue to be based on our earnest desire for the development of friendly relations and cooperation both political and economic, but always on a *quid pro quo* basis. This means tying our economic assistance directly into our political problems with the Soviet Union. This should be faced squarely in our consideration of the fifth protocol.

HARRIMAN

THE AMBASSADOR IN THE SOVIET UNION
(HARRIMAN) TO THE SECRETARY OF STATE

Moscow, April 6, 1945—1 p. m.
[Received April 7—3:23 a. m.]

1061. You request a report on our relations with the Soviet Government in your personal cable No. 777, April 3, 5 p.m. You will recall that on September 18 in Department's No. 2234, 10 p. m. a similar request was made to which I replied in cable No. 3572, September 19, 1 p. m. and No. 3600, September 20, 8 p. m. At that time I pointed out that a telegraphic message was a difficult medium in which to report on as complicated a situation as then existed and suggested that a satisfactory report could only be given if I were directed to return to Washington. The situation today is even more difficult to analyze and explain in a message. It is for this reason that I urgently request that I be permitted to return at once to Washington. However, in the meantime, for such a limited value as it may be, I will attempt to outline the situation as it appears from Moscow.

We have recognized for many months that the Soviets have three lines of foreign policy. (1.) Overall collaboration with us and the British in a World Security Organization; (2.) The creation of a unilateral security ring through domination of their border states; and (3.) The penetration of other countries through exploitation of democratic processes on the part of Communist controlled parties with strong Soviet backing to create political atmosphere favorable to Soviet policies.

We have been hopeful that the Soviets would, as we have, place number 1 as their primary policy and would modify their plans for 2 if they were satisfied with the efficacy of plan 1. It now seems evident that regardless of what they may expect from the World Security Organization they intend to go forward with unilateral action in the domination of their bordering states. It may well be that during and since the Moscow Conference they feel they have made this quite plain to us. You will recall that at the Moscow Conference Molotov indicated that although he would inform us of Soviet action in Eastern Europe he declined to be bound by consultation with us. It may be difficult for us to believe, but it still may be true that Stalin and Molotov considered at Yalta that by our willingness to accept a general wording of the declarations on Poland and liberated Europe, by our recognition of the need of the Red Army for security behind its lines, and of the predominant interest of Russia in Poland as a friendly neighbor and as a corridor to Germany, we understand and were ready to accept Soviet policies already known to us.

We must recognize that the words "independent but friendly neighbor" and in fact "democracy" itself have entirely different meanings to the Soviets than to us. Although they know of the meaning of these terms to us they undoubtedly feel that we should be aware of the meaning to them. We have been hopeful that the Soviets would accept our concepts whereas they on their side may have expected us to accept their own concepts, particularly in areas where their interests predominate. In any event, whatever may have been in their minds at Yalta, it now seems that they feel they can force us to acquiesce in their policies. Since we are resisting, they are using the usual Soviet tactics of retaliating in ways that they think will have the most effect, one of which is the decision not to send Molotov to the San Francisco Conference. They are fully aware of the importance we place on this Conference.

I have evidence which satisfies me that the Soviets have considered as a sign of weakness on our part our continued generous and considerate attitude towards them in spite of their disregard of our requests for cooperation in matters of interest to us.

I am further satisfied that the time has come when we must by our actions in each individual case make it plain to the Soviet Government that they cannot expect our continued cooperation on terms laid down by them. We have recognized that the Soviets have deep seated suspicions of all foreigners including ourselves. Our natural method of dealing with suspicion in others is to show our goodwill by generosity and consideration. We have earnestly attempted this policy and it has not been successful. This policy seems to have increased rather than diminished their suspicions as they evidently have misconstrued our motives. I feel that our relations would be on a much sounder basis if on the one hand we were firm and completely frank with them as to our position and motives and on the other hand they are made to understand specifically how lack of cooperation with our legitimate demands will adversely affect their interests.

I hope that I will not be misunderstood when I say that our relations with the Soviet Government will be on firmer ground as soon as we have adopted a policy which includes on the one hand at all times a full place for cooperation with the Soviet Union but on the other a readiness to go along without them if we can't obtain their cooperation. Up to recently the issues we have had with the Soviets have been relatively small compared to their contribution to the war but now we should begin to establish a new relationship. As you know I am a most earnest advocate of the closest possible understanding with the Soviet Union so that what I am saying only relates to how such understanding may be best attained.

Turning now to practical suggestions, they fall into two general categories. The first relates to policies toward other nations. I feel that we should further cement our relations with our other Allies and other friendly nations, settle our relatively minor differences with them and assist them economically as described in my 1038, April 4, 8 p. m. which I suggest be read in connection with this message. I am in no sense suggesting that in settling our political differences with them we should compromise our principles, but that we should make it our business with energy and understanding to make these countries feel that they are secure in dealing with us, that we will be understanding of their problems and needs.

If such an atmosphere is developed, the people of these countries will feel less dependent politically and economically on Soviet Russia and, as their concepts are much the same as ours, they will be inclined to orient their policies along lines similar to ours. A policy of this kind in itself will have an influence on our relations with the Soviet Union as I believe they fear more than anything else a close understanding among the western nations and I believe they will be more ready to deviate from their unilateral policies if they find that they cannot play one against the other and that they are not indispensable to us.

China is a subject by itself and I will not attempt to deal with it in this telegram.

My suggestions in the second general category relate to our current dealings with the Soviet Union. Although we should continue to approach all matters with an attitude of friendliness we should be firm and as far as practicable indicate our displeasure in ways that will definitely affect their interest in each case in which they fail to take our legitimate interests into consideration by their actions.

In the compass of this message I cannot list the almost daily affronts and total disregard which the Soviets evince in matters of interest to us. Whenever the United States does anything to which the Soviet take exception they do not hesitate to take retaliatory measures. I must with regret recommend that we begin in the near future with one or two cases where their actions are intolerable and make them realize that they cannot continue their present attitude except at great cost to themselves. We should recognize that if we adopt this policy we may have some adverse repercussions in the beginning. On the other hand we have evidence that in cases where they have been made to feel that their interests were being adversely affected we have obtained quick and favorable action. In any event I see no alternative as our present relations are clearly unsatisfactory.

Leaning to the military, General Deane on his return to Washington will present recommendations for a line of policy in which I concur. We both are satisfied that whatever the Soviets do in the Far East will be because of their own interests and not because of any conciliatory policy on our part.

I recognize that I am attempting to discuss in this message most fundamental questions. I feel that regardless of other considerations, serious as they are, I should be ordered home immediately for a very brief stay in order that I may report more fully on developments here and their implications. In spite of recent developments, I am still satisfied that if we deal with the Soviets on a realistic basis, we can in time attain a workable basis for our relations. There is ample evidence that the Soviets desire our help and collaboration but they now think they can have them on their own terms which in many cases are completely unacceptable to us. They do not understand that their present actions seriously jeopardize the attainment of satisfactory relations with us and unless they are made to understand this now, they will become increasingly difficult to deal with.

HARRIMAN

MINUTES OF THE SECRETARY OF STATE'S STAFF COMMITTEE, FRIDAY MORNING, APRIL 20, 1945

RELATIONS WITH THE SOVIET UNION

The United States Ambassador to the Soviet Union, Mr. Harriman, reported on relations with the Soviet Union.

Mr. Harriman said Mr. Molotov had come to see him immediately following President Roosevelt's death. Mr. Molotov was greatly concerned, and questioned Mr. Harriman particularly about President's Truman's attitude. The Russians had respected Mr. Wallace, Mr. Harriman said, and had not understood his being dropped out. Mr. Harriman explained to Molotov that Truman was President Roosevelt's choice.

On the next evening Mr. Harriman saw Stalin, who was very sober and like Molotov asked many questions. It was on this occasion that Stalin (somewhat against Molotov's desires) agreed to Mr. Harriman's proposal that Molotov come to the United States to call on President Truman and then go to San Francisco as an indication to the world of Stalin's stated determination to deal with President Truman as he had with President Roosevelt.

Subsequently Mr. Harriman talked to Stalin about the Polish situation. Mr. Harriman said it was fair to say that since the Crimea Conference the Russians have been greatly disturbed by the fact that for the first time they realized that we were determined to carry through what we said (i.e. in regard to Poland and the Liberated Areas Declaration). We always have dealt directly and fairly and with full candor. This the Russians, accustomed to an atmosphere of suspicion and intrigue, do not understand. Furthermore, they have undoubtedly viewed our attitude as a sign of weakness. For example, they so interpreted our willingness to grant Soviet requests for increased lend-lease in the face of several developments which would have justified refusing their requests.

Mr. Harriman said it was also obvious the Russians after talking with Bierut[1] and Company do not like the agreement with respect to Poland as well as they did at Yalta. This attitude is based principally

[1] Boleslaw Bierut, President of the Polish National Council (National Council of the Homeland), the Communist-dominated legislative body in Soviet-liberated Poland.

on their belief that the Lublin Government[2] could be kept effectively under Soviet domination, but that this would be difficult if any of the old Polish leaders had to be reckoned with. It seemed evident that Mikolajczyk[3] and the other old leaders would be welcomed by the majority of Poles, and thus the Lublin group would be weakened. The Russians seem to be making every effort to make any reorganization of the Polish Government as much of a "white-wash" as possible.

Mr. Harriman said he felt the time had come to eliminate fear in our dealings with the Soviet Union and to show we are determined to maintain our position. He agreed with Mr. Grew that we have great leverage in dealing with the Soviet Union. He said one point worth remembering was that the Soviet Union wants very much to be a respected member of world society. The Russians are more afraid of facing a united west than anything else. In this connection Mr. Harriman thought our relations with the Soviet would be vastly improved if we could settle our differences with Great Britain and France.

Mr. Grew asked to what extent the Soviet leaders are afraid of isolationism. Mr. Harriman said their main problem is keeping internal control. The people were most anxious to have friendly relations with the outside world, particularly the United States. While they have liquidated all opposition, they are still sensitive to public demands and Mr. Harriman doubted they would be willing to face a break with the United States. He said that there were fears that the Russian people might become too internationally minded, and this fear had been responsible for a number of efforts made from time to time to create doubts about the position of the Allies, for example the Cairo separate peace rumors.[4]

[2] By a decree dated July 21, 1944, of the Polish National Council, a Polish Committee of National Liberation was formed. Shortly afterwards, this Committee was established in Lublin and became known as the "Lublin Committee". For an account of the establishment of this Committee, see telegram 2736, July 24, 1944, from Moscow, *Foreign Relations*, 1944, vol. III, p. 1425. On December 31, 1944, the Polish National Council decreed the transformation of the "Lublin Committee" into the Provisional Polish Government. After the capture of Warsaw by the Red Army on January 17, 1945, the Polish Provisional Government moved from Lublin to Warsaw.

[3] Stanislaw Mikolajczyk, Prime Minister of the Polish Government in Exile at London, July 14, 1943–November 24, 1944; leader of the Polish Peasant Party.

[4] The newspaper *Pravda* on January 17, 1944, had published a report from its own correspondent in Cairo based upon assertedly reliable information about a recent meeting in one of the coastal cities of the Iberian Peninsula between two

Mr. Harriman also discussed Soviet information policy. He said it was perfectly clear that the Soviet Government has no intention of loosening its control of the press.

The basic and irreconcilable difference of objective between the Soviet Union and the United States, Mr. Harriman said, was its urge for its own security to see Soviet concepts extend to as large an area of the world as possible. This now arises in connection with their plans to establish friendly governments in bordering countries (e.g. Rumania, Bulgaria and Poland, with Finland temporarily the exception). Such governments are set up with Soviet assistance by leftist groups using secret police and other terroristic and undemocratic methods.

Mr. Harriman expressed the opinion that the Soviet Union, once it had control of bordering areas, would attempt to penetrate the next adjacent countries, and he thought the issue ought to be fought out in so far as we could with the Soviet Union in the present bordering areas.

Asked by Mr. Grew what course of action he would recommend, Mr. Harriman said he would first point out that we would have to face the realities of certain situations. For instance, if we joined the British in backing the present reactionary government in Iran, we would lose out. Each case would have to be studied individually. But, Mr. Harriman said, we must reestablish our respect in Moscow, and we must not tolerate Russian mistreatment of our people and disregard of our interests. He mentioned in this connection the case of an American seaman still being held in a Murmansk jail after his arrest on charges of drunkenness; he also mentioned the holding of a number of American airmen as hostages because the Russians suspected our air force of aiding the Polish Underground, and the closing down of American operations at Poltava. Mr. Harriman said he had recommended, in the case of the Poltava incident, that Soviet planes at Fairbanks be grounded at once, but the U.S. Army had vetoed this.

With regard to air communications routes, Mr. Harriman said there was no reason to accept the Soviet insistence on routing all flights via Tehran. He said that if the British would agree we could stop all out-

responsible British officials and the German Foreign Minister, Joachim von Ribbentrop. The purpose of the meeting was to find out the conditions of a separate peace with Germany. It was presumed that the meeting had not remained without results. Two days later *Pravda* printed a Tass despatch from London reporting that the Reuters Agency had stated that the British Foreign Office had denied the rumors from Cairo.

side air traffic with the Soviet Union. He said we ought now to inform the Russians that as of a certain date Tehran air travel would cease, and that we wished to operate two lines to Russia, one connecting with the Russians at Stockholm and one at Bucharest.

Mr. Harriman emphasized that we ought to take, at the present time, strong stands on minor points at first, to avoid giving the Russians the idea we had made a major change in policy.

With regard to the international security organization, Mr. Harriman said that if we had any basic differences with the Soviet Government, we should make it clear that, while we would be disappointed if the Soviet Union did not go along, we intend to go ahead with those nations which do see the problem as we do. At the same time we would always be ready to welcome full cooperation.

On Poland, Mr. Harriman said we should not recede from our position.

Referring to lend-lease assistance, Mr. Harriman said there had been a perfect case for action in Rumania. At the same time the Russians were stripping Rumanian oil installations and not taking the full advantage of Rumanian potentialities of production, they were asking us to double our lend-lease of petroleum. We had agreed to do this, even though our proposal for a tripartite commission in Rumania had been turned down by the Russians. If we had made an issue of it, we would doubtless have had our way.

At the conclusion of Mr. Harriman's remarks, Mr. Rockefeller referred to what Mr. Harriman had said about the Soviet Union's interpreting our attitude as a sign of weakness and Mr. Rockefeller said he had found this attitude mirrored in many Latin American countries, where governments were losing their respect for the United States for giving in to the Russians so frequently.

Mr. Grew asked Mr. Harriman to attend the next meeting of the Committee.

MINUTES OF THE SECRETARY OF STATE'S STAFF COMMITTEE, SATURDAY MORNING, APRIL 21, 1945

RELATIONS WITH THE SOVIET UNION

The United States Ambassador to the Soviet Union, Mr. Harriman, continued his discussion of relations with the Soviet Union.

Mr. Grew read a telegram from Ambassador Caffery in Paris in which it was indicated the French Government is becoming increasingly worried about Russian expansion in Europe. Mr. Harriman said this represented a change which has developed gradually in the French attitude since General de Gaulle's visit to Moscow. He said it pointed up the desirability (as he had suggested yesterday) of settling our differences with France, as well as any with Great Britain. (In this connection, Mr. Dunn informed Mr. Harriman that the Department is making every effort to improve relations with France, and that we are convincing the French Government we are working on a basis of friendly relations and support. He said the main point of difficulty is Indo-China, a problem now being studied.)

Mr. Harriman went on to say that Russian plans for establishing satellite states are a threat to the world and to us. The excuse offered that they must guard against a future German menace is only a cover for other plans.

Mr. Grew asked if Soviet Government were not establishing more than spheres of influence and if it were not taking complete charge in satellite countries. Mr. Harriman said that this was true.

Some of the areas in which Mr. Harriman suggested Soviet policies might cause further trouble were Macedonia, Turkey, and especially China. If Chiang does not make a deal with the Communists before the Russians occupy Manchuria and North China, they are certainly going to establish a Soviet-dominated Communist regime in these areas and then there will be a completely divided China, much more difficult of uniting. The extent to which the Soviet will go in all directions will depend on the extent of our pressure.

Mr. Grew raised the question of our leverage. He said the Soviet Union appeared to need our money and our supplies, and he asked Mr. Harriman to what extent the Soviet Union was in fact dependent on us; in other words, just how much leverage did we possess? Mr. Harriman said the Soviet Union particularly needed our heavy machinery and machine tools, and our "know-how" in many fields, for example chemical industry, coal mining mechanization, power development, and railroad equipment. In the war, we have been supplying all Russian deficits in essential materials.

Mr. Harriman said it was important not to overestimate Soviet strength. The Army is an extraordinarily effective but disorganized mass of human beings. Almost all of the Army's transport equipment and much of its food is supplied by us. The country is still fantastically backward. There is no road system, railroad mileage is very inadequate, and ninety percent of the people of Moscow live in a condition comparable with our worst slum areas. Mr. Harriman said he was therefore not much worried about the Soviet Union's taking the offensive in the near future. But they will take control of everything they can by bluffing, he added.

Mr. Harriman said one very unfortunate development was the appointment of a Russian as head of the UNRRA Mission to Poland. Thus UNRRA supplies would be used against our policies. He emphasized again the importance of taking a firm stand on the Polish issue.

Mr. Harriman said it was also important for the Department to get control of all the activities of agencies dealing with the Soviet Union so that pressure can be put on or taken off, as required.

Mr. Clayton raised the question of lend-lease assistance. He said that in the discussions now in progress on supplies for liberated areas it had been indicated that if we give the liberated areas the fats, oils, and sugar they need, shipments of these products to the Soviet Union will have to be stopped. Meat shipments will have to be reduced also. Harriman said this should be done—the liberated areas of western Europe should be supplied first.

Mr. Harriman thought there should not be a fifth lend-lease protocol (the fourth, covering the twelve months ending June 30, 1945, was signed April 17, 1945). After the expiration of the fourth protocol, Mr. Harriman said, Russian requests should be dealt with on a supply basis, and we should supply the absolute minimum requirements. He said he was satisfied that up to now the Russians had needed the supplies they had obtained, because of the limitations of available shipping. When the war in Europe ends, however, the Soviet Union should have ample production to meet essential needs in many fields, and our shipments should be reduced accordingly. We should continue to supply legitimate requirements, especially for use in the Far East.

With regard to an agreement under section 3(c) of the Lend-Lease Act, Mr. Harriman said the Russians had the impression we are interested in such an agreement merely to stabilize our own position. Mr. Clayton asked if Mr. Harriman did not think it would be better to avoid opening 3(c) negotiations and to handle the problem in connection with discussions regarding post-war credits.

Mr. Harriman said this procedure conformed to the Soviet view—

the only disadvantage would appear to be that a post-war credit agreement might not be worked out in time to cover certain necessary war supplies, and that it would be difficult to honor certain legitimate Soviet requests without a 3(c) agreement.

Mr. Clayton mentioned that post-war credit arrangements would require legislation—for example, repeal of the Johnson Act and extension of the lending authority of the Export-Import Bank. Mr. Acheson asked whether there was any reason why any such legislative program could not be deferred until mid-July, in order to avoid complicating the current program (Bretton Woods, trade agreements, etc.). Mr. Harriman said it would be quite satisfactory to have negotiations on the question of post-war credits drag along, but that we should begin promptly. He agreed with Mr. Clayton that this was the greatest element in our leverage.

Mr. Harriman also said he hoped that any credits opened would not be for a period of several years (the Russians are asking approval of credits under which they would buy over a several-year period), and he thought that the best method would be to make a one-year arrangement and see how that worked out before expanding it. He also thought we should not renew the offer to negotiate a 3(c) agreement, but explain the disadvantage to them without it. We should then let the Soviet Union take the initiative in this connection.

Mr. Acheson raised the question of the decentralization of the Army throughout the sixteen Soviet republics. Mr. Harriman said he thought that from the standpoint of United States relations with the Soviet Union decentralization of the U.S.S.R., though "phony", was useful to us. It would enable us to have sixteen observation posts in the Soviet Union and it would also increase Soviet knowledge and understanding of the United States if there were sixteen missions in the United States from the various Soviet republics. Mr. Harriman said the Kremlin pays considerable attention to the opinions of Party leaders in the local areas.

Mr. Phillips asked about Soviet-British relations. Mr. Harriman said that in October 1944 Churchill went to Moscow and obtained Soviet agreement to a free hand for Great Britain in Greece in return for his recognition of the importance of Rumania as a supply line for the Red Army. Churchill has assumed, however, that the Allies would be treated at least as well in Rumania as the Russians were in Italy, whereas the Russians had later shown that they had no such intention.

Regarding Yugoslavia it had been agreed that Great Britain and the Soviet Union had completely equal interests, but Tito was now one hundred percent Stalin's man. On Poland Mr. Harriman said the British felt even more strongly than the United States about the need for insisting on the Yalta Agreements. He said that without our support in Europe, however, the British would be forced to work for spheres of influence.

Mr. Harriman concluded by reemphasizing that if this Government is resourceful and firm, it will be possible to check the Soviet Union to a degree.

2

THE TRUMAN DOCTRINE
AND THE MARSHALL PLAN
WALTER LAFEBER

In his message of March 12, 1947, the President explained that the new program sought to promote stability in Western Europe as well as Greece and Turkey by using $400 million of American-controlled military and economic aid to stop Communist-supported rebellions in the two nations. This speech, as well as the many conferences that shaped the doctrine, stressed the growing American concern for the underdeveloped nations. Within twenty-four hours after the receipt of the British note, the State Department's Russian expert, George Kennan, chaired a meeting of specialists on Middle Eastern and African affairs; these policy-makers were relieved that they could now act openly to halt Russia from breaking through Greece and Turkey into the Middle East, Asia, and North Africa. Five days later, Truman, Marshall, and Acheson explained the situation to important Congressmen. It was not a warm audience. The Republicans were busy cutting taxes 20 percent and chopping $6 billion from Truman's already tight budget. The legislators remained unmoved until Acheson swung into the argument that the threat was Russian Communism; its aim the control of the Middle East, South Asia, and Africa; and that this control was a central part of the Communist plan to encircle and capture the ultimate objective of Germany.[1] This argument, coupled with Truman's assurance that the United States would control not only every penny of American aid to Greece, but also run the Greek economy by controlling foreign

[1] Joseph M. Jones, *The Fifteen Weeks* (New York, 1955), pp. 133–134.

Reprinted from *America, Russia, and the Cold War*, pp. 44–53, with permission of John Wiley and Sons, Inc., Publishers.

exchange, budget, taxation, currency, and credits, won over the Congressmen.[2]

Vandenberg and others feared that most Americans, including many Congressmen, might be cool to the program because of a failure to understand the extent of the Soviet danger. Truman and his advisors therefore went to some length to oversell the doctrine ideologically. As Vandenberg advised, the President "scared hell out of the American people," by painting in dark hues the "totalitarian regimes" which threatened to snuff out freedom everywhere. Insofar as public opinion was concerned, this tactic worked well for the Administration, at least until three years later when Senator Joseph McCarthy and others turned the argument around and accused the Administration of too softly handling such a horrible danger.

Inside the State Department, however, the tactic immediately ran into opposition. On March 6, Kennan objected bitterly to the sending of any military assistance to nations such as Turkey which bordered the Soviet Union. Unlike economic aid, arms and ammunition, not to mention possible American military advisers, could be highly provocative. Kennan also protested against the harsh ideological tone and open-ended commitment of American aid in the early drafts of Truman's proposed speech.[3] These criticisms initiated a breach which soon developed into an open and highly significant break between Kennan and Acheson over the matter of military aid to supposed allies. Kennan's objections did not modify the policy that was already in motion. After Truman delivered the message, Robert Taft, the leading Senate Republican, accused Truman of dividing the world into Communist and anti-Communist zones, then objected to the proposed military aid with the words, "I do not want war with Russia." Western European governments joined in this criticism. Henry Wallace, then traveling in Europe, accused Truman of "reckless adventury" that would cost the world "a century of fear." Senator Vandenberg rushed to the defense of the President by calling Wallace an "itinerant saboteur."

Others expressed different, and to the State Department, more troublesome objections. Walter Lippmann led a general attack on the

---

[2] "Draft of President's Policy Statement to the Chief of the American Mission to Greece," by John Snyder, June 3, 1947; Greece and Turkey: Assistance to, Under Public Law 75, Papers of Harry S. Truman, Truman Library.

[3] Jones, *Fifteen Weeks*, pp. 154–155.

Administration's bypassing of the United Nations: "If the pattern of our conduct in this affair becomes a precedent," the columnist warned, "we shall have cut a hole in the Charter which it will be very difficult to repair." Other critics observed that in assisting the governments of Greece and Turkey, the United States was saving reactionary, crumbling social structures unlikely to be of much assistance in making freedom ring throughout the world.[4]

Congress finally completed action on the $400 million request on May 15, and Truman signed the measure a week later. The Soviet response was unpredictably soft. Stalin shrewdly encouraged Tito to handle the job of supporting the Greek Communists, thereby keeping the Yugoslavs and Bulgarians embroiled with the West and freeing Russia of direct responsibility. In an April interview, Stalin expressed hope that Americans and Russians could collaborate in creating a peaceful world, although he followed this with a not indirect comparison of the United States with Hitlerite Germany. During these months, Stalin devoted his major attention to "Zhdanovism," the cleansing of the minds of Soviet intelligentsia who were at odds with his internal policies. The most severe response came at the United Nations. Soviet delegate Andrei Gromyko asked why the United States insisted on acting before the United Nations investigating commission reported, and charged that the United States would destroy Greek and Turkish independence. Gromyko wondered how Turkey, which had sided with the Nazis in World War II, could qualify for such aid. Another, perhaps more significant reaction occurred in Moscow when the first explicitly Cold War, anti-American play, Konstantin Simonov's "The Russian Question" opened in early April.

The Truman Doctrine evolved naturally into the Marshall Plan. On March 5, Senator Vandenberg defined the Greek crisis as "symbolic of the world-wide ideological clash between Eastern Communism and Western Democracy."[5] That same day Acheson initiated a State Department survey to investigate the possibilities of broadening aid to nations other than Greece and Turkey. Two days later, Secretary of Navy James Forrestal sent a highly emotional memorandum to Truman, which warned that the present danger was at least as great as that during World War II. Forrestal urged the President to quit the defensive and "attack successfully" with an all-out economic effort

---

[4] *Washington Post*, March 21, 1947, p. 17.
[5] *Papers of Senator Vandenberg*, p. 340.

which would revitalize Germany and Japan and stabilize the Western world before the "Russian poison" conquered Europe, "South America, and ourselves."[6]

The Doctrine itself suggested no real limitations to the scope of the American effort, but six weeks after Truman's speech, Secretary of State Marshall reoriented policy by concentrating State Department attention upon Europe. The underdeveloped countries would not come back into focus for another seven years. Returning badly shaken from a Foreign Ministers conference in Moscow, the Secretary of State insisted in a nationwide broadcast that Western Europe must receive immediate help. "The patient is sinking," Marshall declared, "while the doctors deliberate." Personal conversations with Stalin had convinced the Secretary of State that the Russians were simply waiting for Europe to collapse. Marshall looked for little help from the weak, embattled European governments. Convinced that the United States must take the lead in restoring Europe, Marshall appointed a Policy Planning Staff under the direction of George Kennan to draw up policies for such a program.

Kennan later explained the basic assumption which underlay the Marshall Plan and, indeed, the entire range of America's postwar policies between 1947 and 1955. Excluding the United States, Kennan observed,

> . . . there are only four aggregations which are major ones from the standpoint of strategic realities [that is, military and industrial potential] in the world. Two of those lie off the shores of the Eurasian land mass. Those are Japan and England, and two of them lie on the Eurasian land mass. One is the Soviet Union and the other is that of central Europe. . . .

> Viewed in absolute terms, I think the greatest danger that could confront the United States security would be a combination and working together for purposes hostile to us of the central European and the Russian military-industrial potentials. They would really create an entity . . . which could overshadow in a strategic sense even our own power. It is not anything, I think, which would be as easy of achievement as people often portray it as being here. I am not sure the Rus-

6 Arnold A. Rogow, *James Forrestal; A Study of Personality, Politics, and Policy* (New York, 1963), pp. 335–337.

sians have the genius for holding all that together.... Still, they have the tendency of political thought, of Communist political expansion.[7]

Building upon this premise, round-the-clock conferences in May, 1947 began to fashion the main features of the Marshall Plan. Kennan insisted that any aid, particularly military aid, be limited and not given to just any area where Communists seemed to be enjoying some success. Lippmann helped solve this problem and also the question of how to minimize American interference in Europe's domestic affairs; he suggested that Europe be encouraged to take the initiative in overall planning by presenting a complete program for American consideration. The all-important question then became how to handle the Russians. Ostensibly, Marshall accepted Kennan's advice to "play it straight" by inviting the Soviet bloc. In reality, the State Department made Russian acceptance improbable by demanding that the economic records of each nation be open for scrutiny; for good measure Kennan also suggested that the Soviets' devastated economy, weakened by war and at that moment suffering from drought and famine, participate in the Plan by shipping Soviet goods to Europe. Apparently no one in the State Department wanted the Soviets included. Russian participation would vastly multiply the costs of the program and eliminate any hope of its acceptance by a purse-watching Republican Congress, now increasingly convinced by Truman of the need to battle Communists, not feed them.

Acheson's speech at Cleveland, Mississippi on May 8 and Marshall's address at Harvard on June 5 revealed the motives and substance of the Plan. In preparing for the earlier speech, Acheson's advisors concluded that American exports were rapidly approaching the $16 billion mark. Imports, however, amounted to only half that amount, and Europe did not possess sufficient dollars to pay the difference. Either the United States government would have to grant credits to European importers or Europe would be unable to buy American goods. The President's Council of Economic Advisers was predicting a slight business recession, and if, in addition, exports dropped in any substantial amount, "the effect in the United States," as one official wrote, "might

[7] U.S. Congress, Senate, Subcommittee to investigate the Administration of the International Security Act . . . of the Committee on the Judiciary, 82nd Congress, 1st Session, *The Institute of Pacific Relations* (Washington, 1951), pp. 1557–1558.

be most serious."[8] Acheson underlined these facts in the May 8th speech.

At Harvard, Marshall urged European nations to create a long-term program that would "provide a cure rather than a mere palliative." On June 13 British Foreign Minister Ernest Bevin accepted Marshall's suggestion and four days later traveled to Paris to talk with French Foreign Minister Georges Bidault. The question of Russian participation became uppermost in their discussions. *Pravda* had labeled Marshall's speech as a Truman Doctrine with dollars, a useless attempt to save the American economy by dominating the markets of Europe. Bidault ignored this; pressured by the powerful French Communist Party and fearful that Russia's absence might compel France to join the Anglo-Saxons in a divided Europe dominated by a resurrected Germany,[9] he decided to invite Molotov. The Russian line immediately moderated.

On June 26, Molotov arrived in Paris with eighty-nine economic experts and clerks, then spent much of the next three days conferring over the telephone with officials in Moscow. The Russians were giving the Plan serious consideration. Molotov finally proposed that each nation individually establish its own recovery program. The French and British proposed instead that Europe as a whole create the proposal for American consideration. On June 30, the West European nations threw their support back of the Anglo-French proposal. Molotov angrily quit the conference, warning that the Plan would undermine national sovereignty, revive Germany, result in American control of Europe and, most ominously, divide "Europe into two groups of states . . . creating new difficulties in the relations between them."[10] Within a week after his return to Moscow, the Soviets set their own "Molotov Plan" in motion. The Poles and the Czechs, who had expressed interest in Marshall's proposal, now informed the Paris conference that they could not attend because it "might be construed as an action against the Soviet Union."

From July 16 until September 22, sixteen European nations hammered out a program. The absence of Russians did not mean an absence of problems. In an interesting preview of a dilemma which would haunt Western Europe in the 1960s, Britain rejected French

---

[8] Jones, *Fifteen Weeks*, p. 207.
[9] See, for example, *The New York Times*, June 19, 1957, p. 1.
[10] Text in *The New York Times*, July 3, 1947, p. 3.

proposals for a supranational body to supervise the Plan. Governed by her Commonwealth ties and her dependence on and ideological links with the United States, Great Britain successfully insisted upon a committee of sovereign nations. Presented with this first opportunity of fulfilling their fervent desire for a closely-knit Europe, American officials appeared confused. They were not prepared to push the British into such a Europe, yet a Europe without England opened possibilities for intra-European friction. "I always thought it odd," one European official observed, "that the descendants of the writers of *The Federalist* were content to be misty on the essentials of policy."[11]

Another problem at the conference was symbolized by the Treaty of Dunkirk, signed by Britain and France in March 1947. This pact pledged cooperation in the containment of a revived, perhaps Communist, Germany. As America's closest Allies demonstrated how green were their memories of World War II, the United States determined to revive Germany quickly. In December 1946, the United States and Great Britain overrode French opposition in order to merge economically the American and British zones in Germany. Administrative duties fell into the hands of Germans. By mid-July 1947, American officials moved so rapidly to rebuild German industry that Bidault finally warned Marshall to slow down or else the French government would never survive to carry through the economic recovery program. Marshall made the Paris conference more serene by bringing the French into the discussion over Germany, but the United States carried on its program to build German nonmilitary industry to the point where Germany would be both self-sufficient and able to aid the remainder of Western Europe. On September 22, the Paris meeting completed its work, pledging increased production, tariff reductions, and currency convertibility in return for American aid. The State Department could view its successes in Germany during the summer as icing on the cake.

The European request for a four-year program of $17 billion dollars of American aid now had to run the gauntlet of a Republican Congress which was dividing its attention between slashing the budget and attacking Truman, both in anticipation of the presidential election only a year away. In committee hearings in late 1947 and early 1948, the

[11] Harry B. Price, *The Marshall Plan and Its Meaning* (Ithaca, New York, 1955), pp. 80, 287.

Executive Department systematically presented its case. Only large amounts of government money which could restore basic facilities, provide convertibility of local currency into dollars, and end the dollar shortage would stimulate private investors to rebuild Europe, Administration witnesses argued. Then, a rejuvenated Europe could offer many advantages to the United States: eradicate the threat of continued nationalization and spreading socialism by releasing and stimulating the investment of private capital, maintain demand for American exports, encourage Europeans to produce strategic goods which the United States could buy and stockpile, preserve European and American control over Middle Eastern oil supplies from militant nationalism which might endanger the weakened European holdings, and free Europeans from economic problems so they could help the United States militarily.

The Administration's plan revolved around a rebuilt and autonomous Germany. As Secretary of State Marshall told Congress, "The restoration of Europe involves the restoration of Germany. Without a revival of German production there can be no revival of Europe's economy. But we must be very careful to see that a revived Germany can not again threaten the European community." The Marshall Plan offered a way to circumvent Allied restrictions of German development, for it tied the Germans to a general European program and then offered vast sums to such nations as France which might otherwise be reluctant to support the rebuilding of Germany.[12]

The Marshall Plan served as an all-purpose weapon for Truman's foreign policy. It charmed those who feared a slump in American exports and who believed, Communist threat or no Communist threat, that American and world prosperity rested on a vigorous export trade. A spokesman for the National Association of Manufacturers, for example, appeared considerably more moderate toward Communism than most government officials when he argued that Europe suffered not from "this so-called communistic surge," but from a production problem" which only the Marshall Plan could solve.[13] Appropriately, Truman named as Administrator of the Plan Paul Hoffman, a proven

[12] U. S. Congress, House, Foreign Affairs Committee, 80th Congress, 1st and 2nd Sessions, *United States Foreign Policy for a Post-War Recovery Program . . .* (Washington, 1948), I, 354–359.
[13] *Ibid.,* I, 680–681.

administrator who, as Dean Acheson once observed, preached a "doctrine of salvation by exports with all the passion of an economic Savanarola."[14] The Plan also attracted a group, including Niebuhr, which placed more emphasis upon the containment of Communism. The Plan offered all things to all people. Or almost all, for Henry Wallace decided to oppose it in late 1947 on the grounds that only by channeling aid through the United Nations could calamitous American-Russian relations be avoided.

The Marshall Plan now appears not the beginning but the end of an era. It marked the last phase in the Administration's use of economic tactics as the primary means of tying together the Western world to stop Communist thrusts. The Plan's approach, that peaceful and positive approach which Niebuhr applauded, soon evolved into military alliances. The Americans for Democratic Action and the American business community came much closer to agreement on Soviet policy than either cared to admit, and both necessarily went along with this new and considerably less-peaceful tactic. Given commonly-shared assumptions of the Russian system, they could do little else but finally admit that the President was correct in saying that the Truman Doctrine and the Marshall Plan "are two halves of the same walnut," and they willingly acquiesced as the military aspects of the Doctrine developed into quite the larger part.

[14] Dean Acheson, *Sketches From Life of Men I Have Known* (New York, 1959), p. 19.

3
FROM KOREA TO VIETNAM: THE FAILURE OF A POLICY ROOTED IN FEAR
STEPHEN E. AMBROSE

On June 24, 1950, American foreign policy in the Pacific was remarkably close to what some of the doves of 1970 want it to be today. At its heart, the policy of 1950 was one of maintaining positions of strength on Asia's offshore islands, especially Japan, Okinawa, and the Philippines, avoiding all entanglements on the mainland, and recognizing the fundamental fact of Asian politics—the emergence of Communist China.

American troops had been withdrawn from South Korea, so there were no American combat units anywhere on the Asian mainland. Mao Tse-tung's troops were preparing an amphibious operation against Chiang Kai-shek's remnants on Formosa, and President Harry Truman and Secretary of State Dean Acheson had warned American ambassadors around the world to be prepared for the repercussions stemming from the final fall of the Chinese Nationalist government.

In Indochina, the French were struggling, without much success, to eradicate the Communist Ho Chi Minh and his Vietminh, while in the Philippines the government faced a serious challenge from the Communist Huks. The United States was giving tidbits of aid to both counterrevolutionary efforts but, in view of the budget restraints at home and what was felt to be the overwhelming need to rearm Europe (not to mention the United States itself), scarcely enough to effect the outcome in Indochina. America's overall policy remained one of holding to its offshore bases, protected by the world's most powerful navy,

From *The Progressive*, November 1970, pp. 14–20. Reprinted by permission.

staying out of the Chinese civil war, and avoiding any involvement on the mainland.

There had been two recent statements by Truman Administration spokesmen making this policy clear. On January 12, 1950, at the National Press Club, Secretary Acheson had drawn a line on a map to indicate the American defensive perimeter—the line excluded South Korea and Formosa. And on May 2, Senator Tom Connally of Texas, chairman of the Senate Foreign Relations Committee, said he was afraid South Korea would have to be abandoned. He thought the Communists were going to overrun Korea when they got ready, just as they "will overrun Formosa." Connally said he did not think Korea was "very greatly important. It has been testified before us that Japan, Okinawa, and the Philippines make the chain of defense which is absolutely necessary."

That remained the American position until June 25, 1950, the day hostilities began in Korea. Then, after only a few hours of meetings with Acheson and a select group of top advisers, without consulting Congress or the United Nations or America's European allies, Mr. Truman announced that he was sending supplies to South Korea, immediately increasing aid to the French in Indochina and to the Philippine government, and ordering the U.S. Seventh Fleet to sail between the Chinese mainland and Formosa to prevent the expected invasion of the island by the Communists. Mr. Truman had, in short, involved the United States in four civil wars at once, and except in the Philippines, all in areas the Americans had previously regarded as outside their sphere of influence. The United States was *on* the Asian mainland.

These were sweeping policy decisions, among the most important of the entire Cold War, carrying with them enormous long-term implications. They were hardly the kind that a government ordinarily makes without deliberation. Yet Mr. Truman later claimed that he made them solely as a result of the Korean War, the outbreak of which astonished him—as it supposedly did General Douglas MacArthur's headquarters in Tokyo—as much "as if the sun had suddenly gone out." For a man who had been surprised, Mr. Truman had recovered with amazing speed.

Actually, as I. F. Stone has shown in his book, *The Hidden History of the Korean War*, there was no surprise. The Americans had a good general idea of what was coming and had their countermeasures prepared. Intelligence reports on North Korean intentions had been specific enough to allow the U.S. State Department, days before the attack, to prepare a resolution to submit to the Security Council of the United Nations condemning North Korea for aggression.

At the time, the Soviet Union was boycotting the United Nations for its refusal to seat Red China; the State Department was prepared to take its resolution to the General Assembly if the Russians came back to the Security Council and exercised their veto. But the Soviets did not return, for they had been caught off guard. Stalin, in fact, seems to have been the most surprised by the outbreak of hostilities; certainly the Americans were much better prepared to move for U.N. action than the Russians were. The resolution the Americans pushed through the Security Council on the day of the attack branded the North Koreans as aggressors, demanded a cessation of hostilities, and requested a withdrawal behind the thirty-eighth parallel. The resolution was a brilliant stroke, for without any investigation at all it established war guilt and put the United Nations behind the official American version.

The speed and scope of the American response to the Korean War were truly impressive. So were the Cold War advantages that accrued. America eventually established a costly hegemony over non-Communist Asia, gained gigantic (and strategically invaluable) military bases for itself in South Korea, Formosa, Indochina, and Thailand, aroused public support for an enormously increased Department of Defense budget (from $13 billion in 1950 to $50 billion the next year), made possible European, including West German, rearmament, and in general put the United States on a permanent Cold War footing. In addition, the Americans saved the governments of Chiang in Formosa and Syngman Rhee in South Korea from certain extinction. After a thorough examination of these and other pieces of circumstantial evidence, Stone, and historian D. F. Fleming, in his work, *The Cold War and Its Origins*, have charged that the South Koreans—with American support—began the war.

Before that accusation can be examined, however, it is necessary to understand the basis of the Truman policy. How did it come about that the United States became committed to the containment of Communism everywhere, whatever the cost? Which is only another way of asking, "How did we get on the Asian mainland?" and "How did we get to Vietnam?"

The United States fights in Vietnam for many reasons, but the chief reason is a set of assumptions about the nature of the world, assumptions given wide currency by our policy-makers. These views were formed largely by the events preceding the Korean War and by the interpretation of the origins of that war. It is to that conflict we must look if we are to understand American policy today.

When Harry Truman became President of the United States, he led a nation anxious to return to traditional civil-military relations and the historic American foreign policy of non-involvement. The public, as it demonstrated by electing a Republican Congress in 1946, wanted an up-dated version of Harding's return to normalcy, with the emphasis on a speedy demobilization from World War II, lower taxes, less Government interference in the economy, and a foreign policy that would rely on the atomic bomb and/or the United Nations to keep the peace. There was no general perception of a threat to America's vital interests.

Mr. Truman and his senior advisers were adamantly opposed to the budding isolationism, primarily because they had a different set of assumptions. They did see a threat, one posed by monolithic Communism directed from the Kremlin, that aimed at world conquest and whose tactics—in the words of George Kennan, a State Department planner and one of the authors of the containment of Communism concept—would be "to make sure that it has filled every nook and cranny available to it in the basin of world power." The Truman Administration was convinced that only the United States could prevent the Kremlin from achieving its victory, but to do so it would have to swing American public opinion to a more "realistic" view of the nature of the world.

In March, 1947, Mr. Truman led the way when he called on Congress to provide aid to the Greek government, the rather shabby rightist monarchy which was threatened by an indigenous guerrilla movement. Mr. Truman assumed that the Greek Communists were directed and aided by Stalin (a judgment almost no historian would accept today). As the then Under Secretary of State Dean Acheson put it, if Greece were lost, Turkey would be untenable. Russia would move in and take control of the Dardanelles, with the "clearest implications" for the Middle East. Morale would sink in Italy, Germany, and France. Acheson was describing what would later be called the domino theory, although—as always—he was more colorful in his choice of symbols. One rotten apple, Acheson said, would infect the whole barrel.

The biggest apple of them all, the United States, would not escape the theory contended. The American economy had become so intimately related to the rest of the world, especially Europe and Latin America, that it could not survive on a hostile globe. "The whole world should adopt the American system," Mr. Truman declared in a speech of March 6, 1947. "The American system can survive in America only if it becomes a world system."

To persuade the American people, and the economy-minded Republican Congress, to pay the cost of containing Communism and spreading the American economic system, Mr. Truman needed a cause more inspiring than one of providing support for the Greek monarchy. He provided it. "We must assist free peoples to work out their destinies in their own way," he declared on March 12, 1947, in asking for aid to Greece, thereby making an unlimited and consequently indiscriminate commitment. "At the present moment in world history every nation must choose between alternative ways of life," he asserted, thereby creating a sense of permanent and universal crisis.

The critics, ranging from Walter Lippmann and publications like *The Progressive* to Senator Robert Taft, warned that such globalism would eventually erode American political institutions, subvert domestic efforts at reform, and ruin the economy, but Mr. Truman ignored them, for he pursued a greater goal. America's mission was "to insure the peaceful development of nations, free from coercion . . . to make possible lasting freedom and independence for all."

The messianic hope of redeeming history drove President Truman. "I believe that it must be the policy of the United States to support free peoples who are resisting attempted subjugation by armed minorities or by outside pressures," he declared, which amounted to a definition of what was to become American policy for the next twenty years. It was a brilliant political speech and it worked, as Congress gave the President the money he wanted.

The following year, 1948, Mr. Truman got the Marshall Plan through the same Republican Congress, thereby starting Western Europe on the road to recovery and insuring that France, Britain, and West Germany would stick to the United States in any confrontation with the Soviet Union. Communism in Europe had been contained, or so it seemed.

The trouble was that, aside from the millions given to Greece and Turkey, and the extensive Marshall Plan aid, Congress was unwilling to provide the funds needed for containment. Mr. Truman could not get Universal Military Training; he could not save the draft; America's armed forces continued to dwindle; the American stockpile of atomic weapons was by no means sufficient to deter the Red Army if it chose to march across the Elbe River; and the Europeans showed no inclination to tamper with their budding prosperity by assuming the cost of rearming. America had a policy in Europe—containment—but it did not have the military muscle to implement it if the 175 Russian divisions marched; nor did the American or Western European peoples show the slightest inclination to pay the heavy costs involved in building that muscle. By June, 1950, the Truman Administration had reached an impasse in Europe.

At home, Truman faced criticism of his earlier foreign policy. The West had lost Czechoslovakia, but Mr. Truman boasted that he had saved Greece, Turkey, Italy, and Western Europe. The use of such concepts as "won" or "lost," however, had serious repercussions. The Republicans had not made an issue of foreign policy in the 1948 elections (only third-party Presidential candidate Henry Wallace did), and by 1950 they tended to believe that their failure to do so was a key factor in their defeat. They began, almost gleefully, to charge the Truman Administration with having "lost" China and with losing the Philippines, Formosa, South Korea, and Indochina. The Republicans, led by Senator Joseph McCarthy, began to insist that the Truman Administration, and most notably Secretary Acheson, was soft on Communism, or worse.

The Democrats were bewildered and angry. With some justice, they wondered what more they could have done to stand up to the Soviets, especially in view of the funds available, funds drastically limited by the very Republicans who now demanded blood for the State Department's shortcomings. Mr. Truman desperately wanted to extend containment to Asia, but he could not even implement it in Europe.

Mr. Truman's frustrations, in the spring of 1950, were great. Foreign and military policy were moving in opposite directions. While Acheson advocated even greater commitments to the non-Communist world, Louis Johnson, a curious kind of Secretary of Defense, was scuttling the Navy's super-carrier and doing everything he could to keep the Defense Department budget under $13 billion, all in accord with Mr. Truman's own policy of balancing the budget. Mr. Truman had commissioned a major study of America's strategic position; the final result reached his desk in early June, 1950, as National Security

Council paper number 68 (thereafter known as NSC 68). Still classified and unpublished twenty years later, it was one of the key historic documents of the Cold War. NSC 68, as Senator Henry Jackson, Washington Democrat, observed, was "the first comprehensive statement of a national strategy."

NSC 68 advocated, in the words of one of its authors, "an immediate and large-scale build-up in our military and general strength and that of our allies with the intention of righting the power balance." It did so on the basis of an analysis of the Soviet Union which held that the Soviets were not only dedicated to preserving their own power and ideology but to extending and consolidating power by absorbing new satellites and weakening their enemies. Implicit in the analysis was the idea that whenever the West lost a position of strength, whether it be a military base or a colony undergoing a war of national liberation, the Kremlin was behind it. This came close to saying that all change was directed by the Communists and should be resisted. The analysis also assumed that if America were willing to try, it could stop change.

The paper was realistic in assessing what it would cost America to become the world policeman. Instead of the $13 billion the Truman Administration was planning on spending annually on defense, NSC 68 wanted to start with $35 billion in fiscal year 1951 and move up to $50 billion a year later. Politically, this was impossible. Truman recognized, as he later wrote, that NSC 68 "meant a great military effort in time of peace. It meant doubling or tripling the budget, increasing taxes heavily, and imposing various kinds of economic controls. It meant a great change in our normal peacetime way of doing things." He refused to allow any publicity about NSC 68 and indicated that he would do nothing about revising the budget until after the Congressional elections in November, 1950. He knew that without a major crisis there was no chance of selling the program to the Congress or to the country.

The contradictory pressures on foreign policy, meanwhile, were almost maddening. While President Truman and Acheson defended themselves from charges of having given China to Mao, they simultaneously had to prepare for even more embarrassments, most notably the expected loss of Formosa and South Korea.

In Korea, all was tension. Postwar Soviet-American efforts to unify the country, where American troops had occupied the area south of the thirty-eighth parallel, and Russia the area to the north, had achieved nothing. In 1947 the United States had submitted the Korean question to the U.N. General Assembly for disposition. Russia, fearful of the implications, had refused to go along. The Soviets reasoned that if the question of Korea could be given to the General Assembly, where the United States controlled a voting majority, nothing would prevent the United States from giving the problem of divided Germany to the Assembly too. The Soviets therefore refused to allow the U.N. Commission on Korea to enter North Korea.

Elections were held in South Korea in May, 1948; Syngman Rhee became president. The Russians set up a government in North Korea. Both the United States and the Soviets withdrew their occupation troops; both continued to give military aid to their respective zones, although the Russians did so on a larger scale.

Rhee was a petty dictator and an embarrassment to the United States. In January, 1950, Philip C. Jessup, U.S. Ambassador-at-large, told the Korean National Assembly that the United States was dissatisfied with the severe restraints on civil liberties which it had imposed. In April, Acheson told Rhee flatly that he either had to hold previously scheduled but consistently delayed elections or lose American aid. Rhee gave in, although on the eve of the elections he arrested thirty of his leading opponents in anti-Communist raids. Still his party collected only forty-eight seats, with 120 going to other parties, mostly on the left. The new Assembly then began to indicate that it wanted to consider unification with the North. Rhee was faced with the total loss of his position.

There was a curious incident shortly after the South Korean elections, one that none of the historians of the Korean War has examined in depth. On June 9 the radio at Pyongyang, North Korea's capital, denounced the recent elections in the South as fraudulent and called for a general election throughout Korea. The North Koreans proposed an election on August 5 of a general legislative organ that would meet in Seoul, capital of South Korea. Rhee, his prime minister, and the U.N. Commission in Korea would all be barred.

Rhee scoffed at the call for elections, dismissing it as "poppycock propaganda" but the U.N. Commission indicated that it was interested, and on June 11, John Gaillard, an American member of the Commission, crossed the thirty-eighth parallel to talk to three North Korean representatives. They gave him copies of the appeal for an election, then crossed the parallel themselves with hundreds of copies of the appeal, which they intended to distribute to the South Koreans. Rhee's police immediately arrested them. There appears to be no evidence that Washington ever explored Pyongyang's suggestion for general elections, and this raises interesting questions about the entire U.S. policy regarding Korea.

Events everywhere in Asia were moving towards a crisis. The British were out of India, revolt was stirring in Malaya, and the Dutch had been forced to leave Indonesia. In Indochina, the French were barely able to hold on. Nearly all the independent Asian governments were hostile to the West. The substitution of native leaders, usually radical, for the white rulers in Asia carried with it terrifying implications for Washington. There was a real possibility that American corporations would lose both their access to the raw materials (especially metals) and to the markets of Southeast Asia. Strategically, none of the new governments would be able to serve as an effective counter to the Chinese, which meant an end to the balance of power in Asia. Only Rhee in South Korea and Chiang in Formosa swam against the powerful tide, and the West did not have the military means available at that time to keep either of its proxies in power. What the Americans liked to call "stability in Asia" was threatened.

The crisis was most acute in China, for if the Chinese Communists drove Chiang off Formosa they would complete their victory and eventually the United States would have to recognize the Communists as the legitimate government of China, which would mean—among other things—giving Chiang's seat on the U.N. Security Council to Mao. The United States would no longer be able to regard Chiang as head of a government or maintain the fiction that he would someday return to his rightful place as ruler of all of China. This in turn would require a new definition of the economic and political relations between China and the United States.

Since late 1949, President Truman had consistently refused to provide aid to Chiang, who had proved to be a poor investment at best. The President insisted—rather late in the game—that the United States would not be drawn into the Chinese civil war. This policy was consistent with the European orientation of the Truman Administration and, in terms of the money Congress had made available for foreign aid, it was realistic. Its only possible outcome, was an end to Chiang's pretensions and an American acceptance of the Chinese Communists among the family of nations.

The domestic political results for the Democrats of such a course of events were frightening to contemplate. Already former President

Herbert Hoover had joined with Senator Taft in demanding that the U.S. Pacific Fleet be used to prevent an invasion of Formosa, while other Republicans advocated using the fleet to carry Chiang's forces back to the mainland for the reconquest of China. If Mr. Truman wished to quiet the McCarthyites at all, he would have to rethink his China policy.

By June, 1950, a series of desperate needs had come together. Mr. Truman had to have a crisis to sell the NSC 68 program of a huge U.S. military build-up. Chiang could not hold on, nor could Rhee, without an American commitment; the U.S. Air Force and Navy needed a justification to retain their bases in Japan; the Democrats had to prove that they could get tough with the Communists. Most of all, the Americans had to establish themselves on the mainland before the white man was driven out of Asia and its islands forever.

The needs were met on June 25, 1950. The outbreak of the Korean War came as a godsend to Chiang, Rhee, and the Truman Administration. Since it "proved" the aggressiveness of international Communism, the war enabled Mr. Truman to push through the NSC 68 program with its vastly increased military budgets, American aid for European rearmament, and an enormously expanded American military presence in Asia.

When President Truman announced that the Seventh Fleet was going to the Formosan Straits, Peiping immediately charged that the Pentagon was seeking to establish a military base on Chinese territory and asked the United Nations to order the Americans to withdraw. Warren Austin, U.S. Ambassador to the United Nations, refuted the charge indignantly, while Mr. Truman declared that the United States "would not seek any special position or privilege on Formosa." Jakob Malik, the Russian delegate, then accused the United States of lusting for bases in Formosa and supported his charge by quoting General MacArthur's statements to the effect that America intended to establish and hold air fields on the island. Mr. Truman rejoined that MacArthur did not speak for the Administration. Yet, as everyone knows, the United States now has enormous air bases on Formosa. By the same token, the Americans declared throughout the Korean War that they had no intention of maintaining troops there once the conflict ended. Lyndon Johnson was to say the same thing about Vietnam.

For more than a decade and a half after the Korean War began, almost no one seriously questioned the Truman Administration's interpretation of the cause of the war, which held that it began because Stalin told the North Koreans to go ahead and attack South Korea. This interpretation strengthened the notion that there was an international Communist conspiracy, centered in the Kremlin, and that therefore all wars of national liberation were carried out by Russian proxies solely to serve the interests of the Soviet Union. This view in turn allowed the Americans to dash into Lebanon at President Eisenhower's orders, to attempt by force, with President Kennedy's approval, to overthrow Castro, to intervene in the Dominican Republic at President Johnson's command, and most of all to involve this country in Vietnam.

The interpretation of the causes of the Korean War, in short, has helped shape American assumptions about the nature of the world. The interpretation may conceivably be correct, but there are questions concerning it that must be asked, and answered, before it can be fully accepted. The standard explanation, for example, as to why the Russians were not in the United Nations during the critical period when the Korean War began, is that Stalin simply made a mistake. He did not think the Americans would return to the Korean peninsula, nor did he expect the United States to go to the United Nations and ask for a condemnation of aggression by North Korea. But Stalin was ordinarily a cautious man who made few mistakes.

The explanation that he was surprised by the American reaction, even if he was, is clearly unsatisfactory, for it leaves unanswered a further query: why did not Stalin send his ambassador back to the Security Council after the first U.S. resolution went through on June 25, the day war broke out, branding North Korea as the aggressor?

The importance of the second question lies in the fact that not until June 27—two days after the outbreak of hostilities—did the United States introduce the second resolution—passed that day—which recommended to the members of the United Nations that they aid South Korea in restoring peace. It was the June 27 resolution which gave the United States U.N. cover for its essentially unilateral action in Korea. Those who wish to maintain that the Russians started the North Koreans on their way south must explain why the Soviets were not in the United Nations to protect their own interests in that world body.

The second mystery about the Soviets is why they took no action elsewhere. President Truman and Acheson assumed from the start that the Korean War was a feint. They reasoned that Stalin wanted them to put America's strength into the Pacific so that he could then march against a defenseless West Europe. The Americans countered this expected strategy by concentrating their military build-up in Europe, not Korea (much to General MacArthur's disgust; indeed, this was a basic cause of the Truman-MacArthur controversy).

Administration supporters have argued that Stalin did not move in Europe only because the United States beat him to the punch. The trouble with that view is that it took months for the Americans to get any strength into Europe; in the meantime, Stalin did nothing. If he started the Korean War as part of a worldwide offensive, as Mr. Truman argued, where was the rest of the offensive?

Finally, if the Russians started the whole thing, where were they at the critical moment? The North Koreans pushed the South Koreans and the small American contingent steadily south until early August, when MacArthur's forces were pinned into a beachhead around Pusan. But the North Koreans were incapable of delivering the final blow and had to watch, more or less helplessly, as MacArthur built up his strength and made his position invulnerable.

Red Army officers must have watched from afar with anguish, for their experience against the Germans only five years earlier had made them the world's leading experts on knocking out defensive positions. If Russia did indeed urge the North Koreans to attack, and if Stalin's aim was in fact to conquer the peninsula, why were no Red Army advisers sent to the North Koreans at the decisive moment? MacArthur himself testified later that no Russians had ever been seen anywhere in the Korean peninsula during the war. Once the Americans had intervened, but before they arrived in great strength, why did not the Russians send a few "volunteer" units to Korea to insure the final push of MacArthur's forces into the sea?

The idea that Russia and China acted in concert in starting the war has, fortunately, long since disappeared. A 1960 RAND Corporation study, *China Crosses the Yalu*, by Allen S. Whiting, concluded that the Chinese were the most surprised of anyone by the outbreak of hostilities in Korea. Mao's two major priorities in June, 1950, were to use his army to reconstruct China and to invade Formosa. His troop dispositions reflected these priorities, and were about as bad as they possibly could have been to support a war in Korea. Indeed, the big losers in the war—aside from the Korean people—were the Chinese, who lost their chance to grab Formosa and who had to divert desperately needed human and material resources from reconstruction and the building of a new society to keep American troops from the Yalu River at China's southern door. The Russians lost too, for Stalin's worst fears were realized as a direct result of the war—West Germany was rearmed and integrated into an anti-Soviet military alliance, and the United States began a massive rearmament program.

The big winners were Chiang, Rhee, and the Truman Administration, which extended containment to Asia, gained additional military bases in the Far East, unilaterally wrote the Japanese peace treaty, retained American markets and access to the natural resources of Southeast Asia, proved to the public that it was not "soft on Communism," and in general reversed the tide of change—at least for a time —that had been running so strongly against the white man in the Far East.

As noted earlier, I. F. Stone and D. F. Fleming have carefully examined the problem of whose needs were met by the Korean War, and who won and who lost, and concluded that the North Koreans were merely responding to aggression by Rhee, an aggression encouraged by Chiang and the United States. But while the circumstantial evidence is strong, these charges almost certainly go too far. The North Korean offensive was too strong, too well coordinated, and too successful to be simply a counterattack.

But granting that the North Koreans were the aggressors does not automatically make the Truman Administration interpretation of the origins of the war correct. There are too many questions that must be answered before it can be accepted.

The most reasonable tentative conclusion is that the North Koreans took matters into their own hands. They decided they could over-run the peninsula before the Americans could reinforce the South Koreans —an assessment that was not far wrong—and they moved. They probably expected that the United States would not intervene at all. Certainly we have had sufficient evidence in the late 1960s of North Korean independence from the Kremlin to make this judgment reasonable.

For our time, the important point is that Mr. Truman seized the opportunity to extend containment to the Asian mainland, thereby reversing entirely—and evidently permanently—America's Pacific policy, on the basis of a highly dubious interpretation of the causes of the conflict, based in turn on a belief in an international Communist conspiracy that never existed. The irony is that of all Mr. Truman's dramatic actions in the last week of June, 1950, the least noticed turned out to be the most important—the increase in U.S. aid to the French in Indochina that demonstrated his determination to prevent Ho Chi Minh from gaining control of Vietnam.

The seeming inevitability of American foreign policy in the postwar period—the Russians act, we react to preserve freedom—rests, in its essentials, on one basic assumption. President Truman, Acheson, and the other architects of the policy of containment (which was never more than a euphemism for the expansion of American influence and dominance) believed—or at least professed to believe—that the Kremlin had a "strategy" for world conquest.

For those who demanded proof of Stalin's intentions, the Administration pointed above all to the supposed Russian influence on and support for the Greek rebels, Ho Chi Minh, and the North Koreans. Historians, however, are finding it extraordinarily difficult to come by any solid evidence of Russian involvement on a significant scale in Greece, Indochina, or even North Korea (after 1948).

The obsessive American fears, in short, not to mention the violent American reaction, were based on assumptions that were almost surely wrong. Taking into account all that flowed from those assumptions—McCarthyism, the Cold War, ABMs, Indochina, and so on—this is the major tragedy of our times.

4
REVISIONIST HISTORIANS
AND THE COLD WAR
HENRY PACHTER

Not only the east has its revisionists. In this country, too, and even more insistently in Western Europe, honest research has led to a thorough and often painful re-appraisal of recent history. The conventional view of the so-called Cold War, as it still appears in such widely used textbooks as Spanier and Lukacz,[1] is under attack. This view may be crudely presented in three propositions:

After World War II the Soviet Union tried to expand its power through military conquest and Communist uprisings in as many countries as possible.

But it was restrained by vigorous counteraction of the Western powers which "contained" the Soviet advance by measures of mutual assistance short of war.

Fortunately, United States opinion had abandoned isolationism and America now was ready to assume its responsibilities as a great world power dedicated to the principle of collective security.

In this view we appear virtuous, restrained, and almost passive; our policy was largely defensive, and if we sent soldiers abroad, it was

[1] John Lukacz, *A History of the Cold War* (Garden City: Doubleday, 1961; rev. ed. 1967); rev. ed. somewhat more critical.
 John Spanier, *American Foreign Policy Since World War II* (New York: Praeger, 1967). Professor Spanier's book is a conventional history; Dr. Lukacz's work is a philosophical history, comparable in scope to the one cited in footnote 2.

From *Dissent*, Nov.-Dec. 1968, pp. 505–518. Reprinted by permission of the author.

only to help the oppressed or to ward off aggression. Moreover, such moves were clearly meant as "deterrence." Only twice were we unfortunate enough to be drawn into military actions—in Korea and in Vietnam, both places where we had to fight under conditions not of our own choosing—and on two occasions we barely avoided military conflict: in Berlin and in Cuba. But on the whole we managed to keep the war "cool" in spite of tempting provocation, as in Hungary, Czechoslovakia, Sinai.

The professional historian will instinctively distrust such a pat presentation. He can hardly remember a twenty-year period in history where right has been consistently on one side and wrong with equal regularity on the other. He is used to the play of force and counterforce with little reference to good and evil, and he expects to see every hero debunked in due time, every patriotic myth destroyed in the light of newly found documents, and every decision which had been deemed "inevitable" or "forced upon us," after diligent research proven avoidable. Therefore, he is not suprised to read, in Mr. Louis Halle's magisterial study of *The Cold War as History* that diametric labels such as "wicked and virtuous," or "aggressor" and "peace-loving nation" have little meaning in a conflict that on both sides was experienced as an irreducible dilemma.[2]

Taking a cool view of the East-West conflict, Mr. Halle pleads for an understanding of the Kremlin's motives and concludes that Stalin was as much afraid of us as we were afraid of him. He does not claim that newly unearthed evidence changed his mind. Rather, his dispassionate view of both sides is a matter of interpretation, and whatever new insight is gained by his method is due to his attitude: having participated in many coldwar decisions as a member of the State Department's Policy Planning staff, he now sits back and reflects on the impact these decisions may have had on the other side, and he comes rather close to the admission that some of the early critics of the containment policy, like Henry Wallace, Walter Lippmann, and P. M. S. Blackett,[3] may have had a point: the Russians refused to play the game according to our rules, and instead of being contained

[2] Louis Halle, *The Cold War as History* (New York: Harper & Row, 1968). A superb work, both personal and scholarly.

[3] Walter Lippmann, *The Cold War* (New York, Harper, 1948). Consists of 12 articles originally printed in the *New York Herald Tribune* in reply to George F. Kennan's "Mr. X." article.

they strained every effort to break out of the "iron curtain" which from their side looked like "capitalist encirclement."

The view that Mr. Halle presents would contrast with the three propositions of the conventional view in the following way:

After the defeat of Hitler, the balance of power was not restored in Europe, and from both sides of its outer fringe, therefore, attempts were made to establish a new equilibrium.

The Cold War, though widened to encompass worldwide conflicts is essentially the continuation of the international power contest which has raged from the time of the Seven Years' War through the Napoleonic wars and the two world wars of this century to the present day.

The U.S. was drawn into this conflict because it is basically a European-Atlantic nation, and this entanglement seems to have been fatefully inevitable; but accidental outbreaks of military hostilities in Asia created a climate of "crusading" which needlessly embroiled the U.S. in areas where it had little interest, less power, and no traditional ties.

Even before Mr. Halle, similar views had been expressed by conservative critics like George Kennan and Hans Morgenthau who warned that the Cold War must not be escalated into a military confrontation, must not be extended to areas outside Europe, and must not be conducted in the name of one ideology against the other.

Mr. André Fontaine, foreign editor of the Paris *Le Monde*, also abandons the black-and-white view of history in his two-volume *History of the Cold War*.[4] Each side, he laments, sees the enemy as an outlaw against whom no holds are barred, and each feels righteous about its cause. Viewing a confrontation of two *righteous* causes makes

---

P. M. S. Blackett, *Fear, War and the Bomb: Military and Political Consequences of Atomic Energy* (London, 1948; New York: McGraw-Hill, 1949). The famous British weapons expert was the first to criticize the concepts of nuclear deterrence.

[4] André Fontaine, *History of the Cold War* (New York: Pantheon, 1968). The scope and point of view of this brave attempt is indicated by its starting date— the October Revolution. Writing from the vantage point of French politics, M. Fontaine usefully reminds us that in 1944 Ho Chi Minh liberated part of Vietnam with the help of the CIA (or its predecessors) and that Maurice Thorez, then the French Communist leader, told the Vietnamese that he "would not like to be considered the liquidator of French positions in Indochina."

tragedy and history close neighbors. But is the Cold War so much past history that we can look at it in this way? We shall see that on the contrary, the revision of our views on the Cold War is no academic exercise—like admitting that George III was a fool rather than a tyrant—but a passionate matter of partisanship. Even the contention that the Cold War is over is a partisan slogan.

To perceive this, a man has to abandon the vantage point of a contestant in the field and view the past with the historian's detachment "It is night when Minerva's owl sets out on its flight." The new view therefore, is somehow associated with deep-seated attitudes of the academic mind. The statesman must act from a conviction of righteousness. But a dispassionate view of our own and a compassionate view of the other side naturally appeal to intellectuals, who not only are more immune to propaganda but also disgusted by its methods and distrustful of its aims. From their vantage point, the Cold War appeared as a contest between two brain-washing crews, and perhaps even as the outgrowth of hate ideologies.

Professor Walter La Feber has rendered a valuable service in tracing the relationship between the domestic and the international phases of the Cold War and in describing the struggle between the cold-war ideology and the critical forces in this country.[5] He shows how much of the cold-war anxieties and of our responses was due not to enemy action but to our interpretation of it. Regrettably, language difficulties and lack of access to Russian documents bar him from attempting a similar study of the cold-war climate in the Kremlin. But like other revisionists, he tends generally to attribute too much of what happened in the last 80 years to American initiatives. *We* did this, *we* did that—as though diplomacy were not an interaction of many powers. Revisionists have justly criticized the self-centered, arrogant view that this country is called to maintain the world order single-handedly. They are no less provincial in assuming that different attitudes in this country alone could at will have changed a course of events that was largely determined by others and by its starting point. Mr. La Feber neither quotes the European promoters and critics of the cold-war policies nor does he analyze the *European* interests and forces that drew or pushed the United States into the Cold War. Revisionists fail

[5] Walter La Feber, *America, Russia and the Cold War 1945–1966* (New York Wiley, 1967). Probably the best of the historical narratives.

to combat but rather tend to amplify the legend that Europe was a mere object of American policies. This is not true. Reading La Feber or any other revisionist book, no one would guess that British Foreign Minister Ernest Bevin did more than anybody else to muddle a postwar settlement in Europe, or that Ernst Reuter single-handedly forced us to fight for the freedom of Berlin. Today our European allies demand that we punish Moscow for the invasion of Czechoslovakia.

Nor would he learn the full measure of Stalin's contribution to the Cold War. Mr. La Feber begins his book with the statement that in October 1945 the magazine *Bolshevik* and President Truman more or less simultaneously ("meanwhile") sounded warlike trumpets. Only in the footnote does he acknowledge that when Truman spoke, *Bolshevik* was already three months old, i.e. it had appeared *before* the end of the war. Even earlier, at the time of Roosevelt's death, two public statements announced a reversal in Kremlin policies: one was Jacques Duclos's "Open Letter" in *Cahiers du Communisme* for April 1945; the letter has been quoted frequently because it denounced the wartime truce between the Allies, deposed Earl Browder as leader of the CP, U.S.A., and reinstated the slogan of fighting capitalism in all its forms. Mr. Christopher Lasch, another revisionist, writing in the *New York Times Magazine*,[6] brushes this letter off as just a quibble about electoral tactics and takes Arthur Schlesinger, Jr., to task for considering it a key document. Mr. Lasch displays ignorance of Communist affairs; an open letter was about the most solemn announcement, next to a speech by Stalin himself, of a shift of policy in Comintern usage. Messrs. Lasch and La Feber also omit Molotov's speech at the opening session of the U.N. April 26, 1945, where he accused the Western powers of complicity with Hitler.

Leaning over backward is a laudable attitude, but this is going rather far. American intellectuals have been angered by cold-war lies; but instead of concluding, like Mr. Halle, that both sides lie, many seem to feel that if we lie, the other side must be telling the truth. Mr. Halle carefully says that in such a great conflict where two historic forces meet, it really does not matter "who started it." In fact, every experienced historian will agree that this is a question for nursery-school teachers. To the younger (and some not so young but equally naive) revisionists, however, this question seems to matter: in order to

[6] *New York Times Magazine*, January 14, 1968.

prove the U.S. government wrong they must prove Stalin right. This calls for three kinds of operations:

Finding a suitable date for the beginning of the Cold War;

Finding documents which disprove Western propaganda claims and prove the claims of Soviet peacefulness;

Re-interpreting or ignoring documents which up to now have formed our view of the Cold War.

This endeavor goes beyond the intentions of moderate critics like Halle and La Feber. They assume that any errors of judgment or mistakes of policy were made in good faith, perhaps under the pressure of circumstances or as the consequence of honest miscalculation, misinformation, and misunderstanding; that even in ideological warfare the participants believed in what they were saying and that indeed the conflict came about rather like a Greek tragedy—through a confusion of the minds wrought by jealous gods. We shall hear about those gods later on; first we must speak of the new revisionists who disclaim to recognize them but charge that vicious men with malicious purposes started the Cold War. For obvious reasons we shall give them the name they prefer, radicals.

If the liberal critic of the Cold War laments the alleged fumbling of our policies,[7] and deplores the fateful but involuntary military and ideological escalation—or if establishment historians impute all criminal initiative to Stalin—the radical says it just was not so. Nor is he content with giving merely his own interpretation to known facts. He cites a different set of facts and he sets out to prove with documents

---

[7] Others have suggested that Truman could have avoided the Cold War if he had not abruptly stopped Lend-Lease operations after V-E Day, or if he had granted Stalin a loan. Lend-Lease was stopped not only to Russia but to England as well since the program's authorization automatically ended when it had fulfilled its purpose—victory in Europe. The U.S. remained at war with Japan while Stalin already was retaining ships loaned to him for war purposes. As to the loan, the Kremlin could have used drawing rights in the amount of $1.5 billion had it ratified the Bretton Woods agreements. Later, Molotov appeared with a large staff of experts to participate in setting up the Marshall Plan machinery; but he was called out of the meeting by a telegram from Moscow and never returned.

that the real course of events was quite different from what people believe. The most impressive and best documented work of this sort has been presented by Gar Alperowitz in his analysis of the Potsdam Conference of August 1945.[8] It will be remembered that President Truman was on his way to Potsdam when he received the "good news" from Almogordo, that the first atomic bomb had been successfully tested. He relayed this top secret to Stalin in such a way as to minimize its importance, and he chuckled when he told Churchill that the Russian apparently had not grasped the significance of the information. In fact he still chuckles when he remembers the incident in his Memoirs.[9] Mindful of the coming election year, eager to "bring the boys home" and also aware that an early victory over Japan would give "Uncle Joe" no chance to claim his part of the spoils, Truman made the fateful decision to use the bomb at once. The world has since questioned the wisdom of this decision but not the alleged reasons. These seem to me quite sufficient to explain Truman's action, given his background and position.

Alperowitz, however, amasses documents to show that the real reason for an early use of the bomb was not victory in Asia over the Japanese, but intimidation of the Russians in Europe. At Potsdam, indeed, where the powers implemented the Yalta arrangements for the future of Europe—we must now say for the partition of Europe—the Western statesmen tried to secure some measure of freedom for their friends in the Eastern countries which they had abandoned to Russian hegemony. Mr. Alperowitz shows how possession of the bomb made the Anglo-Saxons feel much more "confident" that they might be able to negotiate from strength. Lasch flatly maintains that they "asked Stalin to accept hostile governments" or even "tried to force the Soviet

---

[8] Gar Alperowitz, *Atomic Diplomacy: Hiroshima and Potsdam* (New York: Simon & Schuster, 1965). Mr. Alperowitz impresses his point of view on the reader by an excessive display of irrelevant scholarship. However, I have no quarrel with his method. The truth can be known only by careful study of the documents. But so far the results have been meager: the documents Mr. Alperowitz quotes show indeed that the relations between the allies were distrustful throughout the war. This could surprise only Stalin's faithful who had to believe the myth of the anti-fascist, Popular Front coalition. No similarly detailed study exists of the decision to re-arm Germany.

[9] Harry S. Truman, *Memoirs*, Vol. I (Garden City: Doubleday, 1955), p. 419.

Union out of Europe."[10] Alperowitz tells us how: Truman wished to show Stalin his real strength; for that purpose he needed a demonstration of the awesome power of the atom. Therefore he ordered the bombing of Hiroshima—in order to gain room for maneuver in Eastern Europe!

To the odious crime of releasing the djinn that since has hovered over the future of mankind, Alperowitz adds the indictment that this was done wantonly, for an unrelated purpose, in an action that was not even directed against the enemy but against an ally. Since we agree that the use of the bomb was heinous, we are tempted to grant Mr. Alperowitz that the reason for this crime must have been at once sinister and ludicrous. Since Mr. Alperowitz names such a sinister and ludicrous reason, we are further tempted to agree that he must be right, and from there it is only one step to the conclusion that, since all this is so shameful, Truman's hope to save a little democracy in Eastern Europe must also be condemned. On such notions radical revisionism builds its case against the U.S. government's actions in the early months of the Cold War.

But the entire deduction is fantastic. If Truman wished to frighten Stalin why did he chuckle instead of plopping the bomb with all its awful statistics on the conference table? Why does Mr. Alperowitz fail to mention the Oppenheimer-Compton report which recommended the military use of the bomb without any reference to Europe? Why did Secretary of State Byrnes publicly concede that the "Soviet Union has a right to friendly governments along its borders" and Under-Secretary, later Secretary, Acheson even speak of "a Monroe doctrine for Eastern Europe"?[11] Why, in fact, did they all look on meekly while brutal ultimatums expelled their friends from the governments of Bulgaria, Rumania, Poland, Hungary, and later of Czechoslovakia? All this happened while the U.S. still enjoyed its atomic monopoly, and Mr. Halle usefully reminds us that the U.S. demobilized its armies, did not prevent the development of atomic energy elsewhere, and did not try—as I think it should have—to barter its monopoly against the withdrawal of Soviet troops from Eastern Europe. In all the quotations

[10] *New York Times*, January 14, 1968.

[11] *New York Times*, November 1 and 15, 1945. Mr. Alperowitz indeed has an answer: Byrnes was trying to lull Stalin into complacency. That kind of logic can prove anything.

with which Mr. Alperowitz smothers the reader we do not find a shred of evidence for his contention which is based on pure conjecture. Immersed in the documents which have earned him the reputation of scholarship, he neglects to look at the acts of the various governments and to reconstruct the climate of the year 1945. So obsessed is he indeed with the search for secret evidence of evil that he never notices the evil which was being done in plain daylight.

Radical revisionism, we see, is not content with suggesting that wrong may be evenly distributed over both sides; it reverses the roles of hero and villain completely. Where we had pointed an accusing finger at Stalin, charging him with bland disregard of the Yalta agreements, we now find ourselves in the defendant's dock, indicted not with an isolated misdeed but with the consistent, systematic, and—one is tempted to say—congenital pursuit of Empire. Mr. Ronald Steel gives his book the angry title *"Pax Americana—The Cold War Empire,"*[12] and begins by quoting de Gaulle to the effect that the U.S. "feeling that she no longer had within herself sufficient scope for her energies . . . yielded in her turn to that taste for intervention in which the instinct for domination cloaked itself." The general merely was repeating the anguished outcry of his compatriot, Alexis de Tocqueville, 130 years earlier, that "there are today two great peoples which, starting out from different points of departure, advance towards the same goal—the Americans and the Russians. . . . Each of them will one day hold in its hands the destinies of half of mankind."[13]

Tempting as it may be to trace the European roots of revisionism, we must now inquire what is the nature of this American imperialism which has motivated American initiatives in the Cold War. There are three main lines of thought indicating long-term American commitments:

To the first proposition of the conventional view, Professor Denna D. Fleming answers that the world need not be concerned with Soviet expansionism—but with the systematic and consistent encirclement policies of the West, beginning with the interventions of 1917–20, and later methodically enlarged to form coalitions threatening the Soviet

[12] Ronald Steel, *Pax Americana: The Cold War Empire How It Grew and What It Means* (New York: Viking, 1967).
[13] See concluding page of Vol. I of *Democracy in America*.

Union with atomic destruction and organizing the Cold War as a holy crusade.[14] No Soviet actions but the mere existence of the Soviet Union called up Western ire.

To the second proposition Professor William Appleman Williams replies that American interventionism abroad needed no provocation by the Soviets.[15] He maintains that it dates back to well before the October Revolution, to be precise to the Open Door policy of the nineties of the last century, a policy designed to "keep China sovereign for purposes of exploitation by the burgeoning U.S. industrial complex while the Russians who could not compete, tried to assure themselves political leverage by creating spheres of influence."[16]

To the third proposition David Horowitz replies that not idealism led the U.S. into an internationalist policy but the defense of narrow economic interests,[17] to wit those of the rich. He concludes by quoting Arnold Toynbee, that America is today "the leader of a worldwide anti-revolutionary movement in defense of vested interests."[18]

In all the last-named books the scholarship is unbelievably poor. Mr. Fleming's work reads in places like a scrap book of newspaper clippings; he never distinguishes between opinion and document, as he will triumphantly exhibit a silly Letter to the Editor of the *Ashville Courier* as though its author were speaking for the U.S. government, while glossing over the most important statements by Lenin, Stalin, and their successors. Mr. Horowitz requotes Fleming's quotes with admiration and adds nothing but vulgar Marxist explanations or plain misinformation. To show that Stalin was prepared to sacrifice the odious Ulbricht regime in East Germany, he quotes Molotov's unification plan of March 10, 1952. But he fails to mention that Molotov refused to allow free elections under U.N. supervision. Moreover, he

[14] Denna D. Fleming, *The Cold War and Its Origins 1917–1960*, 2 Vols. (Garden City: Doubleday, 1961).

[15] William Appleman Williams, *The Tragedy of American Foreign Policy* (Cleveland: World, 1959).

[16] La Feber, *op. cit*; see also the contributions by Lloyd Gardner and Robert Freeman Smith to the New Left anthology *Towards a New Past*, Barton J. Bernstein, ed. (New York: Pantheon, 1968). All three authors acknowledge W. A. Williams as their master. With the exception of Professor Genovese's contribution, the scholarship in Mr. Bernstein's volume leaves much to be desired.

[17] David Horowitz, *The Free World Colossus* (New York: Hill & Wang, 1965).

[18] Arnold Toynbee, *America and World Revolution* (New York: Oxford University Press, 1961).

fails to mention that the entire "peace plan" was nothing but a desperate, last-minute bait to prevent West Germany from joining NATO. I happen to think that the Western powers should have taken Molotov's offer and trusted the dynamics of further development—the German uprising a year later then might have been a different affair! Had Horowitz analyzed the episode instead of quoting propaganda notes, he would have seen that it provides an argument for, not against cold-war tactics: Molotov had never made even as limited an offer as his March 10 plan until the Germans actually threatened to join NATO! If Acheson needed proof for his theory of "positions of strength," it is here; but though German revisionists have asked why Molotov failed to follow suit, American revisionists remain silent—for good reason; they try to avoid the issue of power.

Mr. Horowitz's treatment of the episode is a rather typical example of the half-truths on which much revisionist writing is based. As for his teacher Fleming, his file of episodes, which throws a bad light on Western governments, may be a good thing to have handy when a government apologist offers nothing but a similar file indicting the Soviet government. But as a serious historical work the Fleming book is beneath discussion. A series of episodes does not show consistency of a policy; by merely suppressing the long periods of coexistence, by ignoring the differences between the attitudes of various Western governments in their relations with the Soviet Union, and by taking the Soviet-Western relationships out of the context of the constantly shifting play of coalitions and constellations, Mr. Fleming misses every point.

Moreover, if Fleming is right, William Appleton Williams must be wrong: if the United States interventions antedate the October Revolution, as Mr. Williams maintains, they cannot have been provoked by it, as Fleming will have it. As George Kennan has shown,[19] Wilson's decision to intervene had no cold-war motivation.

Professor Williams, the most influential writer in this field, ostensibly follows the classical lead of Scott Nearing,[20] in his attempt to reduce U.S. foreign policy to economic causes. He is no Marxist, how-

[19] George F. Kennan, *The Decision to Intervene* (Princeton: Princeton University Press, 1958, paper, New York: Atheneum, 1967).
[20] Scott Nearing and Joseph Freeman, *Dollar Imperialism* (New York: Viking, 1925).

ever but a Christian populist who became a convert to mercantilism. He is fanatically devoted to the idea that closed economic areas are healthy for development and for peace. Whatever disturbs this imaginary idyll is bad, above all the American efforts to prevent any pieces of geography from being fenced off as empire. He calls the Open Door policy "anti-colonialist imperialism" and condemns the Marshall Plan as another attempt to force a door open—an attempt which apparently left Stalin no choice but to save Europe from U.S. control.

As to the economic motive, the trouble is that our China trade never lived up to the expectations of the "100 million lamps,"[21] but remained 1-2 per cent of our total imports and exports. Nor were American capitalists eager to invest in China as the modern theory of the "surplus" would require. At the beginning of the century the State Department vainly tried to encourage American bankers and railway magnates to help in offsetting the Japanese and European influence; but to no avail. Far from practicing "dollar imperialism" the U.S. was not even capable of practicing dollar diplomacy—the use of dollars for political ends. The indifference of U.S. capital made it necessary for Dr. Sun Yat-sen to turn to Lenin for help.

Nor has Professor Williams been very fortunate in the quality of his followers. Robert F. Smith descends to the following trick:[22] to show that U.S. policy was antisocialist even when it seemed to be antifascist, he quotes *Foreign Affairs* for July 1937 to the effect that "capitalism is lost where it is not built on liberalism." On closer inspection, the quoted passage turns out to be by a German exile, editor of a respected

---

[21] Title of a prewar book exhorting America to deny the great Chinese market to the Japanese. Critics of U.S. Asian policies have always argued that we have no substantial "interests" there. If this is true, Professor Williams would have to postulate that potential development of hypothetical interests has the same effect on policy-making decisions as actual interests. I am not contending, of course, that the "Open Door" policy was disinterested or that it was morally superior: in fact, the U.S. demanded no real open door but only equal rights with the Japanese and other colonialists. However, it so happened that U.S. interests coincided with Chinese interests. Many critics of U.S. policies think their job has been done when they can prove an "interest." They forget that all business relations between people, institutions, and states are based on "interest," which may be beneficial either to both or to only one side. Opprobrium should properly be cast not on interests as such but on exploitative interests that subordinate other interests.

[22] Bernstein, *op. cit.*, p. 247.

business magazine, trying to warn American business to beware of Hitler. In the Cold War, too, the economic tools of propaganda and of diplomacy are often mistaken for ends or motivations. Thus professor La Feber quotes A. A. Berle testifying in 1947 that "within four years the world will be faced with surplus production." He then proceeds to interpret this threat as "one paramount motivation" for the Truman Doctrine and the Marshall Plan.[23] It is, of course much more correct to say that the Marshall Plan was the economic arm of the Truman Doctrine. Berle then was Under-Secretary for Economic Affairs, and he was particularly concerned with promoting the "Point Four" program which was designed to win the friendship of underdeveloped countries in the world struggle between the U.S. and the U.S.S.R. for supremacy. The aim of this policy, including its economic measures, was not economic penetration but the preservation of independent states in all areas of the world. So much for "the economic motive," the search for which only shows that American liberals rarely understand power as a motive. Now let us see how power has been understood by U.S. policy-makers.

As originally conceived, the policy of containment meant the creation of strong, self-reliant states along the periphery of the Soviet empire, but especially in Europe. It meant measures short of war, and there was then no premonition of NATO or other military confrontations. Therefore, Bernard Baruch quipped that we were engaged in a "cold war"; he was varying the coinage "dry war," which had been used before World War I.

This policy was consistent with Wilson's policy of creating independent national states in place of the old empires and with F.D.R.'s anticolonial thrust during and after World War II. Long before he had ever heard of Bolshevism, Col. House warned Woodrow Wilson that "an Entente victory would mean domination of Russia on the Continent,"[24] and 30 years later George Kennan expressed the same fear in the now famous "long telegram." As a remedy he recommended the "containment" policy spelled out in the controversial "Mr. X" article.[25]

---

[23] La Feber, *op. cit.*, p. 43.

[24] Quoted by La Feber, from A. S. Link, *Wilson: The Struggle for Neutrality* (Princeton: Princeton University Press, 1960), p. 48.

[25] *Foreign Affairs*, July 1947. Both Documents are now contained in his *Memoirs* (Boston: Little, Brown, 1967).

This indeed has been the red-white-and-blue thread that runs throughout American foreign policy. Shorn of the anti-Communist rhetoric to which Kennan objected, this was the message of the Truman Doctrine of which Kennan approved. It said "hands off" to Stalin, and so did Eisenhower in his first inaugural, as had F.D.R.'s "Quarantine Speech": irrespective of the expansionist's philosophy, the U.S. has been opposed to closed doors indeed, everywhere and at all times. There is something incomprehensibly sectarian in the revisionist charge that all American and indeed all Western policies have always been directed against Russia. The Open Door policy clearly was directed first of all against Japan, second against Western colonialists, and only third against Russia, imperial as well as Soviet. For we are dealing here with the kind of tension between powers that is the usual stuff of history. Its permanence is reflected, for instance, in A. J. P. Taylor's title *The Struggle for the Mastery of Europe* 1848–1914. Ideology has done very little to embitter or alleviate these conflicts. World War I started between nations of like ideology, and World War II saw nations with opposing ideologies allied nevertheless. The U.S. conducted the Cold War by helping Tito, a Communist—but Mr. La Feber can quote senatorial diaries endlessly to the effect that Acheson was staunchly anti-Communist, yet forget to mention that he supported Tito's Communist economy.

In a strange way, revisionists reflect the mirror-image of their opponents: both think that "ideology" was the cause of the Cold War, or that some conspirational power was hiding behind the ideology— be that power the Communist world leadership, or America's military-industrial complex. They find it difficult to admit that conflicts arise out of the fact that "we live in a system of states" (Lenin), and that in such a system of conflicting and converging interests all combinations are possible.

The Cold War is such a conflict for the "mastery of Europe" in which political, diplomatic, psychological and economic pressures are the principal weapons but military deployment is used in a symbolic and logistic fashion short of walike action. It makes no sense to apply the term "cold" war to the hot wars in Korea and Indochina or to areas where no such conflict rages. The Asian and African wars must be explained in terms of their specific origins; they were fought in a different area, with different means, and against a different enemy. But there is not the slightest connection between "Communism" or "anti-Communism," and the quarreling factions in, say, the Congo or Nigeria.

Cold-war ideologists, of course, like to subsume all the post-1945 wars under the heading of anti-Communism or of the "Sino-Soviet bloc." These efforts must be strongly resisted—if only for the practical reason that one may disagree with U.S. conduct in Asia while agreeing with it in Europe, or agree in 1950 but not today. It is regrettable that the revisionists here do not go far enough. Instead of accepting Mr. Rusk's cold-war generalizations—which they denounce in another context—they should analyze each of these wars in terms of its particular condition, its weapons and conduct, its particular ideology, and above all—its particular enemy. It will then be found that the Cold War alone, as we knew it in the forties and fifties, may soon be over. Like many great wars, it was not settled, had no victors or vanquished, but is simmering down. Both sides in that war recognized rather early in the game that its solution could only be a confirmation of the status quo: for all his propaganda antics about the "liberation" of "captive nations" and the "roll-back" of the Iron Curtain, the late John F. Dulles did the most to "freeze" the Cold War where it stood. In Asia, on the contrary, even the most ardent Kremlin partisan of coexistence never wavered in his support of "wars of liberation."

Back to the Cold War. This conflict arose out of the postwar situation: Russia had just emerged from her most excruciating trial. Even without resorting to Stalin's paranoia one must understand his desire for a protective glacis. The U.S., on the other hand, could not allow any power to combine the potential of a reconstructed Europe with the resources of Asia. She is always opposed to the building of empires, as we saw.

But it was not just the actual fear and the recent experience which determined Stalin's expansionism. Rather Mr. Halle impresses on our sympathetic heart, the Russians are suffering from a deep-seated, historical encirclement complex, an anxiety which the Western powers have clumsily fostered instead of allaying. The Cold War, Mr. Halle gravely informs us, cannot be understood unless we go back into history—not to Churchill's Fulton speech that some use as the date of its beginning, nor to Yalta that to me seems the most reasonable date, not even to November 7, 1917, as Messrs. Fontaine and Fleming suggest, and not to the Pan-Slav agitation that led to World War I. No, we must go back to the Day of Creation when Nature failed to endow Russia with frontiers that can easily be defended. The rulers of her wide-open plains we learn, could protect themselves only by seizing adjacent territory, a strategy called "defensive expansionism." What with the understandable reaction of their neighbors the Russians unhappily acquired, over the centuries, that feeling of insecurity and the resulting ferocity which can be appeased only by giving them mastery over other nations. (Never mind how *their* anxiety is to be soothed.) The pattern which the Czars established reproduced itself in the relations of the Bolshevikis with their neighbors and even (I am writing at the peak of the Czechoslovak crisis) with other "socialist" countries. Long before the end of World War II, it was therefore clear to Professor Halle, who then was in the State Department, that ultimately a confrontation between the victors could not be avoided: "The dynamics of the postwar situation produced an expansion of Moscow's tyranny that was not altogether voluntary but provoked a reaction in the West that in turn awoke Moscow's persecution mania. Had it not been for this persecution mania, the Western reaction might have provided the basis for a settlement." The finger of God driving men into mad confusion and conflagration!

With all due respect to Professor Halle's eminence and scholarship, this is history stood on its head. Russia's open plains indeed were invasion roads for Napoleon and Hitler. But the Tartars had come through the inhospitable Urals; the Varangians and the Swedes had come across the sea, and so did the allies in the Crimean War. On the other hand, Russia's open frontiers permitted the Cossacks to invade Poland-Lithuania and to conquer Asia. It was Russia's neighbors who had reason to complain about Nature's disfavor, and Russia's belligerency was a product of her state rather than of her geography. Lenin, and to a geater extent Trotsky, needed no "persecution mania" to conceive of the Soviet state as a revolutionary bastion in a worldwide uprising of the underprivileged proletarians and colonial peoples. Zhdanov revived these conceptions when the power vacuum in postwar Europe opened an opportunity, and Stalin felt "secure" only with Communist governments installed in each European capital. Khrushchev felt encircled by the free city of West Berlin, and today

Brezhnev does not feel secure behind the Carpathian mountains. "In a conquered country," Stalin said after Machiavelli, "each of the hegemonial powers must install its system." As Engels said, no border is ever strategically safe.

An important function of the Cold War is to keep the bloc allies in line. This aspect has been very little commented upon by the revisionists because it is the one which is least likely to disappear so soon, and it is also the one that keeps the cold-war ideology alive. I do not think the Russians had to march into Czechoslovakia because they were afraid of internal reform—after all, the Czech economy is still 100 per cent socialist and Czech agriculture is the most collectivized of all the satellites. What the Russians were unable to tolerate was the softening of Czech relations with West Germany, and for that reason they had to insist on ideological conformity throughout the satellite empire, too.

The revisionists' ability to empathize with Stalin's tender nerves is at times limitless. Christopher Lasch laments that it was inconsiderate of Mikolajczyk to inquire how 4,000 Polish officers came to be buried in a mass grave in Katyn. Could Stalin really be expected to tolerate such a man in a Polish cabinet, even a cabinet totally dominated by Communists? Small nations, on the other hand, have no right to tender nerves. Exalting Stalin's magnanimity, Mr. Brian Thomas reminds us that Groza was not even a Communist.[26] Correct! Nor was Laval a Nazi. Groza was only the man on top of the list of the ministers which Vishinsky handed the king of Rumania with an ultimatum to appoint them within two hours.

The examples of revisionist writers exculpating Soviet policies by psycho-sociological explanations, or even by doing a touch-up job on the events, are as numerous as the apologetic somersaults of our Establishment champions. After all, reasoning from insecurity is available to all parties and every nation may need "defensive expansion."

This is the domino theory in reverse, and we must ask ourselves how far it may lead. Would it not justify a Hitler, too? Strangely enough, some revisionist writers have drawn this uncouth consequence. It is not Dean Rusk who proposes the false analogy between

[26] Brian Thomas, in the *Journal of Contemporary History* (London) January 1968.

Hitler and Stalin or Ho Chi Minh; it is Mr. Robert Freeman Smith, writing in a New Left collection, who suggests that the conformist interpretation of World War II supports the cold-war arguments.[27] Mr. Smith is amused by "simplistic" people who still believe in "the Adolf Hitler syndrome"; he cannot conceive that Hitler and Hirohito had any design to rule the world, and Pearl Harbor to him "revealed the full implication of [Brooks Adams's] imperial logic," which also made the Cold War inevitable. For it was not Japan but the United States which "in 1941 rigidly asserted that any order in Asia would have to be in terms of its objectives."

Professor A. J. P. Taylor, in his turn, author of a book which absolved Hitler of all guilt in unleashing World War II,[28] writes in— of all places!—the New York Review of Books:

"Germans were no more wicked in aspiring to dominate Europe . . . than others were in resolving to stop them. They were in a sense less wicked. For their domination was achieved with little physical destruction and comparatively few casualties, whereas the effort to resist them produced general devastation." The wanton destruction of Guernica in the Spanish Civil War, of Lidice, of Coventry, of Amsterdam and Kharkov—all brought about by the wicked resistance of the victims. The 6 million Jews were so wicked as not to see that Hitler was merely trying to do them a favor. Not the murderer but the victim is guilty! This atrocious statement is followed by more sick jokes and by an interesting aside which reveals the purpose of Taylor's revisionist effort. Citing Poland's Quixotic refusal to become either Hitler's or Stalin's satellite, he says: "Western historians exaggerate Soviet faults as much as they condone Polish ones. This is only to be expected in the era of the cold war, which historians are still loyally fighting when most sensible people have forgotten about it."[29]

Professor Taylor . . . still thinks that in September 1939 the peace might have been preserved if Poland had yielded some territory and in exchange had been compensated, perhaps, with a piece of the Ukraine. The English have always been very generous with land that did not belong to them—but why does the New York Review lend its columns

[27] Bernstein, op. cit., p. 237.
[28] A. J. P. Taylor, The Origins of World War II (New York: Atheneum, 1962).
[29] New York Review of Books, June 6, 1968.

to this kind of 18th-century statecraft? Do the revisionists of World War I, World War II, and of the Cold War have more in common than the name?

It may be possible to point to an aversion which they share—the fear of ideologies and in particular of the idea of collective security. The Astor set had to resist the pressures which came from the Popular Front in the name of both antifascism and collective security. These two themes were intimately linked with each other since the fascist governments were by nature and ideology aggressors, and to resist them was tantamount to the creation of international police forces against the disturbers of the peace.

One needs no imagination to see the trap here: the Cold War, too, has been fought on this side under the ideology of collective security against a power that had openly proclaimed itself as the challenger of the status quo. The New Left, which accepts the arguments of radical revisionism, sees the similarities between the cold-war ideology and the ideologies which were used to bring America into both world wars:

In all three cases the U.S. was defending the status quo against challengers who attacked the traditional power of the Western, colonialist states.

In each case ideology was used more or less deliberately to proclaim a "crusade" against a militant force of change.

In each case the notion of collective security was propagated to justify American involvement in alliances which allegedly were contrary to its interests and which perhaps overtaxed its power.

We can now understand the importance of this ideological identification. To the liberal it matters whether Ho Chi Minh can be compared to Stalin or maybe even to Hitler; to the radical it does not matter at all. He may even find it easier to proclaim his solidarity with a frankly revolutionary Ho Chi Minh than with a pacific one. What matters to him is not whether this country has obligations to come to the aid of others, but that it returns to the isolationist stance which was imparted to it in George Washington's Farewell Address.

Liberals usually know that this is not possible. Conservatives and Radicals cherish the pious legend that once this country lived in a state of innocence but at some point evil spirits, power-hungry politicians and greedy capitalists, contrived to entangle it in foreign alliances and wars. Though a superficial glance at 19th-century history should dispel such fantasies, most criticism of U.S. policies is based on some version of a Fall. A particularly flattering version of the legend is the Woodrow Wilson myth: that a misguided "idealism," an arrogant, puritanical sense of mission drove this country to assume the mantle of world policeman, which sat awkwardly on its shoulders; it had not been created to "take up the white man's burden" and was not fit for empire. The country was able, therefore, to play a role in world politics only if armed with a righteous ideology. The late John Foster Dulles, with his solemn countenance, was ideally suited to make this image plausible. But let us note that for all his talk about brinkmanship Dulles failed to come to the aid of East Berlin in 1953, or Hungary in 1956; he kept Chiang Kai-shek on the leash and made no move to get the Russian armies out of Europe. He concluded armistices in Korea and Vietnam and seemed reasonably happy with a world divided between "theirs" and "ours": his rhetoric was no guide to his politics, which were defensive and unimaginative. While he sought to contain the Communists he also recognized that they were containing us.

Moreover, this policy was bipartisan. Rusk took it over from his predecessor, and Stevenson endorsed it shortly before his death in a letter to Paul Goodman.

The essence of this policy was not ideology or anti-ideology, but collective security (even the Communist scare was mobilized only to make containment acceptable to a reluctant Congress and a war-weary public). As formulated by Niebuhr: *for peace we must risk war.* In the less poetic language of the Secretary of State: "Let no would-be aggressor suppose that the absence of a formal defense treaty . . . grants immunity to aggression."[30]

The "cool," sophisticated postwar generation feels superior to the generation of its parents which stumbled into two or three wars because they either believed in ideas or placed their faith in collective security. The New Left rejects these illusions: containment policy, the Truman Doctrine, the Marshall Plan, and NATO have led to other alliances and to wars in Asia; they have dispelled the world political dream of the liberals that peace can be won by power. Conservative

---

[30] Senate Preparedness Committee, quoted in the *Washington Post*, August 26, 1966.

and radical critics of the Cold War may differ on the precise phase of it which they began to reject: some started the day Henry Wallace was fired, others after the proclamation of the Truman Doctrine, the more moderate would still go along with the European confrontation until after the death of Stalin,[31] or even side with the U.S. government in the first phase of the Korean War[32]—but all share the contempt for "idealism":

> He [Rusk] is a meliorist, a liberalist and moralist . . . the heir to the Wilsonian tradition. . . . Ultimately it was Wilson's effect to convert the First World War, initially a European [!] dynastic and commercial carnage, into a war for the unattainable goal of universal peace and justice. . . . It has escaped notice that the "war to end all wars," that black joke of the Wilson era, has emerged once more in our day as the war to end all insurgency.[33]

It may not be easy to recognize in this caricature the person of the Secretary of State; but it is not difficult to recognize the bastard which conservative *realpolitik* has begotten on Populist pacifism. The noblest principle of American foreign policy, or perhaps the noblest principle in the foreign policy of all ages, has been ridiculed in order to disparage the policies of a particular Secretary of State. Instead of attacking him for misapplying the principle, the principle itself is attacked; instead of denouncing the use of great ideas for petty ends, ideas as such are held up to ridicule.

The revisionists are poor historians if they don't understand the importance of principles and ideas, either in guiding or in moving the men who act.[34] No part of history not even foreign policy, is a game

---

[31] Ronald Steel, *op. cit.*

[32] William Pfaff and Edmund Stillman, *The New Politics* (New York: Harper, 1961), and *The Politics of Hysteria* (New York: Harper, 1964).

[33] Edmund Stillman, "Dean Rusk: In the American Grain," *Commentary*, May 1968, p. 36.

[34] Revisionists of the conservative school reject "ideologies" but at least are aware that "principles" or political concepts are necessary to understand and to shape foreign policy. Such a principle is the old-fashioned "balance of powers." A more modern one would be "collective security"; very ancient ones are "empire" and "hegemony." The New Left, in its general waste land of theory, does not understand the difference between ideologies, which supply rationalizations or justifications for action, and theories or concepts and principles, which are tools. A

on a checker board where every move can be figured out coldly with all its consequences. The responsible statesman is distinguished from the chess player in that he does not see all his enemy's forces on the board and has no way of knowing his true intentions. The revisionist, who can study the archives at a later time, obviously has the advantage over the statesman who was in the middle of the rumble. He knows what each of the acting governments should have done. He can leisurely study all the pertinent documents and ignore the pressures of time, opinion, and other business that act on the statesman. Nor do his documents reveal the anxieties of contemporaries.[35]

Professor Taylor can calmly assure us that we only needed to give Hitler one more country to have eternal peace—he does not choose to remember the anxious moments when Hitler's, Mussolini's, and Hirohito's ultimatums followed each other with the inexorable regularity of a military march. Mr. La Feber may blame Acheson for throwing the Communist scare into the Congress debate when obdurate isolationists like Taft would not grant Greece the aid she needed; fortunately Mr. Halle, writing from personal memories, conveys the sense of urgency that set the pace for those who had to respond to a sudden change of the situation. He also makes it clear that the somewhat confused message which soon was to be called "Truman Doctrine" was hardly conceived as the blistering pronunciamento which it seemed to Kennan in retrospect.

To the orderly mind of the political scientist, historical events always seem to be planned, or at least conceived to suit some idea or conception. In real history nothing ever happens that way. No one had conceived of the "cold war"; the statesmen reacted to situations into which they tumbled. No one seemed to have planned a crusade, many wondered later on how they came to be in one. We have to accept as the lesson of history that forces which were more or less blind and

---

genuine difficulty is that some principles may be used as ideologies. A perfectly good tool of foreign policy, e.g., such as "arbitration," may be used as an excuse for having no policy. But even such debased principles are easy to distinguish from ideologies, such as Communism and anti-Communism, which cannot serve as guides for a policy and never have served so, but merely described an imputed motivation.

[35] There is no more dangerous trap for the inexperienced historian, nor any more dangerous weapon in the hands of the experienced propagandist, than the pseudo-fact: a well-documented record of irrelevant events.

guided by their own dynamism clashed in conflict and therefore had to hate each other. It was the diplomats' business to keep this conflict under control, not to fan it. We must judge them by their success in disentangling the entanglement because they could not avoid it in the first place.

This does not mean, of course, that we must absolve the governments of the charge that they blundered, or that at least some of the blunders were avoidable. But the revisionists have failed to prove that the postwar co-existence could be anything but antagonistic; it might even be possible to argue that the cold confrontation was among the milder forms which that antagonism was capable of taking. In certain respects it might even be said that the phrase "cold war" exaggerates the gravity of the situation. There was no war plan and no concerted effort to achieve well-defined aims; no proof has been given that either Stalin or Truman was having designs for the destruction of the other's power. What we see, rather, is a series of disconnected actions which happened at opportune moments, of opportunities seized and of weaknesses exploited. We also see a certain awareness on both sides to spare the other's susceptibilities and to carry provocations just to the threshold but not beyond. This must be said even of Dulles whose often misquoted simile emphasized the need to step to the brink *and back*.

Speaking of Dulles, finally one remembers the worst feature of the Cold War, its ideological aggressiveness, its crusading spirit, its grandiloquacious militancy. Well, Homer's heroes are hollering at each other when they are not giving battle, and ideology in the Cold War served the most degrading purpose to which an ideology can finally be put—as a cover for inaction. We won all the battles of righteousness but, thank God, the Cold War did not really break out into a hot war. Most of it was shouting.[36]

[36] U.N. Security Council debates provide good examples of "cold-war" language signifying nothing. After the recent invasion of Czechoslovakia by the armies of five Warsaw Pact powers, Mr. George Ball deplored, berated, and condemned the Soviet Union, but carefully avoided key words such as aggression which might have obligated the U.S. to take or support countermeasures. The invasion of Hungary in 1956 was subjected to the same "cold-war" treatment. Yet, some political scientists still seize upon such rhetoric to prove that there is a "cold war." One may criticize this rhetoric on many grounds, except on the assumption that the Russians take it seriously. This they leave to our simpletons on the Right and Left.

Ideologies rarely are the cause of action; they provide rationalizations for actions, they justify the division into parties. Once created, however, ideas may transcend the immediate propaganda purpose and become myths or rigid doctrines which tend to alienate their faithful from reality, freeze hostilities whose real causes have long been forgotten, and prolong loyalties which no longer make sense. By searching for the sources of the Cold War, revisionists might contribute to the thawing-out process, to loosen up the ideological rigidities, and on the whole to deideologize the antagonisms.

Unfortunately, most revisionists are doing the exact opposite: instead of understanding how the ideologies were first manipulated and then began in turn to manipulate the manipulators, the revisionists have become victims of the ideological impact. Instead of separating the cold-war ideologies from the power conflict, they have carried them into more areas of conflict, such as the wars in Africa and in the Middle East. They have fallen down on their self-assigned task; instead of questioning the ideological foundations of the crusade, they have simply changed the labels of villain and victim.

PART 7
POST-1953

INTRODUCTION

The years since 1953 have brought no fundamental changes in American foreign policy. Many of the clichés of the postwar years still have currency, and the rhetoric, although changing with each administration plays mere variations on a theme by HST: that the United States must prevent the spread of communism everywhere in the world. For example, President Eisenhower's Secretary of State, John Foster Dulles, frequently used aggressive terms like "massive retaliation" and "liberation not containment" (discussed in Reading No. 1); yet neither concept led to any basic departure in foreign policy, and the Eisenhower period was one of relative stability in East-West relations. In Europe aid through the Marshall Plan had contributed decisively to economic recovery and political stability, and Dulles sustained his predecessor's policy of including German troops in NATO—a policy disliked by both the French and the Russians.

Although no major crisis with Russia developed in the Eisenhower years, American diplomacy went through some adventurous and trying times. At home Senator Joseph McCarthy, ignoring the change in parties at the White House, continued his attacks on the State Department and American foreign policy. In Asia the administration threatened to "unleash" Chiang against Mao and contemplated direct support to the French in Vietnam, but finally decided against it. In Latin America the United States was more active: it overthrew a "red" government in Guatemala and began to train Cubans to invade their homeland and overthrow Castro. Two incidents greatly embarrassed the national pride; first, in 1957, when the Soviet Union demonstrated its technical superiority by launching the first sputnik and again later, and second, at the close of the Eisenhower era, when the Russians shot down a U-2 spy plane over Soviet territory. This incident, which led Eisenhower to make a public admission of American espionage activities, occurred on the eve of a Paris summit meeting between American and Russian leaders designed to reduce tensions between the two nations. The Suez crisis of 1956 might have led to grave international differences, but in this case the two major powers actually cooperated to restore peace. Two other serious disturbances, the Hungarian uprising against Russian control and the American intervention in Lebanon, also passed without an American-Russian confrontation.

The lull in the political fight with the communists did not imply any slackening in the effort, initiated before Roosevelt's death, to implement an economic policy with the primary objective of protecting and expanding the United States' interests overseas. Two arguments arise over the role played by Americans—officially and privately—in the economic life of foreign nations. Some observers charge the United States with economic imperialism; other insist that without technical aid and a large influx of capital, underdeveloped nations would never enter the twentieth century. Harry Magdoff alleges in Reading No. 2 that American loans and foreign aid programs are designed to advance the political, military and economic objectives of the United States while the real needs of the recipient remain of secondary importance.

The Cuban missile crisis during the Kennedy administration precipitated the most serious confrontation between the United States and Russia. The somber tone of President Kennedy's message to the American people reflects a genuine fear that the country could be facing a nuclear war. (Reading No. 3) Only when the Russians retreated and promised to remove the missiles was the danger of war averted. Paradoxically, the showdown contributed to a detente in American-Russian relations.

After President Kennedy's tragic death, Lyndon Johnson appeared likely to rank among the country's great presidents, in that his ability to get enacted advanced domestic legislation seemed matchless. But an adventurous foreign policy proved his undoing. The military intervention in the Dominican Republic in 1965, being only a transitory venture, did not arouse extensive criticism, but his decision to bomb North Vietnam and to commit a large number of men to a seemingly endless war in South Vietnam caused a divisiveness rarely paralleled in

American history. After 1965 the war became the dominating issue in both the domestic and foreign policy of the United States and led ultimately to President Johnson's retirement from public life.

Testifying before a Senate committee in 1966, Secretary of State Dean Rusk presented the administration's reasons for the military intervention in Vietnam. Invoking the Truman Doctrine as his basic justification, Rusk's statements clearly indicate the continuity in American foreign policy. (Reading No. 4)

The publication of the Pentagon Papers in 1971 clarified innumerable questions that had troubled many Americans. Reading No. 5 incorporates the interpretations presented by *The New York Times* correspondents and some of the supporting documents. Most Americans were disturbed by the information that the commitment really began under President Truman and increased in tempo through the administrations of Presidents Eisenhower and Kennedy. Many other Americans were shocked by the frank evaluations as to why we were in Vietnam. John McNaughton, a high official in the Defense Department, wrote Secretary of Defense McNamara in March 1965 that our troops were there: "Seventy per cent to avoid a humiliating U.S. defeat, 20 per cent to keep South Vietnamese territory from Chinese hands, 10 per cent to permit the people of South Vietnam to enjoy a better, freer way of life."

In the spring of 1970 President Richard Nixon tried unsuccessfully to hasten the end of the Vietnam war by ordering the Cambodian invasion, a commitment that provoked violent protests in the United States. Recently, in response to growing public antipathy toward the war, Nixon withdrew most of the ground troops from South Vietnam, but after the invasion of that country by North Vietnam the President ordered the mining of North Vietnam harbors and the intensification of the bombings in both sections of the country.

Although the war in Vietnam has occupied center stage for the American people in the field of foreign affairs, the Nixon administration has devoted considerable attention to economic foreign policy. To improve the balance of foreign trade the dollar was devalued, and certainly a primary reason for Nixon's dramatic trip to China was a desire to open new markets for American products. When Secretary of State William Rogers addressed a group of American businessmen he stressed the close relationship between foreign trade and American foreign policy. (Reading No. 6)

1
JOHN FOSTER DULLES ON AMERICAN FOREIGN POLICY

HEARINGS

Mr. Dulles. There are a number of policy matters which I would prefer to discuss with the committee in executive session, but I have no objection to saying in open session what I have said before: namely, that we shall never have a secure peace or a happy world so long as Soviet communism dominates one-third of all of the peoples that there are, and is in the process of trying at least to extend its rule to many others.

These people who are enslaved are people who deserve to be free, and who, from our own selfish standpoint, ought to be free because if they are the servile instruments of aggressive despotism, they will eventually be welded into a force which will be highly dangerous to ourselves and to all of the free world.

Therefore, we must always have in mind the liberation of these captive peoples. Now, liberation does not mean a war of liberation. Liberation can be accomplished by processes short of war. We have, as one example, not an ideal example, but it illustrates my point, the defection of Yugoslavia, under Tito from the domination of Soviet communism.

Well, that rule of Tito is not one which we admire, and it has many aspects of despotism, itself; but at least it illustrates that it is possible to disintegrate this present monolithic structure which, as I say, repre-

---

Selected from hearings on Dulles' appointment as Secretary of State and from a speech by Dulles before the Council on Foreign Relations, January 12, 1954.

sents approximately one-third of all the people that there are in the world.

The present tie between China and Moscow is an unholy arrangement which is contrary to the traditions, the hopes, the aspirations of the Chinese people. Certainly we cannot tolerate a continuance of that, or a welding of the 450 million people of China into the servile instruments of Soviet aggression.

Therefore, a policy which only aims at containing Russia where it now is, is, in itself, an unsound policy; but it is a policy which is bound to fail because a purely defensive policy never wins against an aggressive policy. If our only policy is to stay where we are, we will be driven back. It is only by keeping alive the hope of liberation, by taking advantage of that wherever opportunity arises, that we will end this terrible peril which dominates the world, which imposes upon us such terrible sacrifices and so great fears for the future. But all of this can be done and must be done in ways which will not provoke a general war, or in ways which will not provoke an insurrection which would be crushed with bloody violence, such as was the case, for example, when the Russians instigated the Polish revolt, under General Bor, and merely sat by and watched them when the Germans exterminated those who were revolting.

It must be and can be a peaceful process, but those who do not believe that results can be accomplished by moral pressures, by the weight of propaganda, just do not know what they are talking about.

I ask you to recall the fact that Soviet communism, itself, has spread from controlling 200 million people some 7 years ago to controlling 800 million people today, and it has done that by methods of political warfare, psychological warfare and propaganda, and it has not actually used the Red Army as an open aggressive force in accomplishing that.

Surely what they can accomplish, we can accomplish.

SPEECH

It is now nearly a year since the Eisenhower administration took office. During that year I have often spoken of various parts of our foreign policies. Tonight I should like to present an overall view of those policies which relate to our security.

First of all, let us recognize that many of the preceding foreign policies were good. Aid to Greece and Turkey had checked the Communist drive to the Mediterranean. The European Recovery Program had helped the peoples of Western Europe to pull out of the postwar morass. The Western powers were steadfast in Berlin and overcame the blockade with their airlift. As a loyal member of the United Nations, we had reacted with force to repel the Communist attack in Korea. When that effort exposed our military weakness, we rebuilt rapidly our military establishment. We also sought a quick buildup of armed strength in Western Europe.

These were the acts of a nation which saw the danger of Soviet communism; which realized that its own safety was tied up with that of others; which was capable of responding boldly and promptly to emergencies. These are precious values to be acclaimed. Also, we can pay tribute to congressional bipartisanship which puts the nation above politics.

But we need to recall that what we did was in the main emergency action, imposed on us by our enemies.

Let me illustrate.

1. We did not send our army into Korea because we judged in advance that it was sound military strategy to commit our Army to fight land battles in Asia. Our decision had been to pull out of Korea. It was Soviet-inspired action that pulled us back.

2. We did not decide in advance that it was wise to grant billions annually as foreign economic aid. We adopted that policy in response to the Communist efforts to sabotage the free economies of Western Europe.

3. We did not build up our military establishment at a rate which involved huge budget deficits, a depreciating currency, and a feverish economy because this seemed, in advance, a good policy. Indeed, we decided otherwise until the Soviet military threat was clearly revealed.

We live in a world where emergencies are always possible, and our survival may depend upon our capacity to meet emergencies. Let us pray that we shall always have that capacity. But, having said that, it is necessary also to say that emergency measures—however good for the emergency—do not necessarily make good permanent policies. Emergency measures are costly; they are superficial; and they imply that the enemy has the initiative. They cannot be depended on to serve our long-time interests.

This "long time" factor is of critical importance.

The Soviet Communists are planning for what they call "an entire historical era," and we should do the same. They seek, through many types of maneuvers, gradually to divide and weaken the free nations by overextending them in efforts which, as Lenin put it, are "beyond their strength so that they come to practical bankruptcy." Then, said Lenin, "our victory is assured." Then, said Stalin, will be "the moment for the decisive blow."

In the face of this strategy, measures cannot be judged adequate merely because they ward off an immediate danger. It is essential to do this, but it is also essential to do so without exhausting ourselves.

When the Eisenhower administration applied this test, we felt that some transformations were needed.

It is not sound military strategy permanently to commit U.S. land forces to Asia to a degree that leaves us no strategic reserves.

It is not sound economics, or good foreign policy to support permanently other countries; for in the long run, that creates as much ill will as good will.

Also, it is not sound to become permanently committed to military expenditures so vast that they lead to "practical bankruptcy."

Change was imperative to assure the stamina needed for permanent security. But it was equally imperative that change should be accompanied by understanding of our true purposes. Sudden and spectacular change had to be avoided. Otherwise there might have been a panic among our friends and miscalculated aggression by our enemies. We can, I believe, make a good report in these respects.

We need allies and collective security. Our purpose is to make these relations more effective, less costly. This can be done by placing more reliance on deterrent power and less dependence on local defensive power.

This is accepted practice so far as local communities are concerned. We keep locks on our doors, but we do not have an armed guard in every home. We rely principally on a community security system so well equipped to punish any who break in and steal that, in fact, would-be aggressors are generally deterred. That is the modern way of getting maximum protection at a bearable cost.

What the Eisenhower administration seeks is a similar international security system. We want, for ourselves and the other free nations, a maximum deterrent at a bearable cost.

Local defense will always be important. But there is no local defense which alone will contain the mighty landpower of the Communist world. Local defenses must be reinforced by the further deterrent of massive retaliatory power. A potential aggressor must know that he cannot always prescribe battle conditions that suit him. Otherwise, for example, a potential aggressor, who is glutted with manpower, might be tempted to attack in confidence that resistance would be confined to manpower. He might be tempted to attack in places where his superiority was decisive.

The way to deter aggression is for the free community to be willing and able to respond vigorously at places and with means of its own choosing.

So long as our basic policy concepts were unclear, our military leaders could not be selective in building our military power. If an enemy could pick his time and place and method of warfare—and if our policy was to remain the traditional one of meeting aggression by direct and local opposition—then we needed to be ready to fight in the Arctic and in the Tropics; in Asia, the Near East, and in Europe; by sea, by land, and by air; with old weapons and with new weapons.

The total cost of our security efforts, at home and abroad was over $50 billion per annum, and involved, for 1953, a projected budgetary deficit of $9 billion; and $11 billion for 1954. This was on top of taxes comparable to wartime taxes; and the dollar was depreciating in effective value. Our allies were similarly weighed down. This could not be continued for long without grave budgetary, economic, and social consequences.

But before military planning could be changed, the President and his advisers, as represented by the National Security Council, had to take some basic policy decisions. This has been done. The basic decision was to depend primarily upon a great capacity to retaliate, instantly, by means and at places of our choosing. Now the Department of Defense and the Joint Chiefs of Staff can shape our military establishment to fit what is *our* policy, instead of having to try to be ready to meet the enemy's many choices. That permits of a selection of military means instead of a multiplication of means. As a result, it is now possible to get, and share, more basic security at less cost.

2

FOREIGN AID:
INSTRUMENT OF CONTROL
HARRY MAGDOFF

The foreign aid program consists of a wide assortment of loans and gifts, including, in the words of a Presidential Commission, "gifts to prove our esteem for foreign heads of state, hastily devised projects to prevent Soviet aid, gambles to maintain existing governments in power."

These diverse activities can be classified according to their purpose or result as follows:

1. To implement the world-wide military and political policies of the United States.

2. To enforce the open-door policy: for freedom of access to raw materials, trade, and investment opportunities for U.S. business.

3. To ensure that such economic development as does take place in the underdeveloped countries is firmly rooted in capitalist ways and practices.

4. To obtain immediate economic gains for U.S. businessmen seeking trade and investment opportunities.

5. To make the receivers of aid increasingly dependent on the U.S. and other capital markets. (The debts created by the loans extended perpetuate the bondage of aid-receivers to the capital markets of the metropolitan centers.)

. . .

From *The Age of Imperialism*, pp. 117, 142–149. Copyright © 1969 by Harry Magdoff: reprinted by permission of Monthly Review Press. Footnotes omitted.

In carrying out its policies, the United States works in cooperation with such international organizations as the International Monetary Fund (IMF)—a major source of short-term loans for deficit countries —and the International Bank for Reconstruction and Development (hereafter referred to as IBRD or World Bank)—an important source for long-term funds. In addition, there is the coordinating group of the leading industrial nations, called the Development Assistance Committee, and made up of the United States, Canada, Japan and the aid-donor countries of Western Europe. (Among other things, "the DAC . . . establishes working groups for intensive consideration of specific assistance problems, such as how to assess a less-developed country's performance and aid requirements, or how to encourage greater private investment in developing countries."

The cooperation between the U.S. foreign aid program and such international institutions is based on the control that the United States and the other leading industrial nations have in these institutions, and the mutual interest of these leading nations (despite competitive struggles among themselves) in preserving a certain type of relationship with the underdeveloped countries. The impact of these organizations working in harness, often as consortia in aid programs, is to impress the recipient countries that there is no recourse other than to follow the advice and instructions of aid and loan givers. For the United States, working with the other countries often serves as a handy tactic: the imposition of the will of the United States does not appear as ominous when it comes under the auspices of an international organization. Professor Mason, who has had much experience in the foreign aid field, observes that

> it is usually much easier to bring about changes in domestic policies through the mediation of an international agency such as the International Bank or Monetary Fund than through bilateral stabilization agreements in Latin America. The consortium meetings presided over by the International Bank have come to be the most important forums for criticism of the development programs and policies of India, Pakistan, and other countries financed in this manner . . . if the United States, or any other aid-dispensing country, is to exert influence on the domestic policies of an aid-receiving country, either directly or via an international agency, its representatives must have a clear idea, based on careful analysis, of what it wants this country to do. Fre-

quently, such ideas have been lacking. Recently AID has given increased attention to this problem and has attempted to formulate for some of the principal aid-receiving countries a so-called Long-Range Assistance Strategy which spells out U.S. economic, political, and security interests in the countries in question, the conditions necessary to their attainment, and the relevant instruments of foreign policy.

In its own right, the World Bank exercises simple and direct controls. It withholds and grants loans, as any good banker would, according to its opinion of the reliability of the borrower. Recall the above reference to AID expenditures before and after Goulart. The World Bank too "refused to make any loans to Brazil for several years prior to 1964 mainly because of the unsound financial policies of the government preceding the Branco administration."

The Bank sets rigid conditions of control over independent nations as terms for its loans, dictating, as in the case of the Yanhee Power Project in Thailand, that the government set up a separate Power Board apart from the normal government authority; that all key positions in the electric power authority, including general manager, be made with prior consultation with the Bank; and that no contracts be let without approval of the consulting engineers who in turn must be approved by the World Bank.

Aside from pressuring the borrowers to improve the private investment climate, the World Bank also serves as an unabashed conduit for the movement of private capital to the most choice investment opportunities revealed in negotiations with loan applicants. Professor Baldwin, who is not reluctant to use the term "blackmail," describes in general terms, some of the past activities of the Bank:

> The IBRD, in effect, exists to drum up business for its competition, the private investors. In the face of demands from the underdeveloped countries for the maximum amount of capital on the easiest possible terms in the shortest period of time, the IBRD was replying, in effect, that they really did not need as much capital as they imagined; the capital they did need was private, not public; and the reason they were short of private capital was that their governments were following undesirable policies. The solution, therefore, was for the IBRD to withhold loans in a strategic attempt to encourage (blackmail) the government into changing their policies.

To temper the resentment of underdeveloped nations against the heavy-handed control exercised by the World Bank, various new arrangements have been devised, especially the regional development banks. But they too, covered by a façade of "local" control, are subject to the same rigors of economic necessity in the world of finance. The reasons for this are explained by Professor Mikesell:

There is a feeling in many of the less-developed countries that the major international lending institutions are dominated by the United States and other Western Powers and that therefore they seek to impose the policies of the Western industrial countries upon the developing countries of the world. It was partly for this reason that the Latin American republics worked for many years for the establishment of an inter-American financial institution which would be operated by and for Latin Americans. Although to a considerable degree this argument has been based on the dissatisfaction with the lending standards imposed by the International Bank, there may be important political and psychological advantages in channeling a substantial portion of the public capital available for Latin America through the new Inter-American Development Bank. Nevertheless, *because the Inter-American Development Bank must, as must the World Bank, secure its financing from the international capital markets, it must gain the confidence of the U.S. government and the public by means of sound loan operations.* Therefore, if it's to be successful, its policies are not likely to be greatly different from those of the World Bank. (Emphasis added.)

CONTROL VIA THE IMF

The ultimate discipline imposed by the rich nations on the poor arises from the stabilization loans made by the International Monetary Fund. Here we are no longer dealing with development projects or long-term plans for possible growth. The country that applies to the IMF for a loan (a short-term loan to stabilize its currency) is more often than not in desperate, or close to desperate, straits. The usual sequence is that the country's balance-of-payments deficit eats up the reserves of the state treasury or the central bank; the deficit persists; collection notices from foreign sellers cannot be complied with; payments of interest and amortization on past loans from foreign bankers and governments cannot be made; dividends on foreign investments cannot be remitted. As a result, the country faces bankruptcy. Bankruptcy for a country, it should be noted, is not merely a matter of losing one's good name; it signals the breakdown of foreign trade and the inability to import foreign goods necessary for the economic life of the country.

The country affected will try various emergency measures to get out of the box it finds itself in: controls over imports, subsidies for exporters, multiple exchange rates as a device for subsidy and control, etc. But when these fail, or extra cash is needed to give them a chance to work, the country turns necessarily to the IMF: private bankers are not very reliable lenders to a customer who can't meet his bills, especially if the bills are from a fellow banker. The practice of the IMF is to lend the country virtually on demand up to 25 percent of the country's quota in the Fund—this is backed up by the collateral of the country's own gold subscription to the Fund. Beyond this, the deficit country has to justify its request for a loan. And the IMF, like any good banker, uses the period of squeeze to insist that the borrower take action so that he will be a more responsible borrower. A good, conservative banker conserves; in other words, he helps to maintain the traditional business relations, including, of course, the continuing economic and financial dependency of the weaker on the stronger nations.

The classic illustration of the IMF-type of control occurred when the Castro government turned to the IMF and the World Bank to build up foreign currency reserves that had been depleted by the Batista regime, and to initiate serious industrialization and agricultural reform. *The New York Times* explained that Cuba could get economic assistance under certain conditions: "If Dr. Castro is to get large-scale aid for his budgetary and balance-of-payments problems, he will have to agree to a stabilization program proposed by the International Monetary Fund. This would involve credit restraint and a balanced—or nearly balanced—budget."

However, credit restraint and a balanced budget would produce more, not less, unemployment. Even more than that, such rigid restrictions would in effect be a veto on agrarian reform and on measures to eliminate unemployment.

The Cuban response, of course, was to opt out of the imperialist system, seek allies in the socialist camp, and begin to reconstruct its economy along diversified lines, with maximum utilization of its human and natural resources. (It is wrong to confuse economic independence with autarky. The question is not elimination of trade, but the elimination of the extreme reliance on a limited type of trade that serves only to meet the requirements and conditions of the ruling nations.)

But the country that does not seek a wholly different path must be ready to buckle down to the demands of the lender. The IMF as lender to borrowers in distress sets up tough conditions before handing out money, in the best traditions of international banking. IMF circles are not concerned, at least not officially, whether the persistent deficit of some countries may be the necessary consequence of a persistent surplus in other countries and, if so, whether balance can ever be attained if adjustments are not made in the surplus countries (tariff walls, import quotas, and the like) as well as in the deficit countries. By its structure and administrative procedures, the IMF acts only to enforce the rules of the game that governs the existing power relations among countries—*rules that evolved in the very process by which some nations became the rich nations and other nations became the poor nations.* That is why Thomas Balogh, Fellow of Balliol College, Oxford, and since 1964 Economic Adviser to the British Cabinet, evaluates the mechanics of neo-imperialism (as he calls it) thus:

> I believe it can be shown that the automatism [of the market] which evolved represents in itself a severe limitation on the possibility of full development of the weaker partner in the "colonial pact," even if there is no conscious policy which aims at exploitation for the benefit of the metropolitan area. Beyond this, the philosophy of monetary and fiscal soundness itself represents a further handicap to the weaker area. If this analysis is correct, two conclusions follow, both unpalatable to current conventional wisdom. The first is that the present upsurge in the ex-colonial areas provides no guarantee of a stable and steady progress in the future unless special efforts are made to substitute positive stimuli for the negative ending of colonial limitation. The second is that neo-imperialism does not depend on open political domination. The economic relations of the U.S. to South America are not essentially different from those of Britain to her African colonies. *The International Monetary Fund fulfills the role of the colonial administration of enforcing the rules of the game.* (Emphasis added.)

The sound monetary and fiscal policies insisted on by the IMF fall into familiar patterns:

1. Eliminate controls over imports and exports; free exchange rates; devalue the currency to a more realistic exchange rate relative to the dollar. The result of such changes is to reinforce the existing price and trade relationships and all the resulting facets of economic and financial dependency. This is not necessarily by design, or a nefarious plot by a small group of international bankers. This is a straightforward application of "sound" principles of economics and finance: the blind forces of the market place are to work their wonders. However, the blind forces of the market place, when they are efficient, are efficient in reproducing the existing allocation of resources and, equally, in reproducing the inequities of this allocation of resources: inequities within the country and inequities in the relations of the strong nations to the weak.

2. Inaugurate strong money and fiscal controls within the country; institute wage and price controls; balance the budget. Again, sound and responsible economics. But what does this mean in underdeveloped capitalist nations? Balanced budgets are achieved by increasing taxes and reducing government expenditures. What taxes and whose taxes will be increased in countries dominated by a small ruling elite? On reducing expenditures, the easiest items to cut are welfare expenditures. (This should not seem strange to U.S. readers who witnessed the impact of the Vietnam War on welfare spending.) One of the biggest gripes of the IMF and U.S. AID officials concerns the government corporations in the underdeveloped countries (such as public transportation and electric power) that operate on a deficit. One of the chief demands made by the IMF in exchange for assistance in stabilizing currencies is the elimination of such deficits. But usually these deficits are a government subsidy to supply electric power and transportation, for example, at rates which lower-income groups can afford. The elimination of the deficits is accomplished by raising prices to a profitable level. As for wage and price controls, no comment need be made on how these habitually work in capitalist nations.

There is no conflict between the aims of the IMF and of AID activity; in fact they work closely together, as evidenced by a former AID official:

> The Greek stabilization program in the mid-1950's, and agreements with Brazil, Colombia, and Chile have all been supported by U.S. aid

linked to observance of IMF recommendations. In Chile, for example, program loans in 1963 and 1964 were largely conditioned on Chilean compliance with fiscal, monetary, and foreign exchange rate policies defined in Stand-by Agreements with the IMF. More recently, in 1966–67, AID assistance to Ceylon and Ghana was tied to stabilization measures recommended by the Fund. . . .

When the IMF negotiates loans, the imposed conditions get down to very specific commitments the borrowing countries must make. The exchange of letters between the IMF, the United States, and the borrowing country, which reveal the terms dictated, are confidential and difficult for the public to discover. However, one instance that came to the surface is highly illuminating. In 1959 one of the budget-balancing requirements imposed on the Bolivian government was the elimination of superfluities from the budget:

> Both International Monetary Fund stabilization assistance and U.S. government aid were negotiated on condition that the government of Bolivia undertake economic stabilization measures, including specifically the elimination of a $3 million a year subsidy to government commissaries selling consumers' goods to miners.

What this elimination of a subsidy for miners' commissaries must have meant can be inferred from the following story in *The New York Times* by Paul Montgomery, headed "Hunger is Constant Companion of Bolivia Miners":

> Down a creaking, narrow-gauge track, two Indian miners strained to move a rusted cart full of tin ore.
>
> The ore would eventually find its way to Huanuni, in the valley, then to the concentrating mill near Oruro 20 miles away, then to smelters in the United States or Britain, and then, perhaps, to tin cans for the convenience of housewives and, finally, to garbage heaps to be buried again in the earth.
>
> The Indians pushing the cart, whose basic wage is $25 a month, had probably never eaten anything that comes in a tin can. Their cheeks bulged with their staple food—coca leaves, from which cocaine is extracted.
>
> Bolivian miners chew the leaf, which costs 5 cents for a double handful, because it dampens hunger and gives them energy for work in the thin air.

Behind the one cart, a tiny girl no more than 6 years old trudged along. Her infant brother peered out from the tattered shawl that held him to his sister's back. The little girl's feet were bound in mud-caked rags. Her legs were blue.

She was looking along the track for pieces of ore shaken loose from the carts. If the ore is of high grade, it can be exchanged for food in illicit stores.

AID AND INDEBTEDNESS

The economic dependency of the underdeveloped countries as the suppliers of food and raw materials to the developed countries results in financial dependency as well. And this financial dependency serves to cement the economic dependency. This process usually follows the following lines: Fluctuations in the demand for and hence the price of the primary products exported by the underdeveloped countries creates frequent deficits. The deficits are financed by borrowing from the creditor countries. Servicing the debt—payment of interest and amortization—requires that a portion of future exports be devoted to this purpose instead of buying needed imports. Hence, further borrowing is induced to pay for their regular imports. This cycle of economic-financial dependency becomes even more pronounced, paradoxically, as a country tries to advance via the established capitalist path. For then the country imports capital goods from the same creditor nations and goes even further into debt: the capital goods are bought on credit and have to be paid for in the currency of the supplying country.

3

ADDRESS BY PRESIDENT KENNEDY, OCTOBER 22, 1962, ON THE MISSILE CRISIS

Good evening, my fellow citizens. This Government, as promised, has maintained the closest surveillance of the Soviet military build-up on the island of Cuba. Within the past week unmistakable evidence has established the fact that a series of offensive missile sites is now in preparation on that imprisoned island. The purposes of these bases can be none other than to provide a nuclear strike capability against the Western Hemisphere.

Upon receiving the first preliminary hard information of this nature last Tuesday morning (October 16) at 9:00 A.M., I directed that our surveillance be stepped up. And having now confirmed and completed our evaluation of the evidence and our decision on a course of action, this Government feels obliged to report this new crisis to you in fullest detail.

The characteristics of these new missile sites indicate two distinct types of installations. Several of them include medium-range ballistic missiles capable of carrying a nuclear warhead for a distance of more than 1,000 nautical miles. Each of these missiles in short, is capable of striking Washington, D.C., the Panama Canal, Cape Canaveral, Mexico City, or any other city in the southeastern part of the United States, in Central America, or in the Caribbean area.

Additional sites not yet completed appear to be designed for inter-mediate-range ballistic missiles capable of traveling more than twice as far—and thus capable of striking most of the major cities in the Western Hemisphere, ranging as far north as Hudson Bay, Canada, and as far south as Lima, Peru. In addition, jet bombers, capable of carrying nuclear weapons, are now being uncrated and assembled in Cuba, while the necessary air bases are being prepared.

This urgent transformation of Cuba into an important strategic base —by the presence of these large, long-range, and clearly offensive weapons of sudden mass destruction—constitutes an explicit threat to the peace and security of all the Americas in flagrant and deliberate defiance of the Rio Pact of 1947, the traditions of this nation and Hemisphere, the Joint Resolution of the 87th Congress, the Charter of the United Nations, and my own public warnings to the Soviets on September 4 and 13.

This action also contradicts the repeated assurances of Soviet spokesmen, both publicly and privately delivered, that the arms build-up in Cuba would retain its original defensive character and that the Soviet Union had no need or desire to station strategic missiles on the territory of any other nation.

The size of this undertaking makes clear that it has been planned for some months. Yet only last month, after I had made clear the distinction between any introduction of ground-to-ground missiles and the existence of defensive antiaircraft missiles, the Soviet Government publicly stated on September 11 that, and I quote, "The armaments and military equipment sent to Cuba are designed exclusively for defensive purposes," and I quote the Soviet Government, "There is no need for the Soviet Government to shift its weapons for a retaliatory blow to any other country, for instance Cuba," and that, and I quote the Government, "The Soviet Union has so powerful rockets to carry these nuclear warheads that there is no need to search for sites for them beyond the boundaries of the Soviet Union." That statement was false.

Only last Thursday, as evidence of this rapid offensive build-up was already in my hand, Soviet Foreign Minister Gromyko told me in my office that he was instructed to make it clear once again, as he said his Government had already done, that Soviet assistance to Cuba, and I quote, "pursued solely the purpose of contributing to the defense capabilities of Cuba," that, and I quote him, "training by Soviet specialists of Cuban nationals in handling defensive armaments was by no means offensive," and that "if it were otherwise," Mr. Gromyko went on, "the Soviet Government would never become involved in rendering such assistance." That statement also was false.

Neither the United States of America nor the world community of nations can tolerate deliberate deception and offensive threats on the part of any nation, large or small. We no longer live in a world where only the actual firing of weapons represents a sufficient challenge to a nation's security to constitute maximum peril. Nuclear weapons are so destructive and ballistic missiles are so swift that any substantially increased possibility of their use or any sudden change in their deployment may well be regarded as a definite threat to peace.

For many years both the Soviet Union and the United States, recognizing this fact, have deployed strategic nuclear weapons with great care never upsetting the precarious status quo which insured that these weapons would not be used in the absence of some vital challenge. Our own strategic missiles have never been transferred to the territory of any other nation under a cloak of secrecy and deception; and our history, unlike that of the Soviets since the end of World War II, demonstrates that we have no desire to dominate or conquer any other nation or impose our system upon its people. Nevertheless, American citizens have become adjusted to living daily on the bull's eye of Soviet missiles located inside the U.S.S.R. or in submarines.

In that sense missiles in Cuba add to an already clear and present danger—although it should be noted the nations of Latin America have never previously been subjected to a potential nuclear threat.

But this secret, swift, and extraordinary build-up of Communist missiles—in an area well known to have a special and historical relationship to the United States and the nations of the Western Hemisphere, in violation of Soviet assurances, and in defiance of American and hemispheric policy—this sudden, clandestine decision to station strategic weapons for the first time outside of Soviet soil—is a deliberately provocative and unjustified change in the status quo which cannot be accepted by this country if our courage and our commitments are ever to be trusted again by either friend or foe.

The 1930's taught us a clear lesson: Aggressive conduct, if allowed to grow unchecked and unchallenged, ultimately leads to war. This nation is opposed to war. We are also true to our word. Our unswerving objective, therefore, must be to prevent the use of these missiles against this or any other country and to secure their withdrawal or elimination from the Western Hemisphere.

Our policy has been one of patience and restraint, as befits a peaceful and powerful nation, which leads a world-wide alliance. We have been determined not to be diverted from our central concerns by mere irritants and fanatics. But now further action is required—and it is underway; and these actions may only be the beginning. We will not prematurely or unnecessarily risk the costs of worldwide nuclear war in which even the fruits of victory would be ashes in our mouth—but neither will we shrink from that risk at any time it must be faced.

Acting, therefore, in the defense of our own security and of the entire Western Hemisphere, and under the authority entrusted to me by the Constitution as endorsed by the resolution of the Congress, I have directed that the following initial steps be taken immediately:

First: To halt this offensive build-up, a strict quarantine on all offensive military equipment under shipment to Cuba is being initiated. All ships of any kind bound for Cuba from whatever nation or port will, if found to contain cargoes of offensive weapons, be turned back. This quarantine will be extended, if needed, to other types of cargo and carriers. We are not at this time, however, denying the necessities of life as the Soviets attempted to do in their Berlin blockade of 1948.

Second: I have directed the continued and increased close surveillance of Cuba and its military build-up. The Foreign Ministers of the Organization of American States in their communiqué of October 3 rejected secrecy on such matters in this Hemisphere. Should these offensive military preparations continue, thus increasing the threat to the Hemisphere, further action will be justified. I have directed the Armed Forces to prepare for any eventualities; and I trust that in the interests of both the Cuban people and the Soviet technicians at the sites, the hazards to all concerned of continuing this threat will be recognized.

Third: It shall be the policy of this nation to regard any nuclear missile launched from Cuba against any nation in the Western Hemisphere as an attack by the Soviet Union on the United States, requiring a full retaliatory response upon the Soviet Union.

Fourth: As a necessary military precaution I have reinforced our base at Guantanamo, evacuated today the dependents of our personnel there, and ordered additional military units to be on a standby alert basis.

Fifth: We are calling tonight for an immediate meeting of the Organ of Consultation, under the Organization of American States to consider this threat to hemispheric security and to invoke articles six and eight of the Rio Treaty in support of all necessary action. The United Nations Charter allows for regional security arrangements—and the nations of this Hemisphere decided long ago against the military presence of outside powers. Our other allies around the world have also been alerted.

Sixth: Under the Charter of the United Nations, we are asking tonight that an emergency meeting of the Security Council be convoked without delay to take action against this latest Soviet threat to world peace. Our resolution will call for the prompt dismantling and withdrawal of all offensive weapons in Cuba, under the supervision of United Nations observers, before the quarantine can be lifted.

Seventh and finally: I call upon Chairman Khrushchev to halt and eliminate this clandestine, reckless, and provocative threat to world peace and to stable relations between our two nations. I call upon him further to abandon this course of world domination and to join in an historic effort to end the perilous arms race and transform the history of man. He has an opportunity now to move the world back from the abyss of destruction—by returning to his Government's own words that it had no need to station missiles outside its own territory, and withdrawing these weapons from Cuba—by refraining from any action which will widen or deepen the present crisis—and then by participating in a search for peaceful and permanent solutions.

This nation is prepared to present its case against the Soviet threat to peace, and our own proposals for a peaceful world, at any time and in any forum in the Organization of American States, in the United Nations, or in any other meeting that could be useful—without limiting our freedom of action.

We have in the past made strenuous efforts to limit the spread of nuclear weapons. We have proposed the elimination of all arms and military bases in a fair and effective disarmament treaty. We are prepared to discuss new proposals for the removal of tensions on both sides—including the possibilities of a genuinely independent Cuba, free to determine its own destiny. We have no wish to war with the Soviet Union, for we are a peaceful people who desire to live in peace with all other peoples.

But it is difficult to settle or even discuss these problems in an atmosphere of intimidation. That is why this latest Soviet threat—or any other threat which is made either independently or in response to our actions this week—must and will be met with determination. Any hostile move anywhere in the world against the safety and freedom of peoples to whom we are committed—including in particular the brave people of West Berlin—will be met by whatever action is needed.

Finally, I want to say a few words to the captive people of Cuba, to whom this speech is being directly carried by special radio facilities. I speak to you as a friend, as one who knows of your deep attachment to your fatherland, as one who shares your aspirations for liberty and justice for all. And I have watched and the American people have watched with deep sorrow how your nationalist revolution was betrayed and how your fatherland fell under foreign domination. Now your leaders are no longer Cuban leaders inspired by Cuban ideals. They are puppets and agents of an international conspiracy which has turned Cuba against your friends and neighbors in the Americas— and turned it into the first Latin American country to become a target for nuclear war, the first Latin American country to have these weapons on its soil.

These new weapons are not in your interest. They contribute nothing to your peace and well being. They can only undermine it. But this country has no wish to cause you to suffer or to impose any system upon you. We know that your lives and land are being used as pawns by those who deny you freedom.

Many times in the past Cuban people have risen to throw out tyrants who destroyed their liberty. And I have no doubt that most Cubans today look forward to the time when they will be truly free— free from foreign domination, free to choose their own leaders, free to select their own system, free to own their own land, free to speak and write and worship without fear or degradation. And then shall Cuba be welcomed back to the society of free nations and to the associations of this Hemisphere.

My fellow citizens, let no one doubt that this is a difficult and dangerous effort on which we have set out. No one can foresee precisely what course it will take or what costs or casualties will be incurred. Many months of sacrifice and self-discipline lie ahead—months in which both our patience and our will will be tested, months in which many threats and denunciations will keep us aware of our dangers. But the greatest danger of all would be to do nothing.

The path we have chosen for the present is full of hazards, as all paths are; but it is the one most consistent with our character and courage as a nation and our commitments around the world. The cost of freedom is always high—but Americans have always paid it. And one path we shall never choose, and that is the path of surrender or submission.

Our goal is not the victory of might but the vindication of right— not peace at the expense of freedom, but both peace and freedom, here in this Hemisphere and, we hope, around the world. God willing, that goal will be achieved.

4

THE NEED FOR SUPPLEMENTAL
FUNDS FOR VIETNAM
DEAN RUSK

Mr. Secretary, I want to apologize for the procedure which has required you to come so early in the morning. As you know, it has grown out of the difficulty on the floor of the Senate. I had to change our meeting time last night at a very late hour having received word that there might be objection on the floor to our meeting while the Senate is in session.

That, however, is still not definite. You have had very long experience in these affairs, I know. We are very pleased to have you this morning.

Would you care to open up with a statement, a short statement?

STATEMENT OF HON. DEAN RUSK, SECRETARY OF STATE

Secretary RUSK. Thank you very much, Mr. Chairman, and members of the committee; I am pleased to be here this morning, and I understand very fully the circumstances with regard to our schedule. I am especially glad to have Mr. David Bell, Administrator of AID, with me because, among some other things, he has spent some time in southeast Asia; in South Vietnam and in Laos and in Thailand, three countries that make up a very important part of this proposed supplement.

I am pleased to appear before the committee to support the President's request to authorize appropriation of supplemental funds. A major portion of this request, $275 million in supporting assistance funds, arises from the continuing and bitter struggle in Vietnam.

Hearings before the Committee of Foreign Relations, U.S. Senate, 89th Congress. 2nd Session. Jan. 28, 1966.

In March 1947 in connection with our then assistance to Greece, which was under guerrilla attack, President Truman stated:

> I believe that it must be the policy of the United States to support free peoples who are resisting attempted subjugation by armed minorities or by outside pressures.

That is the policy we are applying in Vietnam in connection with specific commitments which we have taken in regard to that country.

The heart of the problem in South Vietnam is the effort of North Vietnam to impose its will by force. For that purpose, Hanoi has infiltrated into South Vietnam large quantities of arms and tens of thousands of trained and armed men, including units of the North Vietnamese Regular Army. It is that external aggression, which the north has repeatedly escalated, that is responsible for the presence of U.S. combat forces.

While assisting the South Vietnamese to repel this aggression, the United States has made persistent efforts to find a peaceful solution. The initiatives for peace undertaken by us and by many other governments during the last 5 years are almost innumerable. You are familiar with the vigorous and far-reaching peace probes which the United States has made during the past month which I have had a chance to discuss with the committee in executive session.

None has brought a positive or encouraging response from Hanoi. Indeed, during this period—and while the South Vietnamese and ourselves refrained from bombing North Vietnam—the infiltrations from the north have continued, and the Communists have continued both their military operations and their campaigns of terror in the south. Even during the TET "cease fire" there were approximately 100 attacks on South Vietnamese, ROK, and U.S. forces.

The United States has a clear and direct commitment to the security of South Vietnam against external attack. The integrity of our commitments is absolutely essential to the preservation of peace right around the globe.

At stake also is the still broader question whether aggression is to be permitted, once again, to succeed. We know from painful experience that aggression feeds on aggression.

A central issue in the dispute between the two leading Communist powers today is to what extent it is effective—and prudent—to use force to promote the spread of communism. If the bellicose doctrines of the Asian Communists should reap a substantial reward, the outlook for peace in this world would be grim indeed.

The steady purpose of the United States is to build a world in which all nations—large and small, rich and poor—can progress in peace, secure against external interference. In Vietnam we shall continue to seek a peaceful solution—but we shall do what is necessary to assist the South Vietnamese to repel the aggression against them.

As President Johnson put it just last week:

> The door of peace must be kept wide open for all who wish to avoid the scourge of war, but the door of aggression must be closed and bolted if man himself is to survive.

The challenge in Vietnam demands the selective application of our U.S. military power in support of the forces of the Government of Vietnam. In the absence of a willingness on the part of the other side to sit down and make peace, there is no alternative—except defeat and surrender—to meeting force with force.

The free Vietnam we seek to preserve through military efforts and sacrifices must not be undermined by economic and social chaos and despair. The expanding scale of Communist aggression and our military response have added new dimensions to the task of AID. Without our AID programs we could win the major military battles in Vietnam and still lose the war and the peace.

For this reason I regard our economic assistance programs in Vietnam as equal in importance with our military assistance. We fully intend to reinforce the economic and social progress that South Vietnam has been making during a brutal war and in spite of unremitting destructive efforts by the enemy.

We can only help those who wish to defend and strengthen their freedom and to build a better future. The struggle—and the choice—is ultimately theirs to make. The South Vietnamese must believe that they and we are fighting for something worth great sacrifice. It is not enough to fight against something. All the people still able to make this choice in South Vietnam—farmers, schoolteachers, merchants, workers, mothers, students, police, soldiers, and government officials—must know that the long struggle is worth their suffering and personal tragedies. They must know that by this hard course their future will be better than their past.

The first essential in Vietnam, of course, is security against Vietcong terror and murder. The second is a unifying spirit or cause to which the people can subscribe, in the hamlets and in the cities. In this spirit, the villager and his local leaders and the security forces can cooperate to build ever-expanding areas of progress and resistance to Communist appeals and threats. In this spirit, the people of the cities can cooperate with their government in devoting their talents and efforts to strengthening the nation against those who would destroy or enslave it.

These essential conditions of success in Vietnam sound commonplace to Americans. In Vietnam their achievement requires performance—now—by Government in responding to the needs of the people and creating a partnership with the people. These are basic needs: security, social justice, a chance to grow and market crops at fair prices, protection of the value of incomes, safe water and medical care, and education for the children.

With our help and that of other free nations, enlightened elements in South Vietnam are bringing about this social revolution in the midst of war. The Government of Vietnam, in Saigon and in the countryside, is struggling with great handicaps to carry out this constructive effort, which it calls "rural construction." This coupled with the military defense against the Vietcong forces, is the heart of our joint strategy.

Without our economic assistance, the entire effort to maintain a sound economy and to build for the future would quickly fail. Destructive inflation would be spawned by the Vietnamese Government's necessarily mounting budget and by the wartime dislocations of the economy. Supplies for the rural development program could not be obtained or shipped. Internal transportation, communications, electricity, and other essential services disrupted or overloaded by the war could not be maintained or expanded. A half million refugees could not be sheltered and fed. Millions of Vietnamese would be without any medical attention. Industry would not be able to import the materials and equipment it needs to operate and grow. The development of effective local government, and agricultural and educational institutions would be handicapped by a lack of expert advisers.

The funds which Congress has appropriated for economic assistance to Vietnam cover less than half the presently estimated requirements for fiscal year 1966.

There are two principal elements in the request for additional funds.

First, to meet the rising and severe threat of inflationary pressures, additional funds are needed to finance imported goods; $175 million are now needed to finance importation for commercial sale of goods such as rice, construction materials, petroleum products, fertilizer, drugs, and many other commodities. In this way we contribute to economic and political stability, by offsetting shortages in local production and maintaining morale essential to the entire effort.

Second, $100 million is needed to fund new or expanded activities to strengthen the Government of Vietnam's work in contested rural areas. These AID operations include refugee relief; provision of medical teams and individual doctors and nurses; building or repairing of hospitals and veterans' rehabilitation centers; leasing of ships for coastal and ocean supply operations; expanding civil airlift capacity; building of warehouses, bridges, and roads; repair of war-damaged rail and other facilities; installation of temporary and permanent electric power services; construction of workers' housing and training centers; police equipment and training—the list grows long.

While we look—and work and fight—for the day when South Vietnam will enjoy peace, we must apply our resources and ingenuity to building the foundation for that future.

We are also requesting additional fiscal year 1966 funds to meet other existing or potentially dangerous situations. The sum of $7.5 million in supporting assistance is for Thailand and Laos each; $25 million is for the Dominican Republic. In addition, $100 million is required to replenish the AID contingency fund which is already exhausted.

Additional funds for Thailand and Laos are necessary to assist these nations in developing and maintaining the economic and political stability to withstand increasingly threatening Communist pressures. These funds are earmarked for nonmilitary security activities and intensified rural development projects in vulnerable areas.

In the Dominican Republic, economic and political instability have followed in the wake of last April's revolution. We are determined to help the provisional government create and maintain a stable environment prior to the coming elections in June. It is equally important that we assist the provisional government in meeting its essential current operations so that the new government will not be saddled with a crippling financial crisis, which would threaten its very existence. Additional economic assistance is needed to cover the gap between existing operating and capital budget costs of the government and tax revenues. These revenues have not increased as quickly as expected because of continued political unrest. We expect these additional funds to alleviate the high level of unemployment, which itself has contributed to Dominican instability.

In addition, as I noted above, the President has requested Congress to provide $100 million in supplemental funds to the AID contingency fund.

The fiscal year 1966 contingency fund was small; it is now depleted. It is absolutely necessary that a sufficient amount of contingency funds be on hand for the remainder of this fiscal year to permit us to respond immediately and effectively to emergency situations or unforeseen requirements which engage the interests of the United States.

It might be well, Mr. Chairman, for the committee in executive session to consider some of those situations which we see potentially on the horizon.

I would also like to note that the President's request includes provision for the transfer of funds required for military assistance to South Vietnam from the account of the military assistance program to the account of the Department of Defense. U.S. and other free world military forces have joined in the defense effort in South Vietnam in large numbers. It is more efficient, and less cumbersome, to program and budget for all U.S. military operations in Vietnam under one unified system. The military assistance program was not created to bear the costs of such combat forces. I commend to the Congress this recommendation.

In conclusion, Mr. Chairman I urge the committee's support of this urgent request in its entirety, and I welcome any questions or comments which you may have.

Thank you, Mr. Chairman.

The CHAIRMAN. [Senator Fulbright] Thank you, Mr. Secretary.

BEGINNING OF AMERICAN INVOLVEMENT

Mr. Secretary, I need not tell you that many of us are deeply troubled about our involvement in Vietnam and it seems to us that since this is the first bill this session dealing with the subject now is an appropriate opportunity for some examination of our involvement there for the clarification of the people of this country.

I know you have had long experience out there. Could you tell us very briefly, when did we first become involved in Vietnam?

Secretary RUSK. I think the first involvement was the assistance that we provided to France during the period of the Marshall plan at a time when France was faced there with the Vietminh movement, a vary large part of which was nationalist but which also had within it a very strong Communist increment.

The CHAIRMAN. What year was that?

Secretary RUSK. That began in 1949–50, Mr. Chairman.

At that time, the attitude of the United States was that it would provide assistance to France in the expectation that France would move promptly to make its own agreement with the nationalist elements in Indochina, and make it clear that the Associated States of Indochina, which later became Vietnam or the two Vietnams, Laos, and Cambodia, would, in effect, be independent.

The political movement by the French Government of that day was slower than the United States had hoped for, and the military operations came to the conclusion of the Geneva Conference of 1954.

The CHAIRMAN. Were you in the State Department at that time, 1950?

Secretary RUSK. Yes, sir; I was.

The CHAIRMAN. In what position?

Secretary RUSK. In the spring of 1950 I became Assistant Secretary for Far Eastern Affairs.

The CHAIRMAN. Were you at that time concerned with the original involvement?

Secretary RUSK. We had been involved in South—in Indochina before that.

The CHAIRMAN. In what respect were we involved before that?

Secretary RUSK. Well, the question of aid to France came up in the spring of 1950, but the policy involvement and the discussions with the French Government over it preceded it by some period. I just wanted to point out that the spring of 1950 was not our first expression of concern about Indochina.

The CHAIRMAN. But it was the first financial commitment, wasn't it?

Secretary RUSK. I believe so.

The CHAIRMAN. Was France at that time trying to reassert her colonial domination of Vietnam? Was that her objective at that time?

Secretary RUSK. I think, just at the conclusion of the war, in that part of the world, the first step that was taken was the restoration of the status quo ante bellum in the broadest sense in India, Burma, Malaysia, Indochina, Indonesia, and indeed in part in the Philippines, although the Philippines moved almost immediately to independence.

In varying degrees each of these areas became independent from her former colonial country, and in different circumstances.

In the case of France, the first step that was made was to work out something like a commonwealth arrangement: Associated States in which France would retain certain authority with respect to defense and foreign affairs. But there was never a firm basis of agreement with most of the Indochinese peoples themselves. So they moved—proceeded inevitably and I think properly—toward a more clear independence.

The CHAIRMAN. I confess I was scarcely conscious about problems of any significance there until the last few years because our attention was directed largely to Europe. But I am puzzled about what moved our Government to assist France to retain her control of Vietnam in contrast to our actions in Indonesia, for example.

Secretary RUSK. The problem there, sir, was—I am trying my best to remember something which happened quite a few years ago—the problem was not just that, or was not at all that, really, of assisting France in establishing and reenforcing a colonial position. Rather it was to give France a chance to work out its political settlement with these states on the basis of their own independence, and without having communism as a basic—without giving to the Communists a basic position in southeast Asia.

After the Communists took over authority in Peiping, we and the British and the French were consulted on this situation and pretty well agreed that the security of southeast Asia was of vital interest to the free world. The joint effort therefore to find an agreement with the nationalists on the one side and to prevent a Communist takeover on the other was a common thread of policy throughout that period.

The CHAIRMAN. Do you remember how much aid we gave France for that struggle in Vietnam, between 1950 and 1954?

Secretary RUSK. I think it was approximately $2 billion.

The CHAIRMAN. You stated in your original statement that we have a very clear commitment.

What is the origin and basis for a clear commitment for the action we are now taking in Vietnam?

COMMITMENT UNDER SEATO

Secretary RUSK. I think, sir there are a combination of components in that commitment. We have the Southeast Asia Treaty, to which South Vietnam was a protocol state.

The CHAIRMAN. What does that commit us to in that regard? This is where there is a good deal of confusion in my mind and I think in the public mind about the nature of that commitment.

Does the southeast treaty, Southeast Asia Treaty Organization commit us to do what we are now doing in Vietnam?

Secretary RUSK. Yes, sir; I have no doubt that it does.

A protocol state has a right to call on the members of the organization for assistance. The obligations of that treaty are both joint and several. That is they are both collective and individual.

So that there seems to be no doubt that we are entitled to offer that assistance. But the underlying legal basis for the assistance is the right of individual and collective self-defense against an aggressor. There is clearly an aggression from the North here which has been persistent and since 1960 has been sharply increased.

The CHAIRMAN. You say we are entitled to do this.

Are we obligated to do this under the treaty?

Secretary RUSK. I would not want to get into the question of whether, if we were not interested in the commitments, policy and principle under the Southeast Asia Treaty, we have some legal way in order to avoid these commitments. I suppose that one could frame some argument which would make that case.

But it would seem to us that the policy, which was discussed and passed upon by the Executive and the Senate of that day, is that we are opposed to aggression against these countries in Southeast Asia: both the members of the Organization and the protocol states.

OTHER ASPECTS OF COMMITMENT

In addition to that, we have bilateral assistance agreements to South Vietnam. We have had several actions of the Congress. We have had the annual aid appropriations in which the purposes of the aid have been fully set out before the Congress. We have had special resolutions such as the one of August 1964, and we have had the most important policy declarations by successive Presidents with respect to the protection of South Vietnam against Communist aggression.

QUESTION OF PAX AMERICANA

The CHAIRMAN. This question arose the other night in your "Meet the Press" appearance last Sunday night, particularly with regard to a question by the British correspondent. I think he suggested that it would be easier for all, for them to understand and for many people to understand this operation if it was put on the basis of straight out containing communism rather than the other way of protecting their right to self-determination.

What would you comment on that?

Secretary RUSK. Well, Mr. Chairman, the particular correspondent invited me to subscribe to the doctrine of Pax Americana.

The CHAIRMAN. Why?

Secretary RUSK. That is not our policy. We do not have worldwide commitments to all 117 countries with whom we have relations. We have some 42 allies, very specific commitments to those allies.

Now, it is true that, in the appropriate way in the United Nations and elsewhere, we would presumably give sympathy and support to those who are victims of the kind of aggression which would have worldwide implications. But we are not putting ourselves in the position of the gendarmes of the universe. There has been a good deal of fighting within this postwar period in which we did not participate. We are not trying to impose a Pax Americana on the world. We are trying to create a situation in which, in accordance with the charter, all nations, large and small, can live unmolested by their neighbors and have a chance to work out their own decisions in their own way. We support that policy in different ways at different times and under different circumstances. In the case of our specific allies and those with whom we have specific commitments if they are subject to an attack from those who declare a policy of aggression as a systematic course in the world, we have on a number of occasions joined with them to meet those attacks.

OBJECTIVE IN VIETNAM

The CHAIRMAN. How do you foresee the end of this struggle? Do you think we are likely to be there, 5, 10, or 20 years.?

What do you foresee as the outcome of this—even if we are successful in the military activities?

Secretary RUSK. Well, I would hate to try to cast myself in the role of a specific prophet in the development of this particular situation.

The CHAIRMAN. Maybe I will put it another way, what is our objective? Can you define our objective in terms of what we seek to achieve?

Secretary RUSK. To put it in its simplest terms, Mr. Chairman, we believe that the South Vietnamese are entitled to a chance to make their own decisions about their own affairs and their own future course of policy: that they are entitled to make these decisions without having them imposed on them by force from North Vietnam or elsewhere from the outside. We are perfectly prepared to rely upon the South Vietnamese themselves to make that judgment by elections, through their own Government, by whatever way is suitable for them to make that decision.

Now, we have indicated a good many points which have a bearing on this matter. We are not, for example, trying to acquire a new ally. If South Vietnam and the South Vietnamese people wish to pursue a nonalined course by their own option, that is an option which is open to them.

If they wish to join in the regional activities in the area, such as Mekong River development and projects of that sort, that is open to them. But we do believe they are entitled not to have these answers decided for them on the basis of military force organized from Hanoi through an aggression initiated from Hanoi, in the leadership of a front which was organized in Hanoi in 1960 for the purpose of taking over South Vietnam by force.

The CHAIRMAN. Do you think they can be a completely free agent with our occupation of the land with 200,000 or 400,000 men?

Secretary RUSK. If the infiltration of men and arms from the north were not in the picture, these troops of ours could come home. We have said that repeatedly. They went in there, the combat troops went in there, because of infiltration of men and arms from the north. That is the simple and elementary basis for the presence of American combat forces.

5

SELECTIONS FROM
THE PENTAGON PAPERS

Mr. McGovern. Mr. President, I yield myself 10 minutes.

Documents are now coming to light, as reported in the New York Times yesterday and again today, which reveal perhaps better than anything else that we have seen to date the way in which our country became so deeply involved in the Indochina war. What those documents tell is a story of almost incredible deception—deception of the U.S. Congress and the American people by the highest official in this Government, including even the President of the United States.

My own personal reaction to this, as one who has long been critical of our involvement is nevertheless a reaction almost of disbelief. That this Government of what we have thought was the greatest country in the world would engage in that kind of cynical deception of its own people and of the Congress is almost beyond belief.

I think we should clearly understand that whatever the causes of our involvement as revealed by these documents, and whatever deception has been practiced aside from that, the reasons for setting a date for the withdrawal of all our forces and for ending U.S. military operations on and over Indochina remain absolutely valid. The best way to secure the return of our prisoners, to insure the safety of our forces during the withdrawal period, to end the menace of drug addiction for American men in Indochina and to bring about a political settlement is to set the date now.

But if these documents were to have any impact at all on the con-

From the *Congressional Record*, June 14, 1971, pp. 8977–8982, 8984–8997.

gressional consideration of the pending amendment, they certainly ought to underscore the need for this amendment—in other words, the need for Congress to assume a greater measure of responsibility and control over American foreign policy.

I think we can learn from the documents that have been released much about our own failures as Members of Congress. We must understand, at long last, that we cannot give to the executive branch the unlimited power to decide on all questions of war and peace.

I really do not see how any Senator reviewing the documents can ever again believe that it is safe, in terms of the national interest, to assume that the executive branch can conduct foreign policy and can make these crucial decisions about war and peace without full participation by Congress as intended by the Constitution of the United States. The system of checks and balances was placed in the Constitution for a good reason, and if we have to learn that lesson the hard way, we need only read these documents for the proof.

What they show, for example, is that the United States deliberately planned to attack North Vietnam long before the Gulf of Tonkin incident and the ensuing resolution. They show that, as a matter of fact, the language of the Gulf of Tonkin resolution itself was drafted by Mr. Bundy, not in August or July, but the previous May, and then efforts were made to provoke the kind of sequence of events that led Congress to pass this resolution and, indeed to the bombing attacks against North Vietnam. These documents show that as early as September 1964, plans had been made to bomb North Vietnam at precisely the same time when top administration officials were ridiculing Senator GOLDWATER for advocating that course. They show that a contingency plan was actually drawn up for finding an incident which could be made into a provocation for American bombing of the North, and for passage of such a document as the Gulf of Tonkin resolution.

One official, the late Mr. McNaughton, former Secretary of Defense McNamara's assistant, made the observation in one of these documents that many people in the United States thought the establishment—that is, the foreign policy establishment—had gone mad; and one wonders, after reading this document, if that was not a legitimate concern. Such a provocation brings to mind all too easily the plan for a simulated Polish attack on German forces which enabled the Nazis to invade Poland and launch World War II. I would have believed that this kind of cynical manipulation was completely unkown in American history. But now we see that it was not.

The leaders of Congress who had every right to know what was happening in Vietnam, who had every right to know exactly what policy they were called upon to support on this floor were clearly duped and misled.

It has been said that the continuing appropriation of funds for the war has represented congressional approval of that war. But now we learn, from a reading of these documents that our congressional leadership has had to recommend support for the war without knowing the facts and, indeed, while being told things that were not true.

To cite just one example with which I am familiar, when I asked Senator FULBRIGHT, on this floor, on July 30, 1964, whether American ships were involved in military operations off the coast of North Vietnam, just prior to the alleged North Vietnamese PT boat attack on our destroyers, Senator FULBRIGHT said, in all good faith, acting as chairman of the Foreign Relations Committee, that he had been assured by the administration that American vessels were not involved in those harassment operations. The truth is that Senator FULBRIGHT had been told a lie, and that is revealed in these documents.

The executive branch, it seems to me, has no right to deceive the Members of Congress, to say nothing of the American public, in such a shameful fashion.

These documents, Mr. President, reaffirm what I have long believed and asserted about our involvement in Indochina. While they do not in any way reflect on the policy of the present administration—I am not making a partisan statement here today; quite the contrary, I am criticizing a previous administration of my own party—I believe that they stand as a warning to those of us now in Congress; and this foreign policy establishment and the Pentagon operation are not all that partisan. It functions with pretty much the same people, from administration to administration; and we would make a serious mistake to assume that the kind of deception revealed in these documents began and ended with a single administration. This whole war has been a misconceived operation from the very beginning, involving some four administrations.

If we do not now act to insure that Congress plays its full constitutional role relating to the war in Indochina, it seems to me that we are making ourselves the accomplices of any who would seek to deceive us again.

Both the President and many in Congress say they want to bring the war to an end. By adopting the McGovern-Hatfield amendment, we in the Senate will be acting in the one way we can act to make further deception and further delay impossible.

I urgently hope that all Senators who have not read these documents will take the time to do so. While admittedly an incomplete record, it is the most revealing record we yet have of the decisions that got us so hopelessly involved in this war.

Mr. President, I ask unanimous consent to have printed in the RECORD the article and the documents published in yesterday's and today's New York Times.

There being no objection, the article and the documents were ordered to be printed in the RECORD, as follows:

VIETNAM ARCHIVE: PENTAGON STUDY TRACES THREE DECADES OF GROWING U.S. INVOLVEMENTS (BY NEIL SHEEHAN)

A massive study of how the United States went to war in Indochina, conducted by the Pentagon three years ago, demonstrates that four administrations progressively developed a sense of commitment to a non-Communist Vietnam, a readiness to fight the North to protect the South, and an ultimate frustration with this effort—to a much greater extent than their public statements acknowledged at the time.

The 3,000-page analysis, to which 4,000 pages of official documents are appended, was commissioned by Secretary of Defense Robert S. McNamara and covers the American involvement in Southeast Asia from World War II to May, 1968—the start of the peace talks in Paris after President Lyndon B. Johnson had set a limit on further military commitments and revealed his intention to retire. Most of the study and many of the appended documents have been obtained by The New York Times and will be described and presented in a series of articles beginning today.

Though far from a complete history, even at 2.5 million words, the study forms a great archive of government decision-making on Indochina over three decades. The study led its 30 to 40 authors and researchers to many broad conclusions and specific findings, including the following:

That the Truman Administration's decision to give military aid to France in her colonial war against the Communist-led Vietminh "directly involved" the United States in Vietnam and "set" the course of American policy.

That the Eisenhower Administration's decision to rescue a fledgling South Vietnam from a Communist takeover and attempt to undermine the new Communist regime of North Vietnam gave the administration a "direct role in the ultimate breakdown of the Geneva settlement" for Indochina in 1954.

That the Kennedy Administration, though ultimately spared from major escalation decisions by the death of its leader, transferred a policy of "limited-risk gamble," which it inherited, into a "broad commitment" that left President Johnson with a choice between more war and withdrawal.

That the Johnson Administration, though the President was reluctant and hesitant to take the final decisions, intensified the covert warfare against North Vietnam and began planning in the spring of 1964 to wage overt war, a full year before it publicly revealed the depth of its involvement and its fear of defeat.

That this campaign of growing clandestine military pressure through 1964 and the expanding program of bombing North Vietnam in 1965 were begun despite the judgment of the Government's intelligence community that the measures would not cause Hanoi to cease its support of the Vietcong insurgency in the South, and that the bombing was deemed militarily ineffective within a few months.

That these four succeeding administrations built up the American political, military and psychological stakes in Indochina, often more deeply than they realized at the time, with large-scale military equipment to the French in 1950; with acts of sabotage and terror warfare against North Vietnam beginning in 1954; with moves that encouraged and abetted the overthrow of President Ngo Dinh Diem of South Vietnam in 1963; with plans, pledges and threats of further action that sprang to life in the Tonkin Gulf clashes in August, 1964; with the careful preparation of public opinion for the years of open warfare that were to follow; and with the calculation in 1965, as the planes and troops were openly committed to sustained combat; that neither accommodations inside South Vietnam nor early negotiations with North Vietnam would achieve the desired results.

The Pentagon study also ranges beyond such historical judgments. It suggests that the predominant American interest was at first containment of Communism and later the defense of the power, influence and prestige of the United States, in both stages irrespective of conditions in Vietnam.

And it reveals a great deal about the ways in which several administrations conducted their business on a fateful course, with much new information about the roles of dozens of senior officials of both major political parties and a whole generation of military commanders.

The Pentagon study was divided into chronological and thematic chapters of narrative and analysis, each with its own documentation attached. The Times—which has obtained all but one of nearly 40 volumes—has collated these materials into major segments of varying chronological length, from one that broadly covers the two decades before 1960 to one that deals intensively with the agonizing debate in the weeks following the 1968 Tet offensive.

The months from the beginning of 1964 to the Tonkin Gulf incident in August were a pivotal period, the study makes clear, and The Times begins its series with this phase.

VAST STUDY OF WAR TOOK A YEAR (BY HEDRICK SMITH)

In June, 1967, at a time of great personal disenchantment with the Indochina war and rising frustration among his colleagues at the Pentagon, Secretary of Defense Robert S. McNamara commissioned a major study of how and why the United States had become so deeply involved in Vietnam.

The project took a year to complete and yielded a vast and highly unusual report of Government self-analysis. It was compiled by a team of 30 to 40 Government officials, civilian and military, many of whom had helped to develop, or carry out the policies that they were asked to evaluate and some of whom were simultaneously active in the debates that changed the course of those policies.

While Mr. McNamara turned over his job to Clark M. Clifford, while the war reached a military peak in the 1968 Lunar New Year offensive, while President Johnson cut back the bombing of North

Vietnam and announced his plan to retire, and while the peace talks began in Paris, the study group burrowed through Government files.

The members sought to probe American policy toward Southeast Asia from World War II pronouncements of President Franklin D. Roosevelt into the start of Vietnam peace talks in the spring of 1968. They wrote nearly 40 book-length volumes backed up by annexes of cablegrams, memorandums, draft proposals, dissents and other documents.

MANY INCONSISTENCIES

Their report runs to more than 7,000 pages—1.5 million words of historical narratives plus a million words of documents—enough to fill a small crate.

Even so, it is not a complete or polished history. It displays many inconsistencies and lacks a single all-embracing summary. It is an extended internal critique based on the documentary record, which the researchers did not supplement with personal interviews, partly because they were pressed for time.

The study emerged as a middle-echelon and official view of the war, incorporating material from the top-level files of the Defense Department into which flow papers from the White House, the State Department, the Central Intelligence Agency and the Joint Chiefs of Staff.

Some important gaps appear in the study. The researchers did not have access to the complete files of Presidents or to all the memorandums of their conversations and decisions.

Moreover, there are other important gaps in the copy of the Pentagon study obtained by The New York Times. It lacks the section on the secret diplomacy of the Johnson period.

But whatever its limitations, the Pentagon's study discloses a vast amount of new information about the unfolding American commitment to South Vietnam and the way in which the United States engaged itself in that conflict. It is also rich in insights into the workings of government and the reasoning of the men who ran it.

Throughout the narrative there is ample evidence of vigorous, even acrimonious, debate within the Government—far more than Congress, the press and the public were permitted to discover from official pronouncements.

But the Pentagon account and its accompanying documents also reveal that once the basic objective of policy was set, the internal debate on Vietnam from 1950 until mid-1967 dealt almost entirely with how to reach those objectives rather than with the basic direction of policy.

The study related that American governments from the Truman Administration onward felt it necessary to take action to prevent Communist control of South Vietnam. As a rationale for policy, the domino theory—that if South Vietnam fell, other countries would inevitably follow—was repeated in endless variations for nearly two decades.

CONFIDENCE AND APPREHENSIONS

Especially during the nineteen-sixties, the Pentagon study discloses, the Government was confident that American power—or even the threat of its use—would bring the war under control.

But the study reveals that high officials in the Johnson Administration were troubled by the potential dangers of Chinese Communist intervention and felt the need for self-restraint to avoid provoking Peking, or the Soviet Union, into combat involvement.

As some top policy makers came to question the effectiveness of the American effort in mid-1967, the report shows, their policy papers began not only to seek to limit the military strategies on the ground and in the air but also to worry about the impact of the war on American society.

"A feeling is widely and strongly held that 'the establishment' is out of its mind," wrote John T. McNaughton, Assistant Secretary of Defense, in a note to Secretary McNamara in early May, 1967. Mr. McNaughton, who three years earlier had been one of the principal planners of the air war against North Vietnam, went on to say:

"The feeling is that we are trying to impose some U.S. image on distant peoples we cannot understand (any more than we can the younger generation at home), and that we are carrying the thing to absurd lengths. Related to this feeling is the increased polarization that is taking place in the United States with seeds of the worst split in our people in more than a century."

At the end of June, 1967, Mr. McNamara—deeply disillusioned with the war—decided to commission the Pentagon study of Vietnam policy that Mr. McNaughton and other high officials had encouraged him to undertake.

Mr. McNamara's instructions, conveyed orally and evidently in writing as well, were for the researcher to pull together the Pentagon's documentary record and, according to one well-placed former official, to produce an "objective and encyclopedic" study of the American involvement.

BROADEST POSSIBLE INTERPRETATION

The Pentagon researchers aimed at the broadest possible interpretation of events. They examined not only the policies and motives of American administrations, but also the effectiveness of intelligence, the mechanics and consequences of bureaucratic compromises, the difficulties of imposing American tactics on the South Vietnamese, the governmental uses of the American press, and many other tributaries of their main story.

The authors reveal, for example, that the American intelligence community repeatedly provided the policy makers with what proved to be accurate warnings that desired goals were either unattainable or likely to provoke costly reactions from the enemy. They cite some lapses in the accuracy of reporting and intelligence, but give a generally favorable assessment of the C.I.A. and other intelligence units.

The Pentagon researchers relate many examples of bureaucratic compromise forged by Presidents from the conflicting proposals of their advisers.

In the mid-fifties, they found, the Joint Chiefs of Staff were a restraining force, warning that successful defense of South Vietnam could not be guaranteed under the limits imposed by the 1954 Geneva accords and agreeing to send in American military advisors only on the insistence of Secretary of State John Foster Dulles.

In the nineteen-sixties, the report found, both Presidents Kennedy and Johnson chose partial measures, overriding advice that some military proposals were valid only as packages and could not be adopted piecemeal.

In examining Washington's constant difficulties with the governments in Saigon, the study found the United States so heavily committed to the regime of the moment and so fearful of instability that it was unable to persuade the South Vietnamese to make the political and economic reforms that Americans deemed necessary to win the allegiance of the people.

Though it ranges widely to explain events, the Pentagon report makes no summary effort to put the blame for the war on any single administration or to find fault with individual officials.

The writers appear to have stood at the political and bureaucratic center of the period, directing their criticisms toward both left and right.

In one section, Senator Eugene J. McCarthy, the antiwar candidate for the 1968 Democratic Presidential nomination, is characterized as "impudent and dovish," and as an "upstart challenger." At another point in the same section the demands of Adm. U.S. Grant Sharp, commander of Pacific forces, for allout bombing of North Vietnam, are characterized as "fulminations."

For the most part, the writers assumed a calm and unemotional tone, dissecting their materials in detached and academic manner. They ventured to answer key questions only when the evidence was at hand. They found no conclusive answers to some of the most widely asked questions about the war, including these:

Precisely how was Ngo Dinh Diem returned to South Vietnam in 1954 from exile and helped to power?

Who took the lead in preventing the 1956 Vietnam elections required under the Geneva accords of 1954—Mr. Diem or the Americans?

If President Kennedy had lived, would he have led the United States into a full-scale ground war in South Vietnam and an air war against North Vietnam as President Johnson did?

Was Secretary of Defense McNamara dismissed for opposing the Johnson strategy in mid-1967 or did he ask to be relieved because of disenchantment with Administration policy?

Did President Johnson's cutback of the bombing to the 20th Parallel in 1968 signal a lowering of American objectives for the war or was it merely an effort to buy more time and patience from a war-weary American public?

The research project was organized in the Pentagon's office of International Security Affairs—I.S.A., as it is known to Government insiders—the politico-military affairs branch, whose head is the third-ranking official in the Defense Department. This was Assistant Secretary McNaughton when the study was commissioned and Assistant Secretary Paul C. Warnke when the study was completed.

'IT REMAINS McNAMARA'S STUDY'

In the fall of 1968, it was transmitted to Mr. Warnke, who reportedly "signed off" on it. Former officials say this meant that he acknowledged completion of the work without endorsing its contents and forwarded it to Mr. Clifford.

Although it had been completed during Mr. Clifford's tenure, "in everyone's mind it always remained Mr. McNamara's study," one official said.

Because of its extreme sensitivity, very few copies were reproduced —from 6 to 15, by various accounts. One copy was delivered by hand to Mr. McNamara, then president of the World Bank. His reaction is not known, but at least one other former policy maker was reportedly displeased by the study's candor.

Other copies were said to have been provided to President Johnson, the State Department and President Nixon's staff, as well as to have been kept for Pentagon files.

The authors, mostly working part-time over several months, were middle-level officials, drawn from I.S.A., Systems Analysts, and the military staffs in the Pentagon, or lent by the State Department or White House staff. Probably two-thirds of the group had worked on Vietnam for the Government at one time or another.

Both the writing and editing were described as group efforts, through individuals with academic qualifications as historians, political scientists and the like were in charge of various sections.

For their research, the Pentagon depended primarily on the files of Secretary McNamara and Mr. McNaughton. William P. Bundy, former Assistant Secretary of State for Far Eastern Affairs, provided some of his files.

For extended periods, probably the most serious limitation of the Pentagon history is the lack of access to White House archives. The researchers did possess the Presidential decision papers that normally circulated to high Pentagon officials, plus White House messages to commanders or ambassadors in Saigon. These provide insight into Presidential moods and motives, but only intermittently.

An equally important handicap is that the Pentagon researchers generally lacked records of the oral discussions of the National Security Council or the most intimate gatherings of Presidents with their closest advisers, where decisions were often reached.

As the authors themselves remark, it is common practice for the final recommendations drafted before a key Presidential decision to be written to the President's spoken specifications on the basis of his reactions to earlier proposals. The missing link is often the meeting of the Administration's inner circle.

Also, because the Pentagon history draws almost entirely on internal Government papers, and primarily papers that circulated through the Defense Department, the picture of so important a figure as Secretary of State Dean Rusk remains shadowy. Mr. Rusk was known as a man who rarely committed himself to paper and who, especially during the Johnson Administration, saved his most sensitive advice for solitary talks with the President.

In the late months of the Johnson Administration, the lack of records of such meetings is a considerable weakness because, as the historians comment, Mr. Johnson operated a split-level Government. Only his most intimate advisers were aware of the policy moves he was contemplating, and some of the most important officials at the second level of government—Assistant Secretaries of State and Defense—were late to learn the drift of the President's thinking.

The Pentagon account notes that at times the highest Administration officials not only kept information about their real intentions from the press and Congress but also kept secret from the Government bureaucracy the real motives for their written recommendations or actions.

"The lesson in this," one Pentagon historian observes, "is that the rationales given in such pieces of paper (intended for fairly wide circulation among the bureaucracy, as opposed to tightly held memoranda limited to those closest to the decision maker), do not reliably indicate why recommendations were made the way they were." The words in parentheses are the historian's.

Another omission is the absence of any extended discussion of military or political responsibility for such matters as civilian casualties or the restraints imposed by the rules of land warfare.

NECESSARILY FRAGMENTED ACCOUNT

The approach of the writers varies markedly from section to section. Some of the historians are analytical and incisive. Others offer narrative compendiums of the most important available documents for their periods, with little comment or interpretation.

As a bureaucratic history, this account is necessarily fragmented. The writers either lacked time or did not choose to provide a coherent, integrated summary analysis for each of the four administrations that became involved in Vietnam from 1950 to 1968.

The Pentagon account divides the Kennedy period, for example, into five sections—dealing with the key decisions of 1961, the strategic-hamlet programs, the build-up of the American advisory mission in Vietnam, the development of plans for phased American withdrawal, and the coup d'état that ousted President Diem.

In the Johnson era, four simultaneous stories are told in separate sections—the land war in South Vietnam, the air war against the North, political relations with successive South Vietnamese government and the secret diplomatic search for negotiations. There is some overlapping, but no single section tries to summarize or draw together the various strands.

The over-all effect of the study, nonetheless, is to provide a vast storehouse of new information—the most complete and informative central archive available thus far on the Vietnam era.

TEXTS OF DOCUMENTS

Following are the texts of key documents accompanying the Pentagon's study of the Vietnam war, for the period December, 1963, through the Tonkin Gulf incident in August, 1964, and its aftermath. Except where excerpting is specified, the documents are printed verbatim, with only unmistakable typographical errors corrected.

McNAMARA REPORT TO JOHNSON ON THE SITUATION IN SAIGON IN 1963

(Memorandum, "Vietnam Situation," from Secretary of Defense Robert S. McNamara to President Lyndon B. Johnson, Dec. 21, 1963.)

In accordance with your request this morning, this is a summary of my conclusions after my visit to Vietnam on December 19–20.

1. Summary. The situation is very disturbing. Current trends, un-

less reversed in the next 2–3 months, will lead to neutralization at best and more likely to a Communist-controlled state.

2. The new government is the greatest source of concern. It is indecisive and drifting. Although Minh states that he, rather than the Committee of Generals, is making decisions, it is not clear that this is actually so. In any event, neither he nor the Committee are experienced in political administration and so far they show little talent for it. There is no clear concept on how to re-shape or conduct the strategic hamlet program; the Province Chiefs, most of whom are new and inexperienced, are receiving little or no direction because the generals are so preoccupied with essentially political affairs. A specific example of the present situation is that General [name illegible] is spending little or no time commanding III Corps, which is in the vital zone around Saigon and needs full-time direction. I made these points as strongly as possible to Minh, Don, Kim, and Tho.

3. The County Team is the second major weakness. It lacks leadership, has been poorly informed, and is not working to a common plan. A recent example of confusion has been conflicting USOM and military recommendations both to the Government of Vietnam and to Washington on the size of the military budget. Above all, Lodge has virtually no official contact with Harkins. Lodge sends in reports with major military implications without showing them to Harkins, and does not show Harkins important incoming traffic. My impression is that Lodge simply does not know how to conduct a coordinated administration. This has of course been stressed to him both by Dean Rusk and myself (and also by John McCone), and I do not think he is consciously rejecting our advice; he has just operated as a loner all his life and cannot readily change now.

Lodge's newly-designated deputy, David Nes, was with us and seems a highly competent team player. I have stated the situation frankly to him and he has said he would do all he could to constitute what would in effect be an executive committee operating below the level of the Ambassador.

As to the grave reporting weakness, both Defense and CIA must take major steps to improve this. John McCone and I have discussed it and are acting vigorously in our respective spheres.

4. Viet Cong progress has been great during the period since the coup, with my best guess being that the situation has in fact been deteriorating in the countryside since July to a far greater extent than

we realized because of our undue dependence on distorted Vietnamese reporting. The Viet Cong now control very high proportions of the people in certain key provinces, particularly those directly south and west of Saigon. The Strategic Hamlet Program was seriously over-extended in those provinces, and the Viet Cong has been able to destroy many hamlets, while others have been abandoned or in some cases betrayed or pillaged by the government's own Self Defense Corps. In these key provinces, the Viet Cong have destroyed almost all major roads, and are collecting taxes at will.

As remedial measures, we must get the government to re-allocate its military forces so that its effective strength in these provinces is essentially doubled. We also need to have major increases in both military and USOM staffs, to sizes that will give us a reliable inde-pendent U.S. appraisal of the status of operations. Thirdly, realistic pacification plans must be prepared, allocating adequate time to secure the remaining government-controlled areas and work out from there.

This gloomy picture prevails predominantly in the provinces around the capital and in the Delta. Action to accomplish each of these objec-tives was started while we were in Saigon. The situation in the north-ern and central areas is considerably better, and does not seem to have deteriorated substantially in recent months. General Harkins still hopes these areas may be made reasonably secure by the latter half of next year.

In the gloomy southern picture, an exception to the trend of Viet Cong success may be provided by the possible adherence to the gov-ernment of the Cao Dai and Hoa Hao sects, which total three million people and control key areas along the Cambodian border. The Hoa Hao have already made some sort of agreement, and the Cao Dai are expected to do so at the end of this month. However, it is not clear that their influence will be more than neutralized by these agreements, or that they will in fact really pitch in on the government's side.

5. Infiltration of men and equipment from North Vietnam continues using (a) land corridors through Laos and Cambodia; (b) the Mekong River waterways from Cambodia; (c) some possible entry from the sea and the tip of the Delta. The best guess is that 1000–1500 Viet Cong cadres entered South Vietnam from Laos in the first nine months of 1963. The Mekong route (and also the possible sea entry) is apparently used for heavier weapons and ammunition and raw materials which

have been turning up in increasing numbers in the south and of which we have captured a few shipments.

To counter this infiltration, we reviewed in Saigon various plans providing for cross-border operations into Laos. On the scale proposed, I am quite clear that these would not be politically acceptable or even militarily effective. Our first need would be immediate U–2 mapping of the whole Laos and Cambodian border, and this we are preparing on an urgent basis.

One other step we can take is to expand the existing limited but remarkably effective operations on the Laos side, the so-called Operation HARDNOSE, so that it at least provides reasonable intelligence on movements all the way along the Laos corridor; plans to expand this will be prepared and presented for approval in about two weeks.

As to the waterways, the military plans presented in Saigon were unsatisfactory, and a special naval team is being sent at once from Honolulu to determine what more can be done. The whole waterway system is so vast, however, that effective policing may be impossible.

In general, the infiltration problem, while serious and annoying, is a lower priority than the key problems discussed earlier. However, we should do what we can to reduce it.

6. Plans for Covert Action into North Vietnam were prepared as we had requested and were an excellent job. They present a wide variety of sabotage and psychological operations against North Vietnam from which I believe we should aim to select those that provide maximum pressure with minimum risk. In accordance with your direction at the meeting, General Krulak of the JCS is chairing a group that will lay out a program in the next ten days for your consideration.

7. Possible neutralization of Vietnam is strongly opposed by Minh, and our attitude is somewhat suspect because of editorials by the New York Times and mention by Walter Lippmann and others. We reassured them as strongly as possible on this—and in somewhat more general terms on the neutralization of Cambodia. I recommend that you convey to Minh a Presidential message for the New Year that would also be a vehicle to stress the necessity of strong central direction by the government and specifically by Minh himself.

8. U.S. resources and personnel cannot usefully be substantially increased. I have directed a modest artillery supplement, and also the

provision of uniforms for the Self Defense Corps, which is the most exposed force and suffers from low morale. Of greater potential significance, I have directed the Military Departments to review urgently the quality of the people we are sending to Vietnam. It seems to have fallen off considerably from the high standards applied in the original selections in 1962, and the JCS fully agree with me that we must have our best men there.

Conclusion. My appraisal may be overly pessimistic. Lodge, Harkins, and Minh would probably agree with me on specific points, but feel that January should see significant improvement. We should watch the situation very carefully, running scared, hoping for the best, but preparing for more forceful moves if the situation does not show early signs of improvement.

.   .   .

CABLE FROM PRESIDENT TO LODGE ON ESCALATION CONTINGENCIES

(Cablegram from President Johnson to Henry Cabot Lodge, United States Ambassador in Saigon, March 20, 1964.)

1. We have studied your 1776 and I am asking State to have Bill Bundy make sure that you get our latest planning documents on ways of applying pressure and power against the North. I understand that some of this was discussed with you by McNamara mission in Saigon, but as plans are refined, it would be helpful to have your detailed comments. As we agreed in our previous messages to each other, judgment is reserved for the present on overt military action in view of the consensus from Saigon conversations of McNamara mission with General Khanh and you on judgment that movement against the North at the present would be premature. We have [sic] share General Khanh's judgment that the immediate and essential task is to strengthen the southern base. For this reason our planning for action against the North is on a contingency basis at present, and immediate problem in this area is to develop the strongest possible military and political base for possible later action. There is additional international reason for avoiding immediate overt action in that we expect a showdown between the Chinese and Soviet Communist parties soon and action against the North will be more practicable after than before a showdown. But if at any time you feel that more immediate action is

urgent, I count on you to let me know specifically the reasons for such action, together with your recommendations for its size and shape.

2. On dealing with de Gaulle, I continue to think it may be valuable for you to go to Paris after Bohlen has made his first try. (State is sending you draft instruction to Bohlen, which I have not yet reviewed, for your comment.) It ought to be possible to explain in Saigon that your mission is precisely for the purpose of knocking down the idea of neutralization wherever it rears its ugly head and on this point I think that nothing is more important than to stop neutralist talk wherever we can by whatever means we can. I have made this point myself to Mansfield and Lippmann and I expect to use every public opportunity to restate our position firmly. You may want to convey our concern on this point to General Khanh and get his ideas on the best possible joint program to stop such talk in Saigon, in Washington, and in Paris. I imagine that you have kept General Khanh abreast of our efforts in Paris. After we see the results of the Bohlen approach you might wish to sound him out on Paris visit by you.

DRAFT RESOLUTION FOR CONGRESS ON ACTIONS IN SOUTHEAST ASIA

(Draft Resolution on Southeast Asia, May 25, 1964, as provided in the body of the Pentagon study.)

Whereas the signatories of the Geneva Accords of 1954, including the Soviet Union, the Communist regime in China, and Viet Nam agreed to respect the independence and territorial integrity of South Viet Nam, Laos and Cambodia; and the United States, although not a signatory of the Accords, declared that it would view any renewal of aggression in violation of the Accords with grave concern and as seriously threatening international peace and security;

Whereas the Communist regime in North Viet Nam, with the aid and support of the Communist regime in China, has systematically flouted its obligations under these Accords and has engaged in aggression against the independence and territorial integrity of South Viet Nam by carrying out a systematic plan for the subversion of the Government of South Viet Nam, by furnishing direction, training, personnel and arms for the conduct of guerrilla warfare within South Viet Nam, and by the ruthless use of terror against the peaceful population of that country;

Whereas in the face of this Communist aggression and subversion the Government and people of South Viet Nam have bravely undertaken the defense of their independence and territorial integrity, and at the request of that Government the United States has, in accordance with its Declaration of 1954, provided military advice, economic aid and military equipment;

Whereas in the Geneva Agreements of 1962 the United States, the Soviet Union, the Communist regime in China, North Viet Nam and others solemnly undertook to respect the sovereignty, independence, neutrality, unity and territorial integrity of the Kingdom of Laos;

Whereas in violation of these undertakings the Communist regime in North Viet Nam, with the aid and support of the Communist regime in China, has engaged in aggression against the independence, unity and territorial integrity of Laos by maintaining forces on Laotian territory, by the use of that territory for the infiltration of arms and equipment into South Viet Nam, and by providing direction, men and equipment for persistent armed attacks against the Government of (words illegible);

Whereas in the face of this Communist aggression the Government of National Unification and the non-Communist elements in Laos have striven to maintain the conditions of unity, independence and neutrality envisioned for their country in the Geneva Agreements of 1962;

Whereas the United States has no territorial, military or political ambitions in Southeast Asia, but desires only that the peoples of South Viet Nam, Laos and Cambodia should be left in peace by their neighbors to work out their own destinies in their own way, and, therefore, its objective is that the status established for these countries in the Geneva Accords of 1954 and the Geneva Agreements of 1962 should be restored with effective means of enforcement;

Whereas it is essential that the world fully understand that the American people are united in their determination to take all steps that may be necessary to assist the peoples of South Viet Nam and Laos to maintain their independence and political integrity.

Now, therefore, be it resolved by the Senate and House of Representatives of the United States of America in Congress assembled:

That the United States regards the preservation of the independence and integrity of the nations of South Viet Nam and Laos as vital to its national interest and to world peace;

Sec. 2. To this end, if the President determines the necessity thereof, the United States is prepared, upon the request of the Government of South Viet Nam or the Government of Laos, to use all measures, including the commitment of armed forces to assist that government in the defense of its independence and territorial integrity against aggression or subversion supported, controlled or directed from any Communist country.

Sec. 3. (a) The President is hereby authorized to use for assistance under this joint resolution not to exceed $—— during the fiscal year 1964, and not to exceed $—— during the fiscal year 1965, from any appropriations made available for carrying out the provisions of the Foreign Assistance Act of 1961, as amended in accordance with the provisions of that Act, except as otherwise provided in this joint resolution. This authorization is in addition to other existing authorizations with respect to the use of such appropriations.

(b) Obligations incurred in carrying out the provisions of this joint resolution may be paid either out of appropriations for military assistance except that appropriations made available for Titles I, III, and VI of Chapter 2, Part I, of the Foreign Assistance Act of 1961, as amended, shall not be available for payment of such obligations.

(c) Notwithstanding any other provision of the Foreign Assistance Act of 1961, as amended, when the President determines it to be important to the security of the United States and in furtherance of the purposes of this joint resolution, he may authorize the use of up to $—— of funds available under subsection (a) in each of the fiscal years 1964 and 1965 under the authority of section 614 (a) of the Foreign Assistance Act of 1961, as amended, and is authorized to use up to $—— of such funds in each such year pursuant to his certification that it is inadvisable to specify the nature of the use of such funds, which certification shall be deemed to be sufficient [words illegible].

(d) Upon determination by the head of any agency making personnel available under authority of section 627 of the Foreign Assistance Act of 1961, as amended, or otherwise under that Act, for purposes of assistance under this joint resolution, any officer or employee so made available may be provided compensation and allowances at rates other than those provided by the Foreign Service Act of 1946, as amended, the Career Compensation Act of 1949, as amended, and the Overseas Differentials and Allowances Act to the extent necessary to carry out the purposes of this joint resolution. The President shall prescribe regulations under which such rates of compensation and allowances may be provided. In addition, the President may utilize such provisions of the Foreign Service Act of 1946, as amended, as he deems appropriate to apply to personnel of any agency carrying out functions under this joint resolution.

.   .   .

THE COVERT WAR

The Pentagon papers disclose that in this phase the United States had been mounting clandestine military attacks against North Vietnam and planning to obtain a Congressional resolution that the Administration regarded as the equivalent of a declaration of war. The papers make it clear that these far-reaching measures were not improvised in the heat of the Tonkin crisis.

When the Tonkin incident occurred, the Johnson Administration did not reveal these clandestine attacks, and pushed the previously prepared resolution through both houses of Congress on Aug. 7.

Within 72 hours, the administration, drawing on a prepared plan, then secretly sent a Canadian emissary to Hanoi. He warned Premier Pham Van Dong that the resolution meant North Vietnam must halt the Communist-led insurgencies in South Vietnam and Laos or "suffer the consequences."

The section of the Pentagon study dealing with the internal debate, planning and action in the Johnson Administration from the beginning of 1964 to the August clashes between North Vietnamese PT boats and American destroyers—portrayed as a critical period when the groundwork was laid for the wider war that followed—also reveals that the covert military operations had become so extensive by August, 1964, that Thai pilots flying American T–28 fighter planes apparently bombed and strafed North Vietnamese villages near the Laotian border on Aug. 1 and 2.

Moreover, it reports that the Administration was able to order retaliatory air strikes on less than six hours' notice during the Tonkin incident because planning had progressed so far that a list of targets was available for immediate choice. The target list had been drawn up in May, the study reports, along with a draft of the Congressional resolution—all as part of a proposed "scenario" that was to build toward openly acknowledged air attacks on North Vietnam.

Simultaneously, the papers reveal, Secretary McNamara and the Joint Chiefs of Staff also arranged for the deployment of air strike forces to Southeast Asia for the opening phases of the bombing campaign. Within hours of the retaliatory air strikes on Aug. 4 and three days before the passage of the Congressional resolution, the squadrons began their planned moves.

PROGRESSIVELY ESCALATING PRESSURE

What the Pentagon papers call "an elaborate program of covert military operations against the state of North Vietnam" began on Feb. 1, 1964, under the code name Operation Plan 34A. President Johnson ordered the program, on the recommendation of Secretary McNamara, in the hope, held very faint by the intelligence community, that "progressively escalating pressure" from the clandestine attacks might eventually force Hanoi to order the Vietcong guerrillas and the Pathet Lao to halt their insurrections.

In a memorandum to the President on Dec. 21, 1963, after a two-day trip to Vietnam, Mr. McNamara remarked that the plans drawn up by the military command in Saigon, were "an excellent job."

"They present a wide variety of sabotage and psychological operations against North Vietnam from which I believe we should aim to select those that provide maximum pressure with minimum risk," Mr. McNamara wrote.

President Johson, in this period, showed a preference for steps that would remain "non-committing" to combat, the study found. But weakness in South Vietnam and Communist advances kept driving the planning process. This, in turn, caused the Saigon Government and American officials in Saigon to demand ever more action.

Through 1964, the 34A operations ranged from flights over North Vietnam by U–2 spy planes and kidnappings of North Vietnamese citizens for intelligence information, to parachuting sabotage and psychological-warfare teams into the North, commando raids from the sea to blow up rail and highway bridges and the bombardment of North Vietnamese coastal installations by PT boats.

These "destructive undertakings," as they were described in a report to the President on Jan. 2, 1964, from Maj. Gen. Victor H. Krulak of the Marine Corps, were designed "to result in substantial destruction, economic loss and harassment." The tempo and magnitude of the strikes were designed to rise in three phases through 1964 to "targets identified with North Vietnam's economic and industrial well-being."

The clandestine operations were directed for the President by Mr. McNamara through a section of the Joint Chiefs organization called the Office of the Special Assistant for Counterinsurgency and Special Activities. The study says that Mr. McNamara was kept regularly informed of planned and conducted raids by memorandums from General Krulak, who first held the position of special assistant, and then from Maj. Gen. Rollen H. Anthis of the Air Force, who succeeded him in February, 1964. The Joint Chiefs themselves periodically evaluated the operations for Mr. McNamara.

Secretary of State Dean Rusk was also informed, if in less detail.

The attacks were given "interagency clearance" in Washington, the study says, by coordinating them with the State Department and the Central Intelligence Agency, including advance monthly schedules of the raids from General Anthis.

The Pentagon account and the documents show that William P. Bundy, the Assistant Secretary of State for Far Eastern Affairs, and John T. McNaughton, head of the Pentagon's politico-military operations as the Assistant Secretary of Defense for International Security Affairs were the senior civilian officials who supervised the distribution of the schedules and the other aspects of interagency coordination for Mr. McNamara and Mr. Rusk.

The analyst notes that the 34A program differed in a significant respect from the relatively low-level and unsuccessful intelligence and sabotage operations that the C.I.A. had earlier been carrying out in North Vietnam.

The 34A attacks were a military effort under the control in Saigon of Gen. Paul D. Harkins, chief of the United States Military Assistance Command there. He ran them through a special branch of his command called the Studies and Observations Group. It drew up the advance monthly schedules for approval in Washington. Planning was done jointly with the South Vietnamese and it was they or "hired personnel," apparently Asian mercenaries, who performed the raids, but General Harkins was in charge.

The second major segment of the Administration's covert war against North Vietnam consisted of air operations in Laos. A force of propeller-driven T-28 fighter-bombers, varying from about 25 to 40 aircraft, had been organized there. The planes bore Laotians Air Force markings, but only some belonged to that air force. The rest were manned by pilots of Air America (a pseudo-private airline run by the C.I.A.) and by Thai pilots under the control of Ambassador Leonard Unger.

.   .   .

ATTACK ON TWO ISLANDS

At midnight on July 30, South Vietnamese naval commandos under General Westmoreland's command staged an amphibious raid on the North Vietnamese islands of Hon Me and Hon Nieu in the Gulf of Tonkin.

While the assault was occurring, the United States destroyer Maddox was 120 to 130 miles away, heading north into the gulf on the year's second De Soto intelligence-gathering patrol. Her sailing orders said she was not to approach closer than eight nautical miles to the North Vietnamese coast and four nautical miles to North Vietnamese islands in the gulf.

The account does not say whether the captain of the Maddox had been informed about the 34A raid. He does state that the Maddox altered course twice on Aug. 2 to avoid a concentration of three North Vietnamese torpedo boats and a fleet of junks that were still searching the seas around the islands for the raiders.

The destroyer reached the northernmost point of her assigned patrol track the same day and headed south again.

"When the [North Vietnamese] PT boats began their high-speed run at her, at a distance of approximately 10 miles, the destroyer was 23 miles from the coast and heading further into international waters," the study says. "Apparently," it explains "these boats . . . had mistaken Maddox for a South Vietnamese escort vessel."

In the ensuing engagement, two of the torpedo boats were damaged by planes launched from the aircraft carrier Ticonderoga, stationed to the south for reasons the study does not explain. A third PT boat was knocked dead in the water, sunk by a direct hit from the Maddox's five-inch guns.

NEW ORDERS FOR MADDOX

The next day, Aug. 3, President Johnson ordered the Maddox reinforced by the destroyer C. Turner Joy and directed that both destroyers be sent back into the gulf, this time with instructions not to approach closer than 11 nautical miles to the North Vietnamese coast. A second aircraft carrier, the Constellation, on a vsit to Hong Kong, was instructed to make steam and join the Ticonderoga as quickly as possible.

The study terms these reinforcing actions "a normal precaution" in the light of the first attack on the Maddox and not an attempt to use the destroyers as bait for another attack that would provide a pretext for reprisal airstrikes against the North. "Moreover," it comments, "since the augmentation was coupled with a clear [public] statement of intent to continue the patrols and a firm warning to the D.R.V. that a repetition would bring dire consequences, their addition to the patrol could be expected to serve more as a deterrent than a provocation."

The study gives a clear impression that the Administration at this moment did not believe the North Vietnamese would dare to attack the reinforced destroyer patrol.

For on the night of Aug. 3, while the De Soto patrol was resuming, two more clandestine 34A attacks were staged. PT boats manned by South Vietnamese crews bombarded the Rhon River estuary and a radar installation at Vinhson. This time the Maddox and the Turner Joy were definitely warned that the clandestine assaults were going to take place, the documents show.

Apparently expecting the President to order a resumption of the patrol, the admiral commanding the Seventh Fleet asked General Westmoreland on Aug. 2 to furnish him the general location of the planned raids so that the destroyers could steer clear of the 34A force. There was a good deal of cable traffic back and forth between the two commanders through the Pentagon communications center in Washington to modify the patrol's course on Aug. 3 to avoid any interference with the raiders.

On the night of Aug. 4, Tonkin Gulf time, approximately 24 hours after this second 34A assault, North Vietnamese torpedo boats then attacked both the Maddox and the Turner Joy in what was to be the fateful clash in the gulf.

MOTIVES STILL UNCLEAR

The Pentagon account says that Hanoi's motives for this second attack on the destroyers are still unclear. The narrative ties the attack to the chain of events set off by the 34A raids of July 30, but says that

Hanoi's precise motive may have been to recover from the embarrassment of having two torpedo boats damaged and another sunk in the first engagement with the Maddox, without any harm to the American destroyer.

"Perhaps closer to the mark is the narrow purpose of prompt retaliation for an embarrassing and well-publicized rebuff by a much-maligned enemy," the narrative says. "Inexperienced in modern naval operations, D.R.V. leaders may have believed that under the cover of darkness it would be possible to even the score or to provide at least a psychological victory by severely damaging a U.S. ship."

The study does not raise the question whether the second 34A raid on the night of Aug. 3, or the apparent air strikes on North Vietnamese villages just across the Laotian border on Aug. 1 and 2 by T-28 planes, motivated the Hanoi leadership in any way to order the second engagement with the destroyers.

Marshall Green, then the Deputy Assistant Secretary of State for Far Eastern Affairs, mentioned the apparent bombing of the villages in a lengthy memorandum to William Bundy dated Nov. 7, 1964, on United States covert activities in Indochina.

Listing complaints that North Vietnam had been making to the International Control Commission over the T-28 operations with Thai pilots, Mr. Green noted charges by Hanoi that "T-28s have violated North Vietnamese airspace and bombed/strafed NVN villages on Aug. 1 and 2, and on Oct. 16 and 17 and again on Oct. 28. The charges are probably accurate with respect to the first two dates (along Route 7) and the last one (Mugia Pass area)." The words in parentheses are Mr. Green's.

RAIDS POSSIBLY INADVERTENT

The context of the memorandum indicates that the raids on the North Vietnamese villages may have been inadvertent. But neither the narrative nor Mr. Green's memorandum says whether Hanoi thought this at the time the air strikes occurred.

Whatever the North Vietnamese motives for the second clash, President Johnson moved quickly now to carry out what the analyst calls "recommendations made . . . by his principal advisers earlier that summer and subsequently placed on the shelf."

Because of the Pacific time difference, the Pentagon received the first word that an attack on the Maddox and the Turner Joy might be imminent at 9:20 A.M. on the morning of Aug. 4, after the destroyers had intercepted North Vietnamese radio traffic indicating preparations for an assault. The flash message that the destroyers were actually engaged came into the communication center at 11 A.M.

The Joint Chiefs' staff began selecting target options for reprisal air strikes from the 94-target list, the first version of which was drawn up at the end of May. Adm. U.S. Grant Sharp, who had replaced Admiral Felt as commander in chief of Pacific forces, telephoned from Honolulu to suggest bombing the coastal bases for the torpedo boats.

Within 10 minutes, Mr. McNamara convened a meeting with the Joint Chiefs in his conference room on the third floor of the Pentagon to discuss possibilities for retaliation. Secretary Rusk and McGeorge Bundy came over to join them.

MEETING ALREADY SCHEDULED

Twenty-five minutes later the two secretaries and Mr. Bundy left for a previously scheduled National Security Council meeting at the White House. They would recommend reprisal strikes to the President, while the Joint Chiefs stayed at the Pentagon to decide on specific targets.

At 1:25 P.M., two and a half hours after the flash message of the engagement and possibly while Mr. McNamara, Mr. Rusk, Mr. McCone and McGeorge Bundy were still at lunch with the President, the director of the Joint Staff telephoned Mr. McNamara to say that the Chiefs had unanimously agreed on the targets. Fighter-bombers from the carriers Constellation and Ticonderoga should strike four torpedo boat bases at Hongay, Lochau, Phucloi and Quangkhe, and an oil storage depot near Vinh that held some 10 per cent of North Vietnam's petroleum supply.

At a second National Security Council meeting that afternoon, President Johnson ordered the reprisals, decided to seek the Congressional resolution immediately and discussed with his advisers the swift Southeast Asia deployment of the air strike forces designated in Operation Plan 37–64 for the opening blows in a possible bombing campaign against the North. His approval for these preparatory air deployments, and for the readiness of Marine Corps and Army units planned to meet any Chinese or North Vietnamese retaliation to a bombing campaign, was apparently given later that day, the study shows.

Mr. McNamara returned to the Pentagon at 3 P.M. to approve the details of the reprisal strikes, code-named Pierce Arrow. An execution order was prepared by the Joint Staff, but at 4 P.M. Mr. McNamara learned from Admiral Sharp in a telephone conversation that there was now confusion over whether an attack on the destroyers had actually taken place.

The Secretary told Admiral Sharp that the reprisal order would remain in effect, but that the admiral was to check and make certain that an attack had really occurred before actually launching the planes. At 4:49 P.M., less than six hours after the first message of the attack had flashed into the Pentagon communications center, the formal execution order for the reprisals was transmitted to Honolulu. Admiral Sharp had not yet called back with confirming details of the attack. The order specified that the carriers were to launch their planes within about two and half hours.

The admiral called back at 5:23 P.M. and again a few minutes after 6 o'clock to say that he was satisfied on the basis of information from the task group commander of the two destroyers, that the attack had been genuine. The study says that in the meantime Mr. McNamara and the Joint Chiefs had also examined the confirming evidence, including intercepted radio messages from the North Vietnamese saying that their vessels were engaging the destroyers and that two torpedo boats had been sunk.

By now Mr. McNamara and the Chiefs had moved on to discussing the prepositioning of the air strike forces under Operation Plan 37–64.

At 6:45 P.M., President Johnson met with 16 Congressional leaders from both parties whom he had summoned to the White House. He told them that because of the second unprovoked attack on the American destroyers, he had decided to launch reprisal air strikes against the North and to ask for a Congressional resolution, the study says.

The Pentagon study gives no indication that Mr. Johnson informed the Congressional leaders of United States responsibility for and command of the covert 34A raids on July 30 and Aug. 3.

Nor does the history give any indication that Mr. Johnson told the Congressional leaders of what the historian describes as "the broader purpose of the deployments" under Operation Plan 37–64, which Mr. McNamara was to announce at a Pentagon news conference the next day and describe as a precautionary move.

"It is significant," the analyst writes, "that few of these additional units were removed from the western Pacific when the immediate crisis subsided. In late September the fourth attack aircraft carrier was authorized to resume its normal station in the eastern Pacific as soon as the regularly assigned carrier completed repairs. The other forces remained in the vicinity of their August deployment."

PLANES LEAVE TICONDEROGA

At 8:30 P.M. on Aug. 4, Mr. McNamara returned to the Pentagon and at 11:30 P.M., after several telephone calls to Admiral Sharp, he learned that the Ticonderoga had launched her bomb-laden aircraft at 10:43 P.M. They were expected to arrive over their targets in about an hour and 50 minutes.

The carriers had needed more time to get into launching position than the execution order had envisioned. The Constellation, steaming from Hong Kong, was not to launch her planes for another couple of hours.

The President did not wait. Sixteen minutes after Mr. McNamara's last phone call to Admiral Sharp, at 11:36 P.M., he went on television to tell the nation of the reprisal strikes. He characterized his actions as a "limited and fitting" response. "We still seek no wider war," he said.

Almost simultaneously, the air deployments under Operation Plan 37–64 had begun.

The first F-102 Delta Dagger jet fighters were landing at Saigon's airport around the time Mr. McNamara described the deployments at a Pentagon news conference on Aug. 5. He had given a brief post-midnight conference the same day to describe the reprisal strikes. He reported now that 25 North Vietnamese patrol craft had been destroyed or damaged along with 90 per cent of the oil storage tanks near Vinh.

"Last night I announced that moves were under way to reinforce our forces in the Pacific area," he continued. "These moves include the following actions:

"First, an attack carrier group has been transferred from the First Fleet on the Pacific coast to the western Pacific. Secondly, interceptor and fighter-bomber aircraft have been moved into South Vietnam. Thirdly, fighter-bomber aircraft have been moved into Thailand. Fourthly, interceptor and fighter-bomber squadrons have been transferred from the United States into advance bases in the Pacific. Fifthly, an anti-submarine task force group has been moved into the South China Sea. And finally, selected Army and Marine forces have been alerted and readied for movement."

. . .

VIETNAM ARCHIVE: A CONSENSUS TO BOMB DEVELOPED BEFORE 1964 ELECTION, STUDY SAYS (BY NEIL SHEEHAN)

The Johnson Administration reached a "general consensus" at a White House strategy meeting on Sept. 7, 1964, that air attacks against North Vietnam would probably have to be launched, a Pentagon study of the Vietnam war states. It was expected that "these operations would begin early in the new year."

"It is important to differentiate the consensus of the principals at this September meeting," the study says, "from the views which they had urged on the President in the preceding spring. In the spring the use of force had been clearly contingent on a major reversal—principally in Laos—and had been advanced with the apparent assumption that military actions hopefully would not be required. Now, however, their views were advanced with a sense that such actions were inevitable."

The administration consensus on bombing came at the height of the Presidential election contest between President Johnson and Senator Barry Goldwater, whose advocacy of full-scale air attacks on North Vietnam had become a major issue. That such a consensus had been reached as early as September is a major disclosure of the Pentagon study.

The consensus was reflected, the analysis says, in the final paragraph of a formal national security action memorandum issued by the President three days later, on Sept. 10. This paragraph spoke of "larger decisions" that might be "required at any time."

The last round of detailed planning of various political and military strategies for a bombing campaign began "in earnest," the study says, on Nov. 3, 1964, the day that Mr. Johnson was elected President in his own right.

Less than 100 days later, on Feb. 8, 1965, he ordered new reprisal strikes against the North. Then, on Feb. 13, the President gave the order for the sustained bombing of North Vietnam, code-named Rolling Thunder.

This period of evolving decision to attack North Vietnam, openly and directly, is shown in the Pentagon papers to be the second major phase of President Johnson's defense of South Vietnam. The same period forms the second phase of the presentation of those papers by The New York Times.

The papers, prepared by a team of 30 to 40 authors in 1967–68 as an official study of how the United States went to war in Indochina, consist of 3,000 pages of analysis and 4,000 pages of supporting documents. The study covers nearly three decades of American policy on Southeast Asia. Yesterday The Time's first report on this study, and presentation of key documents, covered the period of clandestine warfare and planning before the Tonkin Gulf incidents in 1964.

In its glimpses into Lyndon B. Johnson's personal thoughts and motivations between the fateful September meeting and his decision to embark on an air war, the Pentagon study shows a President moving and being moved toward war, but reluctant and hesitant to act until the end.

But, the analyst explains, "from the September meeting forward, there was little basic disagreement among the principals (the term the study uses for the senior policy makers) on the need for military operations against the North. What prevented action for the time being was a set of tactical considerations."

The first tactical consideration, the analyst says, was that "the President was in the midst of an election campaign in which he was presenting himself as the candidate of reason and restraint as opposed to the quixotic Barry Goldwater," who was publicly advocating full-scale bombing of North Vietnam. The historian also mentions other "temporary reasons of tactics":

The "shakiness" of the Saigon Government.

A wish to hold the line militarily and diplomatically in Laos.

The "need to design whatever actions were taken so as to achieve maximum public and Congressional support. . . ."

The "implicit belief that overt actions at this time might bring pressure for premature negotiations—that is negotiations before the D.R.V. (Democratic Republic of (North) Vietnam) was hurting."

Assistant Secretary of Defense John T. McNaughton, the head of the Pentagon's Office of International Security Affairs, summed up these tactical considerations in the final paragraph of a Sept. 3 memorandum to Secretary of Defense Robert S. McNamara, in preparation for the crucial White House strategy session four days later:

"Special considerations during the next two months. The relevant audiences of U.S. actions are the Communists (who must feel strong pressures), the South Vietnamese (whose morale must be buoyed), our allies (who must trust us as 'underwriters'), and the U.S. public (which must support our risk-taking with U.S. lives and prestige). During the next two months, because of the lack of 'rebuttal time' before election to justify particular actions which may be distorted to the U.S. public, we must act with special care—signaling to the D.R.V. that initiatives are being taken, to the G.V.N. (Government of (South) Vietnam) that we are behaving energetically despite the restraints of our political season, and to the U.S. public that we are behaving with good purpose and restraint." The words in parentheses are Mr. McNaughton's.

6

FOSTERING THE U.S. ROLE IN AN OPEN WORLD ECONOMY
WILLIAM P. ROGERS

It is a privilege to be here this morning and to address the annual meeting of the Chamber of Commerce. President Nixon has asked me to convey to you his greetings and best wishes for what will surely be a successful and significant meeting. Your program is most timely in that it quite properly connects national progress—and in a very real sense, international progress—with the success of American business enterprise.

Your theme is "The World is Your Main Street." Two generations ago Sinclair Lewis wrote a book called "Main Street" in which he dwelt on the provincialism of American life as he had known it growing up in Sauk Centre, Minnesota.

Nowadays, few social critics write about small towns, or at best they write about them with a sense of nostalgia. In a relatively short time many of our towns have become cities or suburbs of cities, and many of our Main Streets have lengthened into interstate highways. Electronic communications and jet travel take little notice of frontiers and national boundaries, and the provincialism of "Main Street, U.S.A." has given way to the assured sophistication of the theme of your meeting here today.

It is quite surprising that all of us have made the practical and psychological adjustment as well as we have. I venture to suggest that this adjustment was possible because we applied to the world, as our horizon expanded, many of the principles of Main Street, U.S.A. They are the same principles that President Nixon is applying to our international economic policy.

This speech was given in Washington, D.C., on May 1, 1972.

PRINCIPLES FOR GLOBAL ECONOMICS

The first is a sense of community responsibility. I believe that we have shown this responsibility in the Marshall plan, which helped revive a war-ravaged Europe; in our efforts to assist Japan; in our aid to less developed countries; and in our willingness to join with others to stimulate international economic well-being and social improvement. Now that other countries have made good use of their opportunities and have achieved unprecedented prosperity, it's a new ball game—or if they prefer, a new soccer match. Thus it is that we expect them more fully to share with us the responsibility for the free community as a whole.

A second principle is a sense of fairness among neighbors. Good neighbors recognize the necessity of shared responsibility. International behavior must be governed according to rules of fair trade and good international business practice. We intend to insist on this.

A third principle for any dynamic community, local or international, is a determination and zest to grow. In a nation an important role of government is to give encouragement and scope to the human initiative, creativity, and energy which produce growth. In the world the role of the international economic system is to give to rich countries and poor countries alike similar encouragement and scope to develop and grow in an interdependent environment.

Thus these principles—a sense of common responsibility, a sense of fair treatment, a determination to encourage constructive growth— are as sound for international economics as they are for business on Main Street. They helped to build the postwar international economic system from which all have benefited.

Today that system is in need of repair. It was created at a time when the United States had few economic competitors and when our help was essential to stimulating the economies of others. Now that these conditions have changed, the continuing inertia of the system has put both our trade and our payments position on the critical list.

Nineteen seventy-one proved that abrupt and major adjustments were needed. President Nixon's new economic policy, which was announced on August 15, was followed by the so-called Smithsonian agreement of December 18. Thus it is that today we have a new pattern of exchange rates more favorable to the United States, a change which was long overdue. We recognize, of course, that it will take time to improve our balance of payments. And we must not forget that the key to a substantive and lasting improvement is increased productivity, efficiency, and ingenuity by American private enterprise. Without these no amount of government effort will prevail. But now that the exchange rate adjustment has been made, we have the opportunity, and it is up to American business to take full advantage of it. I have every expectation that you will.

U.S. STAKE IN THE WORLD ECONOMY

It is right that Americans should take our international economic problems seriously, but it is also right that we should put them in the perspective of our overall economic success. There is a lot of hand-wringing about America's economic future. I don't subscribe to it. Since becoming Secretary of State, I have traveled to 42 countries, and there is no doubt that our economic system and our economy—whatever their problems and however much those problems are in need of solution—are the envy of virtually every nation and of most thoughtful people in the world. And no wonder, when you look at the facts. For example:

With only one-twentieth of the world's population the United States accounts for one-third of its total output of goods and services. Our annual gross national product is twice that of the second-ranking country, the Soviet Union.

Our annual exports are only 4 percent of our GNP, but those exports alone are more than the total annual GNP of all but nine of the world's nations. One dollar out of every seven generated by world trade comes to this country in payment for American exports.

U.S. direct foreign investment totals nearly $80 billion. It is four times that of Great Britain, the next largest foreign investor, and 60 percent of all worldwide direct foreign investment. According to one estimate of all the goods and services produced outside the United States, the foreign operations of U.S. firms account for fully one-eighth.

It is difficult even to grasp the magnitude of such an economic performance. And we are still growing. During 1971, despite inflation, unemployment, and our international problems, our GNP *in real terms* grew by $30 billion, a figure itself higher than the annual GNP of 90 percent of the countries in the world.

As we set about the task of restructuring the international economic system, therefore, there is as little room for recrimination as there is for complacency. The task is too important for either.

With three million American jobs directly dependent on exports, with our increasing import needs—for example, in petroleum and minerals—and with our enormous investments abroad, we have a large stake in a world economy which is both expanding *and* equitably regulated. Over a year ago, in my first foreign policy report to Congress, I said that economic policy would play a far larger and more vital role in U.S. foreign policy. It is playing such a role, and there can be no doubt that the trend will continue throughout this century.

President Nixon's visits to the People's Republic of China and the Soviet Union, his determination to reach a SALT [Strategic Arms Limitation Talks] agreement, his troop withdrawal policy in Viet-Nam, his successful efforts in bringing about a cease-fire in the Middle East, his fidelity to U.S. commitments throughout the world—all these have created greater opportunities for a more peaceful and stable world. But we simply cannot maintain a constructive foreign political policy unless it is based on a sound American economy.

ASSURING COMPETITION AND COOPERATION

Some segments of the American business community may still believe that the State Department tends to represent foreign interests at the expense of American interests. Nothing could be further from the truth. We are the people who sit where domestic and foreign considerations intersect. I have—and I believe my associates have—a deep conviction that a healthy and competitive American economy is our number one asset in U.S. foreign relations. Thus, the fundamental objective of our foreign economic policy is to assure the international conditions of competition and cooperation which can keep our economy strong.

To accomplish this, we must pay greater attention to economic matters and pay particular attention to our relations with our major economic partners—Canada, Japan, Mexico, and the states of western Europe. These countries are at once our friends, our allies, and our competitors. They are the best customers for our exports, and they sell us most of our imports. They are the host countries to two-thirds of our overseas investments.

These extraordinarily close economic ties grew up in a postwar period distinguished by a rapid growth in the flow of goods and capital across national borders. During the postwar period tariffs worldwide were cut by 75 percent. Let us not forget what this openness meant to our economy. Between 1950 and 1970 U.S. exports increase fourfold. U.S. direct investment abroad increased sixfold.

. . .

DEPARTMENT AID TO U.S. COMMERCE

The State Department is deeply engaged in the effort to strengthen the international aspects of the American economy.

First, we are stepping up our efforts on behalf of U.S. exports. We now have some 450 officers in our missions abroad engaged specifically in commercial and economic activities. A number of your overseas members have testified to the value of their work. To cite only one example, it was largely due to the initiative and followthrough of the U.S. Embassy in Tokyo that the American coal industry obtained agreements resulting in sales to Japan of over $1 billion of coal over a 10-year period.

In this regard, I should note the efforts we have been making within the Government to improve trade with Eastern Europe and the Soviet Union. As many of you know, the Department is now negotiating with the Russians a settlement of their old lend-lease debts. If we can get a reasonable settlement, then we can look forward to a serious examination of the prospects for increased trade with the Soviet Union—where I think there are very substantial markets for our technology and heavy equipment. And we look forward to the day when trade with the People's Republic of China will develop and grow.